1301220 4

D0582150

Market Matters

Also by Christina Garsten

LEARNING TO BE EMPLOYABLE: New Agendas for Work, Responsibility and Learning in a Globalizing World (*co-edited with Kerstin Jacobsson*)

NEW TECHNOLOGIES AT WORK: People, Screens and Social Virtuality (*co-edited with Helena Wulff*)

APPLE WORLD: Core and Periphery in a Transnational Organizational Culture

Also by Monica Lindh de Montoya

PROGRESS, HUNGER AND ENVY: Commercial Agriculture, Marketing and Social Transformation in the Venezuelan Andes

Market Matters

Exploring Cultural Processes in the Global Marketplace

Christina Garsten

and

Monica Lindh de Montoya

SUSSEX LIBRARY

Selection and editorial matter © Christina Garsten and
Monica Lindh de Montoya 2004

Individual chapters © contributors 2004

All rights reserved. No reproduction, copy or transmission of this
publication may be made without written permission.

No paragraph of this publication may be reproduced, copied or transmitted
save with written permission or in accordance with the provisions of the
Copyright, Designs and Patents Act 1988, or under the terms of any licence
permitting limited copying issued by the Copyright Licensing Agency,
90 Tottenham Court Road, London W1T 4LP.

Any person who does any unauthorized act in relation to this publication
may be liable to criminal prosecution and civil claims for damages.

The authors have asserted their rights to be identified
as the authors of this work in accordance with the Copyright,
Designs and Patents Act 1988.

First published 2004 by
PALGRAVE MACMILLAN
Houndmills, Basingstoke, Hampshire RG21 6XS and
175 Fifth Avenue, New York, N.Y. 10010
Companies and representatives throughout the world

PALGRAVE MACMILLAN is the global academic imprint of the Palgrave
Macmillan division of St. Martin's Press, LLC and of Palgrave Macmillan Ltd.
Macmillan® is a registered trademark in the United States, United Kingdom
and other countries. Palgrave is a registered trademark in the European
Union and other countries.

ISBN 1–4039–1757–4

This book is printed on paper suitable for recycling and made from fully
managed and sustained forest sources.

A catalogue record for this book is available from the British Library.

Library of Congress Cataloging-in-Publication Data
Market matters : exploring cultural processes in the global marketplace /
    edited by Christina Garsten and Monica Lindh de Montoya.
       p.   cm.
    Includes bibliographical references and index.
    ISBN 1–4039–1757–4 (alk. paper)
    1. Economic anthropology.   2. Globalization—Economic aspects.
    3. Capitalism.   4. Markets.   I. Garsten, Christina.   II. De Montoya,
    Monica Lindh.
    GN448.2.M37 2004
    306.3—dc22   2004046887

10   9   8   7   6   5   4   3   2   1
13   12   11   10   09   08   07   06   05   04

Printed and bound in Great Britain by
Antony Rowe Ltd, Chippenham and Eastbourne

1 3 0 1 2 2 0

UNIVERSITY OF
SUSSEX LIBRARY

Contents

Notes on the Contributors

Christina Garsten is Associate Professor and Senior Lecturer at the Department of Social Anthropology, Stockholm University, and Research Director at Score (Stockholm Center for Organizational Research) at Stockholm University and Stockholm School of Economics. Her research interests are in the anthropology of organizations and markets. Recent books include *Learning to be Employable: New Agendas on Work, Responsibility and Learning in a Globalizing World* (co-edited with Kerstin Jacobsson, 2004) and *New Technologies at Work: People, Screens and Social Virtuality* (co-edited with Helena Wulff, 2003).

Anna Hasselström received her PhD in Social Anthropology at Stockholm University and has studied economic history and psychology. Her PhD was an ethnographically based investigation into certain aspects of 'the global economy', asking specifically how financial market knowledge is learned, developed, organized and distributed. Her next project revolves around financial actors who produce instruments for the ranking of corporations and nations, as a step towards providing global standards for credit rating. With Christina Garsten she is the author of the article 'Risky Business' (*Ethnos* 68:2, 2003).

Monica Lindh de Montoya is Assistant Professor of Social Anthropology at Stockholm University. She has a number of published articles on the subjects of markets, entrepreneurship, and stock market investors, including 'Driven Entrepreneurs: A Case Study of Taxi Owners in Caracas' (forthcoming in *New Practices of Entrepreneurship*, edited by Daniel Hjort and Chris Steyaert) and 'Looking Into the Future: Anthropology and Financial Markets' (in *Economic Development: An Anthropological Approach*, edited by Jeffery Cohen and Norbert Dannhaeuser, 2002). At present she is working as a consultant for IBM Business Consulting Services on a project in Sarajevo, Bosnia–Herzegovina.

Marianne Elisabeth Lien is Associate Professor at the Department of Social Anthropology, University of Oslo, is trained in nutrition and anthropology and has previously done consumer research with a focus on food habits, nutrition policy, and marketing in Norway. Her current research interests include economic anthropology, globalization, food consumption, and marine farming. Publications include *Marketing and Modernity* (1997) and *The Politics of Food* (co-edited with B. Nerlich, 2004).

Michele Micheletti is Associate Professor of Political Science, Stockholm University. She has done research on corporatism, the role of civil society in politics, democratic auditing, and has recently published *Political Virtue and Shopping: Individuals, Consumerism, and Collective Action* (2003) and jointly edited a volume entitled *Politics, Products, and Markets: Exploring Political Consumerism Past and Present* (2003).

Brian Moeran is Professor of Culture and Communication at the Copenhagen Business School, and has previously held chair professorships at the Universities of London (School of Oriental and African Studies) and Hong Kong. A social anthropologist by training, he has published widely on various aspects of Japanese society and culture. Books include *A Japanese Advertising Agency* (1996), and *The Business of Ethnography* (forthcoming), together with two edited works: *Asian Media Productions* (2001) and, with Timothy de Waal Malefyt, *Advertising Cultures* (2003).

Miguel Montoya is Assistant Professor of Social Anthropology at Stockholm University, and is currently working on a study of transparency in the process of the negotiation of the Free Trade Area of the Americas agreement. He has previously done research on forced migration due to a hydroelectric scheme. Other interests include the anthropology of emerging markets, development, frontiers, and the political processes. He is the author of 'Emerging Markets, Globalization and the Small Investor: The Case of Venezuela' (in *Economic Development: An Anthropological Approach*, edited by Jeffery Cohen and Norbert Dannhaeuser, 2002).

Gustav Peebles holds a post-doctoral fellowship at Columbia University's Department of Anthropology. His dissertation provided an anthropological analysis of Sweden's debate over entering the European Monetary Union. His next project concerns the history and impact of credit and debt regulations in Europe. He also likes to write occasional pieces for more popular audiences.

1

Introduction: Exploring Cultural Processes in the Global Marketplace

Christina Garsten and Monica Lindh de Montoya

Point of entry: ethnographies of contemporary markets

This book is about how people – individuals, organizations, and governments – make use of the market in modern capitalist cultures. Our intention is to provide some insight into the cultural processes taking place in modern markets; showing how people employ the market to solve problems, create capital, gain particular political ends, pose pertinent arguments, question economic processes, and delineate moral values and responsibilities. By focusing on ethnographic material collected in a number of different cultures – all members of the modern global economy in one way or another – we hope not only to add to the ethnography of the market in western societies and to the analysis of contemporary economic processes, but also to provide an anthropological perspective on phenomena more frequently written about by economists, historians, political scientists, or scholars in the field of business studies.

Anthropologists and others have contributed substantially to the ethnography and understanding of market processes in more traditional societies; the focus of this work has mainly been on non-market trans-actions and small-scale systems of distribution. The issues of rationality and self-interest in non-capitalist societies have been widely examined (Mauss 1954 [1924]; Polanyi, 1944, 1957; Sahlins, 1974). Ethnographic studies of the market itself have been oriented around the production and flow of goods within and between societies, and the roles of middlemen – seen as entrepreneurs or ethnic groups – within particular markets or marketplaces. Several different perspectives have been used in studies of trade: while most analyses use neo-classical economic concepts to illuminate their material, indicating that even in exotic settings people are self-interested, rational and seek to maximize valued ends (Plattner, 1989a, b), ideas from political economy have also been used to discuss work processes, control of labour and resources, and the articulation of local economies with the world economic system (Rapp and Schneider, 1995), leading to a greater understanding of the relationships between power and material production.

Contemporary markets – heavily mediated and dependent upon modern technology – constitute something of an unexplored area within anthropology, however. The discipline has not otherwise been hesitant in exploring modern society, yet the vast majority of research in economic anthropology concerns small communities in 'non-western' societies. Often they are in the process of 'developing' – of assimilating western economic practices, or currencies, although these are frequently adapted locally, thereby acquiring different meanings, and outcomes (Parry and Bloch, 1989; Taussig 1980). Even those studies that anthropologists have conducted on contemporary economies in urban areas tend to be set in the so-called developing countries – for example, in India and China – rather than in those core capitalist countries which see themselves as driving worldwide economic growth and integration. Exceptions, however, are recent studies of consumption that focus on consumers and/or marketing in some industrial economies (see, inter alia, de Grazia, 1996; Howes, 1996; Lien, 1997; Moeran, 1996; Slater, 1997), studies on the media and culture industry, and some pioneering work on the cultural component in market relations in modern, complex societies. We believe, however, that it is fair to say that the interest in market aspects has increased in recent years in research on modern society, as a natural offspring of the growing interest in the organization of complex, modern society, and in documenting the uneven development, flow, and distribution of knowledge and ideas.

Fortunately, then, the modern market has recently begun to receive a share of attention from anthropologists as well. As Lien, and also Garsten and Hasselström (this volume) point out, Michel Callon (1998) urges us to recognize that the calculations of so-called 'rational economic man' are both a technical and an ethical practice, and that *Homo Economicus* is constructed by, enmeshed in, and aided in his practices by knowledge, conventions and tools produced by economics. This, Callon argues, opens up new fields for social science, which should explore 'calculative agencies' forms and distributions' (1998: 51). Hasselström (this volume, see also Hasselström, 2003) takes a step in this direction with her work on the construction of knowledge among brokers, traders and analysts working in central nodes of financial markets.

Anthropologists are perhaps better placed than other social scientists to penetrate the meanings people construct about their economic worlds. As Moeran (this volume) points out, the anthropologist can build up a sense of mutual trust and easily move from the formal to the informal, and from observation to participation in the course of fieldwork. This opportunity, inherent in the basic methods of the discipline, enables anthropologists to illuminate market processes from different angles than others in the social sciences, exposing meanings hidden behind the façade of everyday practices.

Financial markets are often taken to be the ultimate form of modern markets, characterized by abstraction, calculation, and rationality. However, recent work by anthropologists has shown that even these markets are shaped by cultural processes and social structures of wider reach. The interest that financial markets are attracting among and for social scientists more broadly is rapidly being recognized, with a number of publications in recent years, from forerunners Abolafia (1996) and Hertz (1998) to the more recent Fligstein (2001), Hasselström (2003), Hägglund (2000, 2001), Knorr Cetina and Bruegger (2000, 2002a and b), Miyazaki and Riles (2004), and Norberg (2001). Works about the modern market that do not deal directly with finance, but focus on the cultural dynamics of modern markets of different kinds, are also beginning to appear; Carrier (1997), Carrier and Miller (1998), Lien (1997) Hart (2001), Miller (1997, 2001), Malefyt and Moeran (2003) and Moeran (1996) are some intriguing examples. Whilst they differ in the empirical material used and the perspectives taken, these works all contribute towards deconstructing the seemingly anonymous, rational and virtual character of markets, and revealing the cultural logics at work.

Another useful theoretical entry into the ethnographic study of market processes, however, is suggested by Gudeman's (2001) observation that market activity does not occur in a sphere independent of culture, but, rather, is grounded on and built by means of all the accomplishments of culture. Entrepreneurship and financial systems, for example, are based on contract law and accounting conventions, transportation and communication systems, and social codes, taboos and traditions (to name only a few bases), all of which have been, and continue to be, negotiated within society via a public discussion – sometimes carried out in the political sphere, but just as likely to be conducted within a religious, or bureaucratic frame. Morality can thus be seen as an integral consideration of any market activity, whether overtly expressed or not, and community as an integral player.

These days, these times

Globalization, the growth of trading blocks such as the European Union, organizational change, the privatization of state services, and the spread of fast and inexpensive communications are all increasing the impact of the market in peoples' lives, making an examination of social and cultural uses of the modern market all the more relevant at this time. The increasing emphasis on market mechanisms, and their elevation to a kind of 'mantra' leading to greater prosperity and development, seems to characterize our times and further encourages us to examine the nature of 'the market'.

The wide range of economic transformations underway today thus spur a need to investigate the interaction of social and economic values. At a historical moment when alternatives to the free market have failed and, for the most part, disappeared from the world arena, western economies are adjusting to new conditions, including competition with industrializing developing countries and the restructuring of hard-won social programmes. Large-scale planned economies have proved untenable in practice, yet they have left a legacy and, one might suggest, they drew much of their original force from moral tensions inherent in economic life: those between the individual and the community, between the desire to realize one's potential, and the need to recognize socially legitimated boundaries. How do recent socioeconomic changes influence peoples' ways of thinking about the relationships that exist between the interests of economic actors and the larger society? How do people re-evaluate their own position as paradigms change, how do knowledge and habits change, and in what ways do people learn, as Bourdieu (1990) suggests, to want that which is possible?

Cultural economics provide a fruitful point of entry into a discussion of the nature of the market. Cultural economics examine the ways in which non-market societies, as well as certain groups within the market economy, model their economic activities using metaphors – for example, via concrete local images such as family relationships, or images of the Other (Gudeman 1986). Market activities and the ideas surrounding them are seen as an integral part of society, understandable only through the analysis of the social context in which they operate. Universal models – used in the discipline of economics – are recognized as being, themselves, the products of particular communities' attempts to model their economic practices.

Although western economic thought is regarded as generating universal models with a broad applicability, anthropologists argue that peoples' conceptions of the economy take a variety of forms, which spring out of their environment, history, and daily practices of economic life. Stephen Gudeman (1986) calls such socially based economic models 'local models'. In this book, contributors examine certain market actors' models of the economy and their activities in today's market, precisely from the standpoint that modern economic life is also made up of local models that spring out of a tension between the market and the community.

In modern capitalist societies, markets and market processes are generally taken to be inevitable, pervasive and unproblematic, as simply a part of everyday life, whose form and function is seldom questioned (see, for example, Carrier, 1997; Garsten and Hasselström, 2003). The fall of the socialist regimes in the former USSR and Eastern Europe has reinforced the view of markets as necessary, efficient, and munificent; and alternative ideas of provisioning society have come to be regarded with doubt. Yet with the decline of ideology, ethics and morality have found a home in the marketplace. Certainly modern markets have never been free of friction and contestation, but today we take note of a greater questioning of market processes, their logic and ethics, and of demands for responsibility and accountability in the marketplace. Simultaneously, markets are increasingly becoming arenas for political statements and action and for the self-definition of individuals and groups, as the enormous swell in global flows of capital and goods now integrates culturally diverse and widely dispersed populations into each other's agendas and aspirations.

It has been said that in social science there exists a gap in knowledge, or zone of ignorance, between micro- and macrostructures. In a presentation at a conference on globalization held by the Swedish Council for Planning and Coordination of Research (FRN) in Stockholm in 1998, sociologist Saskia Sassen called for ethnographic studies that focus on specific areas, or nodes of activity, where the processes of globalization impinge on peoples' lives. There is a need to study the links between social structures, the lives of individuals, and the processes that create and transform them. Today, when we see the market as organizing more and more of daily life, we seek to understand how such trends effect peoples' basic views and feelings about the market and how these are linked to financial actors and organizations.

During recent years, the market as a conception of the world has gained increased relevance worldwide as an organizing principle and ideal model for social life (Gustafsson, 1994). In Sweden, where the ethnographic work for some of the chapters in this volume was conducted, the adjustment of the public sector to the market has had a dramatic impact on the context of daily life; and a shift in discourse, away from the duality of the public and the private, towards an increased influx of concepts and terms from the sphere of private business, is occurring. Financial crises and an accompanying transformation of the social climate are often said to be brought about by the impact of the market on organizations, politics, and the everyday life of people. In Europe as a whole, political and ideological conceptions of a common European market, with an accompanying free flow of money, has to a large extent steered the creation and administration of the European Union and continues to guide policy decisions at both European and national level (see, for example, Shore, 2000). Likewise, in discussions of globalization and the growing power of transnational corporations (TNCs), market forces have been attributed considerable powers of explanation. Markets are generally seen as promoters of globalization processes, or as arenas where globalization takes off. A 'mythology of the market' may be said to exist in the media, where the functioning of the market explains complex relations with little discrimination. Such a mythology, however, speaks to a new constellation of power, in which market transactions and a plethora of new competencies, skills, and frames of mind are assumed to play an increasingly influential role.

Although the notion of the market may refer to practices and institutions in the world, we think it is important to remember Polanyi's point that the market is a conception of the world, rather than the world itself. It should not be unreflectively conflated with those aspects of the world that it labels. Moreover, the market has come to be an expansive notion, the measure against which areas of life beyond markets are to be assessed and subordinated. The idea that market logic ought to predominate is contained aphoristically in the notion of 'the bottom line'. Like all good aphorisms, this one contains not just exhortation, but also resignation: Not only ought we to keep our eyes on the bottom line, we must do so, for those who do not will go under.

Granovetter (1985) points out that it has long been the majority view among sociologists, anthropologists, political scientists and historians that economic behaviour is heavily embedded in social relations in pre-market societies but became more autonomous with modernization. This view sees the economy as an increasingly separate, differentiated sphere in modern society, with economic transactions defined no longer by the social or kinship obligations of those transacting but by rational calculations of individual gain. The concept of embeddedness, as formulated by Granovetter (1985), offers a useful approach to an analysis of market relations: social relations are central, not peripheral or disruptive features of market processes in contemporary societies. It is also through a focus on concrete ongoing social relations that we can gain a fuller understanding of the links between micro- and macro-level social change, and of markets to modernities. The modern and the global often appear as flip sides to the same coin. And with globalization, the argument for disembeddedness as a feature of market relations in modern society seems to gain the upper hand. But globalization, as a process of intensified relations across space, is in fact also embedded locally, or springs out of local practices. Sometimes these local practices take on a translocal character, extending across space. Mass media, migration and digital financial flows make for the uneven and more unstable translocal distribution of resources, ideas and images. Ulf Hannerz (1992, 1996) has shown social interaction in markets to be frameworks for globalization – frameworks within which commodities with cultural content, tangible and intangible, are produced and distributed, setting up more or less centring relationships between consumers and producers, trying expansively to bring more and more of culture into its framework. It is a framework characterized by competition, asymmetry, and a great deal of built-in instability.

Reflections on the relation of markets and communities also involve the role of the nation-state. Nation-states, viewed as modern political forms or units in a complex interactive system, have to a relatively large extent been playing the role of arbiters of the relationship between market, globality, and modernity. The question is, what role will the nation-state play in the future regulation of markets, in organizing the flow of ideologies, moneys and goods, in the distribution of democratic rights, and such things? How will relations between markets and nation-states be modelled in a system of 'fragmented political authority' (Palan, 2000: 17)? This discontinuity between polity and economy is a central point of departure for understanding the ways in which markets influence social life at both global and local levels, and has spurred a great deal of interest among social scientists. Garsten (this volume) discusses how the role of corporate power in this context is discussed and how the shifting lines of responsibility between the nation-state and the market actors – that is, corporations – are being negotiated. The delicate balancing act between national interests and market capitalism is also often evident in empirical studies of media organizations, news production, and marketing. There may, for example, be regulations in relation to advertising that mediate between the interests of corporations treating the world as a single homogenous market, and the ideological positions of nation-states.

In the study of western markets, there has long been a concern with the supply side of the economic factor, with the organization and work that goes with the production and offering for sale of economic goods. Social scientists, including Slater (1997), Featherstone (1991), and Bauman (2000), point to the increasingly important theme of consumerism in the overall trend of globalizing markets. From the point of view of consumption, and the regulation of consumption by the nation-state, we may also gain insights into the making of modern society. Modernity has entailed the construction of a certain type of individual, with certain tastes and habits of consumption, a certain modal personality. If economic models take little heed of the emotional side of economic life, the advertising agency, which is intimately involved in day-to-day economic transactions, must cope with the multifaceted human. In his analysis of the intricate process of negotiation between facts and images involved in the production of a marketing campaign, Moeran (this volume) demonstrates the fortuitous, felicitous ways in which such campaigns can evolve.

Bauman (1995) says that the coming of postmodernity entails the loss of a certain kind of Utopia, the loss of the modernist belief in progress, designed on the national level. This leaves consumerism as the only choice for individuals to seek out meaning, on an individual as well as on a collective level. Consumption provides a means for individuals to create and assert identity, to manifest their interests, and it may take on political overtones, as a form of political action, as Michele Micheletti (this volume) explains. From the angle of consumption, then, we also enter issues of democracy, political participation and the like, issues at the very core of discussions of the social changes underway today.

We believe that by drawing upon and integrating insights generated from within different disciplines in social science, we are better equipped to understand the dynamics of markets and modernities, and perhaps even the relations between the two. The original point of departure for this volume of articles was a multidisciplinary workshop entitled 'Markets and Modernities – Zones of Interplay in the Social Sciences', which was held in Uppsala, Sweden, at the Swedish Collegium for Advanced Study in the Social Sciences (SCASSS), in October 2000. The workshop, exploratory in nature, was organized through a research programme called 'Cultural Models of the Market: Trust, Risk and Social Change', then underway at the Department of Social Anthropology at Stockholm University, financed primarily by the Bank of Sweden Tercentenary Foundation. The four participants in the programme, Christina Garsten, Anna Hasselström, Monica Lindh de Montoya and Miguel Montoya, all anthropologists, were involved in independent, but tightly linked and often interwoven research on modern financial markets. They shared a conviction that anthropology had much to contribute to the understanding of modern market phenomena, and a desire to gain insights from colleagues working on similar themes in other areas of the social sciences. The SCASSS workshop served to bring together anthropologists with scholars from a variety of disciplines – including business studies, economic history, and political science – to examine the concepts of market and modernity. Two of the chapters presented in this volume (Moeran, Micheletti) were originally presented in the workshop, others (Garsten, Garsten and Hasselström, Hasselström, Lindh de Montoya, Montoya) emerged out of the 'Cultural Models of the Market' research programme, and still others (Lien and Peebles) were added along the route.

Consumers and marketing

Moeran demonstrates how advertising plays to the complex rational/ emotional way in which consumption decisions are made. His chapter, which introduces the part on consumers and marketing, is based on extensive fieldwork within the Japanese advertising industry (Moeran, 1996, 2000; Malefyt and Moeran, 2003). In it he reflects on the ways in which anthropology and marketing both differ and resemble each other as practices, and considers whether they might, in the future, enrich each others' knowledge and methods. While anthropology stresses the importance of in-depth fieldwork for the understanding of cultures, marketing also stresses field research (albeit a much more rudimentary process, now referred to as 'ethnography') as an important basis for gathering knowledge about consumers, the marketing target. Moeran clearly demonstrates how this research is the basis for the sale of the campaign to the client, and for the actual advertising campaign that eventually takes shape through a complex process of negotiation between product and consumer information, the client, the agency, and the different members of the campaign team. Thus we have two disciplines based on interpreting what is 'out there' to a wider audience, both of which, it should also be said, have to consider their prospective audiences, and the life their creations will lead out in the public arena.

Moeran points out the problematic interfaces that advertising agencies face as they formulate and execute campaigns: these include that between the marketing and creative departments within the agency in the analysis of data, and in the transposition of analysis into a creative product; between the agency and the client in the selling of a campaign, and the problem of having to appeal to more than one potential consumer target. One could further point out that anthropologists have to negotiate comparable interfaces and deal with similar tensions as they cull and interpret their field data in the preparation of an anthropological product, be it text, film, or exhibition; and that this is a creative process that has been under considerable scrutiny during the last two decades (Aull Davies 1999; Clifford and Marcus, 1986; Gupta and Ferguson, 1997; Marcus and Fischer, 1986; Olwig and Hastrup, 1997; Ortner, 1997).

While Moeran focuses on the dialogue and bargaining that take place as meanings are produced for consumers, Lien analyses the specific search for information that is the point of departure of any marketing campaign. She points out that in marketing, information is never considered to be enough or 'complete' – again, a view with which anthropologists can empathize – and she questions the way in which marketers construct the knowledge that they use to mount advertising campaigns. Lien identifies a *bias of temporality*, in marketing discourse – a focus on the novel, news, the future and anticipated change, which she discusses in light of the fact that life is, after all, primarily continuous; and most novelties never manage to penetrate the market and become the substance of daily life. The focus on change requires a continuous dis-identification with life as lived routinely from day to day; something that is further reflected in marketers' view of consumers as strangers 'out there'. Consumers do not pass through the doors of the marketing department except for the occasional focus group, and personal experience is not considered a valid component of research.

Lien finds part of the answer to this conundrum in the marketing industry's need to establish itself by separating 'marketing knowledge from marketing practices' (Cochoy 1998: 189). The challenge the industry continuously faces is to maintain the level of abstraction that legitimizes it as a discipline (and valuable knowledge product) while maintaining its invaluable connection with the problems and needs of contemporary business practice; it must present itself as simultaneously theoretical and applied – no easy task. But the end product of the exercise, the 'consumer' as seen by marketers, is a person removed from social reality and stripped of social meaning. The 'consumer' is disembedded from life as it is lived, and constructed for the sole purpose of consumption, while consumption, as Lien emphatically points out, is about relationships, about peoples' feelings for and duties to one another; and as such, it is likely to be similar across cultures and over time.

Conceptualizing modernity in the marketplace

Since the fall of the Iron Curtain and the dissolution of the former Soviet Union, political ideologies have decreased in importance as a source of moral discourse and moral action. Production and consumption, the free market vs the controlled market, are no longer thought and argued about in quite the same way. Morality's intrinsic connection to human endeavours, and to the market and its role in provisioning, remain intact, however; and are gradually becoming socially articulated in new ways. It is interesting to discover that market processes, assumed to be rational and self-serving, in fact provide excellent arenas for expressing moral relationships and for moral action, creating, as Micheletti and Garsten show, new varieties of political action. In the part on conceptualizing morality in the marketplace, two anthropologists and a political scientist discuss how market processes are becoming moral meeting grounds, arenas for political action, and generators of social change.

With the de-regulation of markets, non-governmental organizations and grassroots movements are now pushing for re-regulation, and a variety of voluntary forms of regulations have appeared. Christina Garsten explores the growing field of 'corporate social responsibility' as one where the voluntary regulation of markets is shaped, and where bottom line reasoning and social accountability are negotiated among a variety of organizational actors. The field of corporate social responsibility also reflects demands for greater transparency and accountability in corporate actions by state representatives, grassroots movements and organized consumers. In some sense, it may be viewed as a social battlefield, in that it provides an arena for different actors with different interests and priorities to put pressure onto each other, where roles and expectations may be challenged and changed, and where lines of responsibilities are continuously shifting. In these processes, the intricate ways in which markets are in fact entangled in social structures, cultures, and politics, are made evident. As Michael Addo (1999: 21) points out, the social responsibility of corporations recognizes the interactive relationship in which corporations work. As privileged members of society, they are expected to contribute to the advancement of the wider community of which they are a part. This is often not a compelling legal requirement but a moral one, from which the corporation can expect to benefit in the long run.

The placing of social responsibility on the corporate agenda (although historically not a new phenomenon) thus reflects larger structural changes in society and the problematization of the allocation of social responsibilities. These processes also bring to the fore the question of the scope of corporate activity and influence. Exactly how, and by whom, social responsibility is to be defined and put to action, and to whom corporate actors are to be accountable, is often an issue of debate and conflict. Furthermore, the abstract character of codes of conduct, norms, and standards in the area of social accountability renders them open to definition. They exist within a large zone of interpretation and they have the capacity to contain within them a large number of differential understandings.

Markets often operate with the assistance of motivational concepts and mobilizing metaphors (Carrier, 1997), and the area of corporate social responsibility is no exception. 'Talking the talk' of social responsibility is to some extent a way of 'doing' social responsibility. Keywords serve to open up avenues to the future and to place actors within a temporality organized by humane ends as much as by profit and the contingencies of uncontrolled events. These keywords may function as Trojan horses that introduce market notions into discussions of social issues, as seemingly apolitical and neutral tools for fashioning the workings of global market processes.

Miguel Montoya's contribution deals with morality in political life, and focuses on the political transformations that have been underway in Venezuela since the end of the 1990s. In the public discourse being carried out around the ascent of Hugo Chávez to power, morality is a central issue, and is linked to the issues of both political corruption and foreign trade. Pointing out that the majority of Venezuela's population are relatively recent migrants from rural areas and maintain a rural nexus, Montoya goes on to note that the state has not been able to integrate most of these migrants into the economic life of the nation, other than on the lowest rungs; they lead a fragile existence in the shantytowns of the major cities. Using the model of the 'house economy' versus the 'corporate economy' introduced by Stephen Gudeman and Alberto Rivera (1990), Montoya goes on to argue that the shantytown dwellers that make up the core of Chavez' supporters have a basically rural, 'house' view of economic life, where thrift and 'making do' with meagre resources are valued survival strategies. They are suspicious of market exchange, where they seldom hold the upper hand. Thus, Chavez' rhetoric, which first emphasized traditional country values, savings in the public sector, and fighting corruption held a strong appeal for these groups, and their basically anti-market, domestic values remain an important tool for Chavez as he attempts to consolidate his power.

Michele Micheletti takes another approach to morality and market, contributing a thorough assessment of the market as an arena for political action via political consumerism. Pointing out that money and politics have always been intermingled, with political parties positioning themselves on an ideological continuum based on wealth and monetary distribution, she goes on to discuss past and present forms of hands-on political action in the marketplace: boycotts, socially responsible investing, labelling schemes, and public discourse. Boycotts are perhaps the best-known way of expressing political will in the marketplace, but socially responsible investing and labelling schemes are increasing in importance; and ranking systems might be added here, as they also aim at directing consumers in one way or another. Discursive political consumerist action, says Micheletti, is growing as a mode of putting pressure on market actors – particularly among the young – and modern methods of communication enable this global conversation to have far-reaching impact.

Micheletti argues that political consumerist action is increasing today because globalization has weakened the ability of states, institutions and other actors to regulate, solve problems, and to assure citizens' welfare. As economic globalization and political globalization move at unequal speeds, regulatory vacuums arise and are taken advantage of by economic actors. Citizens, along with a wide variety of institutions: governmental, semi-governmental, non-governmental and private, leap into the breach. The political landscape changes, offering citizens new opportunities for moral/political engagement. Micheletti notes that the flow of new motivations, agendas, and goals can be seen as part of the process of postmodernization, where basic social values are in flux, moving generally away from efficiency, authority and rationality towards autonomy, diversity and self-expression (Inglehart, 1997: 12). New political-actor categories are being forged, as individuals and organizations innovate ways to exert agency on peoples' lives by intervening with the market.

Strategies and legitimacies in capital flows

Processes of globalization, then, are gradually transforming our worlds. Sometimes the changes are disruptive, uneven, and hotly contested. In other arenas they pass without greater notice, as part of the routines of daily life. In the part on Strategies and Legitimacies in Capital Flows, three anthropologists examine a variety of economic processes which take place in an arena seemingly beyond the influence of, but certainly with considerable impact on, the lives of ordinary citizens: how knowledge is constructed in financial markets, pension plan reform, and currency crises.

Anna Hasselström writes about the different arenas of action in which particular financial market actors – brokers, traders, and analysts – learn their trades, and how they learn to evaluate knowledge. Basing her observations on fieldwork carried out both on and off trading floors in

Stockholm, London and New York, she discusses the ways in which these financial actors are eased into their professions through a period of observation and of learning by doing; how they go about figuring out whom they can trust, and how they gain vital self-confidence, or 'a feel for the market'. She notes that 'learning' is not so much acquiring a fixed structure of knowledge, as it is acquiring an increased access to legitimate participation in the marketplace though the successful enactment of particular roles. Perhaps one could say that novices are thrown headfirst into a fast-moving, aggressive environment into which they are gradually socialized, and learn the social codes of the natives in much the way an anthropologist does in the field. As Hasselström notes, financial market knowledge is learned by engaging with the market – hour after hour, day after day – and it is a knowledge which is rarely discussed or analysed, and neither kept secret nor shared. Like culture, market knowledge seems to be something free for the taking, and regarded by practitioners as a given. Perhaps this method of socialization also gives market actors their air of chutzpah and hubris – having been socialized into the financial world, they have a difficult time stepping back and questioning it.

The pension plan reforms that are currently being debated and gradually implemented in various countries across Europe are the theme of Lindh de Montoya's chapter. She focuses on the situation in Sweden, which was one of the first countries to reform a generous state pension system due to demographic pressures. As birth rates fall and people choose to retire earlier in their lives, pension systems need to be adjusted to reflect the changing economic base for paying them out. Changes can be implemented in a variety of different ways, however, and the new schemes that take shape are a reflection of ideologies, abilities, and particular political and economic conjunctures. In Sweden, brutal pension cuts were implemented behind the scenes with little public discussion, while the media focused on the introduction of a mutual fund investment segment of the basically pay-as-you go state plan. At the end of the 1990s, at a time of rising stock market valuations, Swedes were given the opportunity to choose a number of funds in which to invest a part of their accumulated pension capital, and they were encouraged to take an active role in this process, rather than allowing the state to make the choice for them. Activity in the scheme has not been high, however, and Lindh de Montoya discusses the reasons for this, based on her earlier research on those Swedes who invest in the stock market. The abstract nature of mutual funds and the fact that they are run by experts who are regarded as having superior knowledge makes fund investing very different from investing in individual stocks, and is thus more difficult for people to engage with.

Peebles' contribution brings the part to an end with more ethnography from Sweden, a discussion of the Swedish currency crisis that took place in the early 1990s. Through careful attention to what was written in the Swedish and foreign press during and after the crisis, he is able to unravel some of the meanings that money, as national currency, holds; and he shows how the power over these meanings is in flux.

As devaluation fears brought the Swedish krona under pressure repeatedly between 1990 and 1992, capital flowed out of the country. A series of metaphors were invoked in the national press – the krona was 'sick', it needed a 'cure', and 'medicine' had to be swallowed. Peebles points out that countries fighting over (or for) the value of their money are often negotiating other things as well, in these confrontations. As is generally the case in currency crises, the Swedish economy was struggling in the beginning of the 1990s. The crisis was one important element that enabled the more conservative government then in power to rush a series of crisis packages through the legislature, making important inroads on the 'welfare state' that its citizens value highly. And the welfare model, once challenged, was further contested in coming years, as Lindh de Montoya shows in her chapter on pension reform.

Confidence – in the currency and the state that issues it – was viewed by Swedes as being the crucial underlying factor that would make or break the krona. If the Swedish state could convince the world that they would never devaluate, the krona would maintain its value; but this, however, also meant convincing the population, and the political parties representing them, that the economic sacrifices necessary were legitimate. Most interesting, perhaps, is the silence that Peebles remarks upon; the way in which the opposition parties went along with the government's interpretation of the situation and their unprecedented budget cuts, and how the financial sector backed up the government policy. While Swedes are known for trying to establish consensus and avoiding open conflict, the united front that was maintained in the political and financial is surprising, considering the fact that there was substantial criticism from abroad and, many who, in retrospect, voiced the doubts they had about the policy. In the end, those who could act on their doubts did, and some of the larger Swedish companies (either intentionally or inadvertently) were able to profit from the crisis. Large sums of money changed hands, from the public to the private sectors. Peebles notes that while national currencies build barriers, capital breaks them down; and placed in between the exigencies of state and those of the economic rationality demanded by capital, financial actors voted with capital. Thereby, says Peebles, the national government's hegemony over currency value ended; and indeed, since the 1990s the idea that governments are subordinate to markets has become quite commonplace.

All in all, the contributors to this volume wish to show how markets matter, how markets are used by people in a variety of settings, and how social ties and patterns of culture influence and fashion people's engagements with markets. In a Postscript, Garsten and Hasselström propose that we move beyond the fictive notion of *Homo Economicus*, by asking: Who are the actors involved in the fashioning of markets? They do so by introducing the idea of *Homo Mercans* as a way of understanding the contemporary construction of markets and market actors, and by discussing the ways in which market man is entangled in market processes. Compared with *Homo Economicus, Homo Mercans* has a greater repertoire of alternative actions to choose from. *Homo Mercans* also calculates, but, it is not always predictable what kind of calculation *Homo Mercans* makes – it is not necessarily always an instrumental one.

Into the future

What, then, can one absorb from a reading of these analyses of modern market processes? We think that one conclusion is that we are living through fascinating economic times, with several streams of change in full progress. Planned economies fell by the wayside in the 1990s and some variety of capitalism became the economic system instituted across most of the globe, but as capitalism 'wins' as a system, it is coming under increasing challenges from different quarters, and by democratic means. Garsten (this volume) shows us how the large actors in the market, the corporations, are finding that they have to respond to calls for a responsibility to society, and that they may have a larger role to play, one which can also strengthen their sales, image, and brand. The recent movements to increase the transparency of companies – especially in the wake of financial disasters such as those at Enron and Worldcom – are another aspect of change in the corporate world, with citizens taking action to protect their interests by regulating companies' operations. To these efforts are added those of the political consumers that Micheletti writes about in her chapter. These consumers are using a variety of organizations, market actions and discourse to regulate business, and to inform and awake consumers worldwide. The environmental movement is another loose grouping that frequently actively challenges current morals and practices of capitalism, and other market-related social trends that carry the potential to change our lives are those that impact peoples' working lives, such as more flexible workplaces and terms and conditions. On the other hand, Peebles shows how markets – in this case the financial market – can act against states, requiring certain market-friendly policies to be in place if they are to be granted legitimacy. Thus we see how states, markets, companies and consumers are enmeshed in conflicts and compromises that are shifting lines of responsibility and power, and new models for how relationships should look are coming into being.

In an article discussing the problem of visualizing modernity, Björn Wittrock (2000: 37) suggests that it is grounded in conceptual changes that have occurred throughout history, and are brought about through institutional projects premised on new assumptions about human beings' rights and agency. The conceptual changes he discusses have their origins deep in history – one example being the separation of the church and the state. The issues we are struggling over today as we attempt to demarcate the frontiers of state, market, and citizens' rights do have their origin far in the past. Wittrock introduces the concept of 'promissory notes'; or generalized reference points which arise through public debates, affiliation formation, and the emergence of new institutional forms. They show how conceptual shifts regarding relationships between the state and the market, the individual and the community may take place, as proposals about the nature of man and society navigate around such generally held assumptions and expectations, or arise in confrontations with them. Departing from Wittrock's perspective, perhaps one could say that the 'promissory notes' having to do with the relationships between individuals, communities, and capital are still under negotiation, and the norms and doctrines that we will take for granted one day are in the process of being established. Some of them have to do with the potential and the limits of markets.

References

Abolafia, M. 1996. *Making Markets: Opportunism and Restraint on Wall Street.* Cambridge, MA: Harvard University Press.
Addo, Michael K. 1999. 'Human rights and transnational corporations – an introduction'. In M. K. Addo (ed), *Human Rights Standards and the Responsibility of Transnational Corporations*. The Hague: Kluwer Law International, 1–20.

Aull Davies, Charlotte. 1999. *Reflexive Ethnography: A Guide to Researching Selves and Others*. London. Routledge.

Bauman, Zygmunt. 1995. *Life in Fragments: Essays in Postmodern Morality*. Oxford: Blackwell.

Bauman, Zygmunt. 2000. *Liquid Modernity*. Cambridge: Polity.

Bourdieu, Pierre. 1990. *The Logic of Practice*. Stanford: Stanford University Press.

Callon, Michel, ed. 1998. *The Laws of the Markets*. Oxford: Blackwell Publishers.

Carrier, James, ed. 1997. *Meanings of the Market: The Free Market in Western Culture*. Oxford: Berg.

Carrier, James and David Miller, eds. 1998. *Virtualism: A New Political Economy*. Oxford: Berg

Clifford, James and George E, Marcus, eds. 1986. *Writing Culture: The Poetics and Politics of Ethnography*. Berkeley: University of California Press.

Cochoy, Franck 1998. 'Another discipline for the market economy: marketing as a performative knowledge and know-how for capitalism'. In M. Callon (ed.), *The Laws of the Market*. Oxford: Blackwell, 94–221.

De Grazia, Victoria, ed. 1996. *The Sex of Things: Gender and Consumption in Historical Perspective*. Berkeley: University of California Press.

Featherstone, Mike. 1991. *Consumer Culture and Postmodernism*. Newbury Park, CA: Sage.

Fligstein, Neil. 2001. *The Architecture of Markets: An Economic Sociology of Twenty-First-Century Capitalist Societies*. Princeton: Princeton University Press.

Garsten, Christina and Anna Hasselström. 2003. 'Risky business: discourses of risk and (ir)responsibility in globalizing markets'. *Ethnos* 68(2): 249–70.

Granovetter, Mark. 1985. 'Economic action and social structure: the problem of embeddedness'. *American Journal of Sociology* 91(3): 481–510.

Gudeman, Stephen. 1986. *Economics as Culture: Models and Metaphors of Livelihood*. London: Routledge and Kegan Paul.

Gudeman, Stephen. 2001. *The Anthropology of Economy*. Oxford: Blackwell Publishers.

Gudeman, Stephen and Alberto Rivera. 1990. *Conversations in Colombia: The Domestic Economy in Life and Text*. London: Routledge & Kegan Paul.

Gupta, Akhil and James Ferguson, eds. 1997. *Anthropological Locations*. Berkeley: University of California Press.

Gustafsson, Claes. 1994. *Produktion av allvar: Om det ekonomiska förnuftets metafysik* [*The Production of Seriousness: About the Metaphysics of Economic Reason*]. Stockholm: Nerenius & Santérus Förlag.

Hägglund, Peter. 2000. 'The value of facts: how analysts' recommendations focus on facts instead of value'. In H. Kalthoff, R. Rottenburg and H.-J. Wagenes (eds), *ökonomie und Geschellschaft, Jahrbuch 16 – Facts and Figures: Economic Representations and practices*. Marburg: Metropolis Verlag, 313–37.

Hägglund, Peter. 2001. *Företaget som investeringsobjekt: hur placerare och analytiker arbetar med att ta fram ett investeringsobjekt* [*The company as object for investment: how investors and analysts work to create an investment opportunity*]. Stockholm: EFI, Stockholm School of Economics.

Hannerz, Ulf. 1992. *Cultural Complexity: Studies in the Social Organization of Meaning*. New York: Colombia University Press.

Hannerz, Ulf. 1996. *Transnational Connections: Culture, People, Places*. London: Routledge.

Hart, Keith. 2001. *Money in an Unequal World*. London: Thompson Texere.

Hasselström, Anna. 2003. *On and Off the Trading Floor: An Inquiry into the Everyday Fashioning of Financial Market Knowledge*. Doctoral dissertation, Department of Social Anthropology, Stockholm University.

Hertz, Ellen. 1998. *The Trading Crowd: An Ethnography of the Shanghai Stock Market*. Cambridge: Cambridge University Press.

Howes, David, ed. 1996. *Cross-Cultural Consumption: Global Markets, Local Realities*. London: Routledge.

Inglehart, Ronald 1997. *Modernization and Postmodernization: Cultural, Economic, and Political Change in 43 Societies*. Princeton: Princeton University Press.

Knorr Cetina, Karin and Urs Bruegger. 2000. 'The market as an object of attachment: exploring post-social relations in financial markets'. *Canadian Journal of Sociology* 25(2): 141–68.

Knorr Cetina, Karin and Urs Bruegger. 2002a. 'Global microstructures: the virtual societies of financial markets'. *American Journal of Sociology* 107(4): 905–50.

Knorr Cetina, Karin and Urs Bruegger. 2002b. 'Inhabiting technology: the global lifeform of financial markets'. Paper prepared for *Current Sociology*.

Lien, Marianne. 1997. *Marketing and Modernity: An Ethnography of Marketing Practice*. London: Berg.

Malefyt, Timothy and Brian Moeran, eds. 2003. *Advertising Cultures*. Oxford: Berg.

Marcus, George and Michael J. Fischer, eds. 1986. *Anthropology as Cultural Critique*. Chicago: The University of Chicago Press.

Mauss, Marcel. 1954 [1924]. *The Gift*. Transl. Ian Cunnison. London: Cohen & West.

Miyazaki, Hirokazu and Annelise Riles. Forthcoming 2004. 'Failure as an endpoint'. In Aihwa Ong and Stephen Collier (eds), *Global Assemblages: Technology, Politics, and Ethics as Anthropological Problems*. London: Blackwell. Chapter 17.

Miller, Daniel. 1997. *Capitalism: An Ethnographic Approach*. Oxford: Berg.

Miller, Daniel. 2001. *The Dialectics of Shopping*. London: University of Chicago Press.

Moeran, Brian. 1996. *A Japanese Advertising Agency: An Anthropology of Media and Markets*. London: Curzon.

Moeran, Brian. 2000. 'The split account system and Japan's advertising industry'. *International Journal of Advertising* 19: 185–200.

Norberg, P. 2001. *Finansmarknadens amoralitet och det kalvinska kyrkorummet. En studie i ekonomisk mentalitet och etik*. Doctoral Dissertation. Stockholm: EFI, Stockholm School of Economics.

Olwig, Karen Fog and Kirsten Hastrup, eds. 1997. *Siting Culture*. London: Routledge.

Ortner, Sherry B. 1997. 'Fieldwork in the postcommunity'. *Anthropology and Humanism*, 22(1): 61–80.

Palan, Ronen. 2000. 'New trends in global political economy'. In R. Palan (ed.) *Global Political Economy: Contemporary Theories*, London: Routledge, 1–18.

Parry, Jonathan P. and Maurice Bloch, eds. 1989. *Money and the Morality of Exchange*. Cambridge: Cambridge University Press.

Plattner, Stuart. 1989a. 'Markets and marketplaces'. In S. Plattner (ed.), *Economic Anthropology*. Stanford: Stanford University Press, 171–208.

Plattner, Stuart. 1989b. 'Economic behavior in markets'. In S. Plattner (ed.), *Economic Anthropology*. Stanford: Stanford University Press, 209–21.

Polanyi, Karl. 1944. *The Great Transformation.* New York: Farrar & Rinehart.
Polanyi, Karl. 1957. *Trade and Market in the Early Empires: Economies in History and Theory.* New York: Free Press.
Rapp, Reyna and Jane Schneider, eds. 1995. *Articulating Hidden Histories: Exploring the Influence of Eric R. Wolf.* Berkeley: University of California Press.
Sahlins, Marshall. 1974. *Stone Age Economics.* London: Tavistock.
Shore, Cris. 2000. *Building Europe: the Cultural Politics of European Integration.* London: Routledge.
Slater, Don. 1997. *Consumer Culture and Modernity.* Cambridge: Polity Press.
Taussig, Michael. 1980. *The Devil and Commodity Fetishism in South America.* Chapel Hill, NC: University of North Carolina Press.
Wittrock, Björn. 2000. 'Multiple modernities'. *Daedalus* 129(1): 31–60.

Part I
Consumers and Marketing

2
Marketing Ethnography: Disciplines and Practices

Brian Moeran

As Marianne Lien (1997: 11) noted some years ago, marketing is both a discipline and a practice. As a discipline, it might be defined most simply, perhaps, as 'the art or science of most efficiently relating production to consumption through distribution' (de Groot, 1980: 4), although there are plenty of alternative views.[1] As practice, it has been defined by the American Marketing Association as: 'The process of planning and executing the conception, pricing, promotion, and distribution of ideas, goods, and services to create exchanges that satisfy the perceived needs, wants and objectives of the customer and the organization' (Wells, Burnett and Moriarty, 2000: 62). In marketing-speak, this is summarized as 'customer satisfaction through product market harmonization' (Kotler, 1986: 3).

Anthropology and marketing (together with consumer research) were described a few years ago as 'linchpin disciplines in parallel intellectual domains' (Sherry, 1995: 10). To judge from the prevalent literature, however, this view is not shared by many anthropologists, who tend to look at markets (for example, Carrier, 1997) rather than at marketing *per se* (Lien, 1997 is the obvious exception here). For their part, marketers, always open to new ideas, have over the decades made use – albeit eclectic (de Groot, 1980: 131) – of the work of anthropologists such as Claude Lévi-Strauss (1966, 1969) and Mary Douglas (1973), even though the latter's aims when they put forward their theories of binary opposition, totemism, and grid and group were far removed from the endeavour of marketing both as a discipline and as practice. Can anthropology really be of use to marketing? Can the discipline market itself as an effective potential contributor to solve the problems faced by marketing people in their practices? There is no reason why it should not. After all, anthropologists of material culture study the relationship between people and things, in much the same way that marketers analyse target audiences and commodities. Economic anthropologists, too, have long been interested in notions of reciprocity and exchange that underpin markets (cf., among many others, Parry and Bloch, 1989). It is they who point out that there is more than one kind of market and that these markets, like the free market beloved by economists, are all sociocultural constructions. In this respect, what they have to say about the social costs of markets, as well as about the non-market social institutions upon which markets depend and the social contexts that shape them (cf. Carruthers and Babb, 2000: 219–22), should be of great relevance to marketers anxious to come up with definitive answers about why certain people buy certain products and how to persuade the rest of the world to do so.

The fact that marketing people in general do *not* pay all that much attention to current developments in anthropology, however, suggests one of two things. Either marketers prefer not to think about anthropology because its fieldwork method of participant observation tends to lay bare how anthropologists arrive at understandings and analyses of people interacting that marketers prefer to keep to themselves. If their clients really knew what marketers did not know about consumers, their wants, needs and desires, they might get a bit of a shock. Or anthropology may *not* be able to be of direct use to marketing practices at all.

We might start, therefore, by asking what the similarities and differences between these two groups of professionals are. As Timothy Malefyt and I have outlined in the introduction to a recent book (Malefyt and Moeran, 2003), what both anthropologists and marketers have to say is driven by experience, politically mediated, historically situated and shaped by specific practices in their respective traditions. Both zigzag back and forth between the observation of situations and theoretical reasoning, as they try to make sense of what does not immediately make sense and pass on their understandings to others (academic peers and clients) who in one way or another then vet their analyses. Both thus make a living by trying to convince their clients that they know how the 'natives' think and, in so doing, present a front of hard assurance in which their findings are 'results'.

Such 'results' are obtained through fieldwork, or what is often nowadays and imprecisely referred to as 'ethnography', and it is fieldwork that underpins this particular study of marketing practices in Japan. In spite of its apparent practical imprecision, in spite of all the differing inter-pretations of what it should be, so-called 'ethnography' drives both the disciplines and the practices of anthropology and marketing. It is, therefore, worth examining theoretically, and seeing what kind of results it produces in practice. The fact that my own experiences in the marketing 'field' – which have included studies of department stores' cultural marketing and women's international fashion magazines, as well as the advertising agency described here – have convinced me of the value of 'ethnography'. That should explain the *double entendre* of this chapter's title.

Anthropology has always put great emphasis on fieldwork as *the* most important and effective way to go about finding out how and why a particular collectivity of people does what it does. For marketers, too, 'ethnography' has become a fashionable, catch-all buzzword that suggests an imprecise – though hinting at 'quality' and 'depth' – upgrading of their consumer research. Ethnography is thus part of marketers' persuasive strategy, as they present 'objective', scientific, and speedy results. They see ethnography as a tool for conducting essentially quantitative research and analysis. To anthropologists, however, things appear rather different. Ethnography has become a qualitative experience that cannot ultimately be systematized or properly structured. Yet, in spite of these differences in approach to their research, both groups of professionals engage in interpretation of the data that they gather during the course of their ethnographic practices.

One major difference in the kinds of ethnography practised by anthropologists and marketers, therefore, is related to the time spent 'in the field'. Anthropologists believe in the value of long-term immersion in the lives of those whom they are studying – a luxury that marketers can never afford in their world of rushed projects and immediate deadlines. As a result, the latter never really get to know what it is like 'being there' (Watson, 1999). In the eyes of the anthropologist, marketers do not have the opportunity to distinguish between what people say they do and what they actually do. Because of the constraints of time and the pressing need to meet deadlines, they are unable to build up a sense of mutual trust, or to move with ease from formality to informality, from observation to participation, and from mere enactment to both enactment and embodiment, during the course of their interaction with their informants.

There are other differences between the two groups. Marketers need results that are oriented to action, not to ivory tower contemplation. To this end, they usually work as a team, unlike the lone anthropologist who rarely (unless engaged in applied anthropology) enters into the kind of collaborative fieldwork, discussions, analyses, and negotiations conducted by marketers. Moreover, the kind of knowledge developed by marketers tends to be cutting edge, sophisticated and much more aware of social and cultural change. This can lead to their constructing, rather than merely reflecting, social groups (like yuppies, generation X or, in Japan, the *shinjinrui* 'new breed') in their interaction with clients. The fact that they may also shape and direct consumer information to achieve marketing and inter-personal ends would make most anthropologists – determined to maintain their own reflective representations of someone or something 'out there' – cringe.

I include such reflections here because, personally, I am convinced that anthropologists and marketers should be talking more to one another. Each group has much to learn from the other and to adopt as part of its own practices. In the rest of this essay, therefore, I want to make use of my own fieldwork experience to analyse the marketing practices that I witnessed during a year spent in a large advertising agency in Japan. My aims are many and reveal, I think, the complexity of anthropological analysis based on extensive ethnography. Some of my findings are related to the social organization of an advertising industry and of the institutions that comprise it. Others are concerned with the curious mix of economic, artistic and personal factors that pervade advertising and other 'creative industries' (Caves, 2000). Hopefully, I will take a few tentative steps towards developing a comparative theory of advertising as a marketing system (cf. Arnould, 1995: 110), even though my research is based on the cultural relativity of a specific set of marketing practices in one Japanese advertising agency.

The discipline, organization and practice of marketing

The Marketing Division is the engine room of the Japanese advertising agency in which I conducted my research in 1990. At the time, this agency handled more than 600 accounts a year, their value varying from only a few thousand to several million dollars. The Marketing Division was almost invariably involved in some way in the ad campaigns, cultural and sporting events, merchandising opportunities, special promotions, POP (Point of Purchase) constructions, and various other activities that the agency carried out on behalf of its clients. Exceptions were those accounts involving media placement or certain kinds of work expressly requested by a client – like, for example, the organization of a national sales force meeting for a car manufacturer. Even here, however, there was often information that could be usefully relayed back to the Marketing Division (the number and regional distribution of the manufacturer's sales representatives, as well as possible advance information on new products and/or services to be offered in the coming year).

The main aims of the Agency's Marketing Division as both discipline and practice were (and, of course, still are): firstly, to acquire as much information as possible from *consumers* about their clients' products and services; secondly, to acquire as much information as possible, too, from *clients* about their own products and services; and, thirdly, to use *strategically* both kinds of information acquired to develop new accounts. In a number of important respects, marketing provided those working in the Marketing Division with the *dispassionate* data that account executives needed in their *personal* networking with (potential) clients whom they cajoled, persuaded, impressed and pleaded with to part with (more) money.

In order to achieve the three overall objectives outlined above, the Agency established a certain set of organizational features to enable marketing practice to take place. Firstly, the Marketing Division, which at the time consisted of almost 90 members, was structured into three separate, but interlocking, sub-divisions. These consisted of Computer Systems; Market Development and Merchandising; and Marketing.[2]

The last was itself sub-divided into three departments, each of which was broken down into three or four sections.[3] Sections were managed by Section Heads (SH) who reported to their Department Head (DH), who in turn reported with other department heads to the Divisional Chief. Each section consisted of between six and a dozen members who worked in teams of two to three on an account under the guidance of their SH. These teams were not fixed. Thus one member, A, might work with another, B, under the Section Leader (SH) on a contact lens advertising campaign, but find herself assigned to work with C under the SH on an airline company's business class service account, and with D under the SH on a computer manufacturer's consumer survey. In this respect, the daily life of members of the Marketing Department was similar to that of product managers described by Lien (1997: 69), who described their work as involving 'frequent shifts from one activity to another, a wide network of communications, and a considerable amount of time spent in meetings or talking on the telephone'.

Secondly, tasks (or accounts) were allocated *formally* through the hierarchical divisional structure – by departments first, then by sections – according to their existing responsibilities and perceived suitability for the job in hand. Each SH then distributed these tasks to individual members on the basis of their current overall workloads. At the same time, however, there was an *informal* allocation of accounts involving individuals. Each SH or DH could take on a job directly from account executives (AEs) handling particular accounts on behalf of their clients. Here, prior experiences and personal contacts were important influences on AEs' decisions as to whether to go through formal or informal channels of recruitment.[4] The account executive in charge of the NFC contact lens campaign described below (see also Moeran, 1996), for example, went directly to a particular SH in the Marketing Department because of some smart work that the latter had done for the AE on a different account some months previously. Mutual respect had been established and the contact lens campaign provided both parties with an opportunity to assess and, in the event, positively validate their working relationship.

There were certain organizational advantages to the ways in which accounts were distributed in the manner described here. Firstly, by freely permitting interpersonal relations between account executives and marketers, the Agency ensured that there was competitiveness at each structural level of department and section. Such competition was felt to be healthy for the Agency as a whole, and to encourage its continued growth. Secondly, by assigning individual members of each section in the Marketing Department to accounts involving different combinations of people in different tasks, the Agency ensured that each member of the Marketing Department received training in a wide variety of marketing problems. It also obliged each to interact fully with fellow section members, thereby promoting a sense of co-operation, cohesion and mutual understanding (vital prerequisites in the organization of Japanese companies generally). This in itself meant that each section developed the broadest possible shared knowledge of marketing issues, because of the knowledge gained by individual members and the interaction among them.

And now let us turn to marketing practice. Accounts were won by the Agency primarily through the liaison work conducted with a (potential) client by an account executive (who might be a very senior manager or junior 'salesman' recruited only a few years earlier). Once an agreement was made between Agency and client – and such an agreement might be limited to the Agency's participation in a competitive presentation, the outcome of which might then lead to an account being established – the AE concerned would put together an account team. This usually consisted of the AE in charge (possibly with assistants); the Marketing Team (generally of two persons under a Marketing Director [MD], but sometimes much larger, depending on the size of the account and the work to be done); the Creative Team (consisting of Creative Director

[CD], Copywriter, and Art Director [AD] as a minimum, but usually including two ADs – one for print-, the other for TV-related work); and Media Planner/Buyer(s).

The job of the account team was to carry out successfully the task set by the client. To this end, it would meet initially for an orientation meeting in which the issues and problems faced by the client were explained by the AE before being discussed by all concerned.[5] Prior to this, however, the AE would have provided the marketing team with all the information and data that he had been able to extract from the client (a lot of it highly confidential to the company concerned). The marketing team, therefore, tended to come prepared and to have certain quite specific questions regarding the nature of the statistics provided, the target market, retail outlets, and other factors directly relating to the advertising campaign on which they had embarked. If it had done its homework properly – which was not always the case, given the number of different accounts on which the team's members were working and the pressure of work that they were under – the marketing team often had several pertinent suggestions for further research.

It was on the basis of these discussions that the AE then used to ask the MD to carry out such research as he thought necessary for the matter in hand. In the meantime, the creative team was asked to mull over the issues generally and to think of possible ways of coping 'creatively' (that is, linguistically and visually) with the client's marketing problems.

Back in the Marketing Department, the MD would tell his subordinates to carry out specific tasks, such as a consumer survey to find out who precisely makes use of a particular product and why. This kind of task was fairly mechanical in its general form – since the Agency did this sort of work for dozens of clients every year – but had to be tailored to the present client's particular situation, needs and expectations. The MD would therefore discuss what had to be done with his subordinates, make some suggestions to ensure that all points were covered (and that might well include some additional questions to elicit further information from the target audience that had taken on importance during their discussion), and then give them permission to have the work carried out.

All surveys of this kind were subcontracted by the Agency to marketing firms and research organizations of one sort or another. This meant that the marketing team's members were rarely involved in direct face-to-face contact or interaction with the consumers of the products that they wished to advertise,[6] *except* when small 'focus group' interviews took place (usually in one of the Agency's buildings).[7] The informal nature of such groups, the different kinds of insights that they could yield, and the need to spot and pursue particular comments meant that members of the marketing team had to be present to listen to and, as warranted, direct the discussion so that the Agency's particular objectives were achieved. In general, however, the only evidence of consumers in the Agency was indirect, through reports, statistics, figures, data analyses and other information that, paradoxically, were always seen to be insufficient or 'incomplete' (cf. Lien, 1997: 112). It was by adding new marketing data to this information that the Agency sought to differentiate itself from its competitors and thereby to establish its own market niche in the advertising industry.

Once the results of the survey were returned, the marketers used to enter them into their computers (since all such information was stored and could be used to generate comparative data for other accounts as and when required). They could make use of particular programmes to sort and analyse such data, but ultimately they needed to be able to present their results in readily comprehensible form to other members of the account team. Here again, the MD tended to ensure that the information presented at the next meeting was to the point and properly hierarchized in terms of importance. This led to the marketing team's putting forward things like: a positioning statement, slogan, purchasing decision model (high/low involvement; think/feel product relationship), product message concept, and creative frame.

One of the main objectives of this initial – and, if properly carried out, only – round of research was to discover the balance between what were termed product, user and end benefits, since it was these factors that determined the way in which an ad campaign was to be presented. This in turn directed the creative team in terms of how it should visualize the marketing problems analysed and cope with ensuing suggestions from the marketing team.

It is here that we come to the crux of marketing as practised in an advertising agency (whether in Japan or elsewhere). Creative people tended to be suspicious of marketing people and vice versa.[8] This was primarily because marketers believed that they worked rationally and that the creative frames that they produced were founded on objective data and analyses. Creative people, for their part, believed that their work should be 'inspired', and that such inspiration could take the place of the data and analyses provided for their consideration.

As a result, when it came to producing creative work for an ad campaign, copywriters and creative directors tended not to pay strict attention to what the marketing team had told them. For example, attracted by the idea of a particular celebrity or filming location, they would on occasion come up with ideas that in no way met the pragmatic demands of a particular ad campaign requiring emphasis on product benefits which were irrelevant to the chosen location or celebrity suggested for endorsement. This did not always happen, of course. A good and professional creative team – and such teams were not infrequent – would follow the marketing team's instructions. In such cases, their success was based on a creative interpretation of the data and analyses provided.

If there was some indecision and argument among different elements of the account team – and it was the presiding account executive's job to ensure that marketers and creatives did not come to blows over their disagreements – they almost invariably banded together when meeting and presenting their plans to the client. Such meetings used to take place several – even more than a dozen – times during the course of an account team's preparations for an ad campaign. At most of them the MD would be present, until such time as it was clear that the client had accepted the Agency's campaign strategy and the creative team had to fine-tune the objectives outlined therein. Very often, therefore, the marketing team would not stay on a particular account long enough to learn of its finished result, although a good AE would keep his MD abreast of creative developments and show him the (near) finalized campaign prior to the client's final approval. But marketers did not get involved in the production side of a campaign (studio photography, television commercial filming, and so on) – unless one of those concerned knew what was going on when, happened to be nearby at the time, and dropped in to see how things were going. In other words, the marketing team's job was to see a project through until accepted by the client. It would then dissolve and its members would be assigned to new accounts.

Advertising campaigns: a case study

To illustrate in more detail particular examples of marketing practice in the Agency, let me describe, as a case study, the preparation of a contact lens campaign in Japan. This example is illuminating because it reveals a number of typical problems faced by an advertising agency in the formulation and execution of campaigns on behalf of its clients. These include the interface between marketing and creative people within an agency and the interpretation of marketing analysis and data; the trans-position of marketing analysis into 'creative' (for example, linguistic, visual and design) ideas; the interface between agency and client in the 'selling' of a campaign proposal; and the problems of having to appeal to more than one 'consumer' target.

When the Nihon Fibre Corporation asked the Agency to prepare an advertising campaign for its new *Ikon Breath O$_2$* oxygen-passing GCL hard contact lenses in early 1990, it provided a considerable amount of product information with which to help and guide those concerned. This information included the following facts: firstly, with a differential coefficient (DK factor) of 150, *Ikon Breath O$_2$* had the highest rate of oxygen permeation of all lenses currently manufactured and marketed in Japan. As a result, secondly, *Ikon Breath O$_2$* was the first lens authorized for continuous wear by Japan's Ministry of Health. Thirdly, the lens was particularly flexible, dirt and water resistant, durable, and of extremely high quality.

The client asked the Agency to confirm that the targeted market consisted of young people and to create a campaign that would help NFC capture initially a minimum 3 per cent share of the market, rising to 10 per cent over three years. The Agency immediately formed an account team, consisting of eight members all told.[9] Their first step was to arrange for the marketing team to carry out its own consumer research before proceeding further. A detailed survey – of 500 men and women – was worked out in consultation with the account executive and the client, and was executed by a market research company subcontracted by the Agency. Results confirmed that the targeted audience for the *Ikon Breath O$_2$* advertising campaign should be young people, but particularly young women, between the ages of 18 and 25 years, since it was they who were most likely to wear contact lenses.

At the same time, however, the survey also revealed that there was little brand loyalty among contact lens wearers so that, with effective advertising, it should be possible to persuade users to shift from their current brand to *Ikon Breath O$_2$* lenses. It also showed that young women were not overly concerned with price provided that lenses were safe and comfortable to wear, which meant that *Ikon Breath O$_2$*'s comparatively high price in itself should not prove a major obstacle to brand switching or sales.

On a less positive note, however, the account team also discovered that users were primarily concerned with comfort and were not interested in the technology that went into the manufacture of contact lenses (thereby obviating the apparent advantage of *Ikon Breath O$_2$*'s high DK factor of which NFC was so proud); and that, because almost all contact lens users consulted medical specialists prior to purchase, the advertising campaign would have to address a second audience consisting mainly of middle-aged men.

All in all, therefore, *Ikon Breath O$_2$* lenses had an advantage in being of superb quality, approved by medical experts and recognized, together with other GCL lenses, as being the safest for one's eyes. Its disadvantages were that NFC had no 'name' in the contact lens market and that users knew very little about GCL lenses or contact lenses in general. This meant that the advertising campaign had to be backed up by point of purchase sales promotion (in the form of a brochure) to ensure that the product survived. Moreover, it was clear that *Ikon Breath O$_2$*'s technical advantage (the DK 150 factor) would not last long because rival companies would soon be able to make lenses with a differential coefficient that surpassed that developed by NFC.

As a result of intense discussions following this survey, the account team moved slowly towards what it thought should be as the campaign's overall 'tone and manner'. Ideally, advertisements should be information-oriented: the campaign needed to put across a number of points about the special product benefits that differentiated it from similar lenses on the market (in particular, its flexibility and high rate of oxygen-permeation). Practically, however – as the marketing team had to emphasize time and time again – the campaign needed to stress the functional and emotional benefits that users would obtain from wearing *Ikon Breath O$_2$* lenses (for example, continuous wear, safety, release from anxiety and so on). This meant that the advertising itself should be emotional (and information left to the promotional brochure) and stress the end benefits to consumers, rather than the lenses' product benefits.

Because the marketing team had concluded that the product's end benefits should be stressed, the copywriter and the art director opted for user imagery rather than product characteristics when thinking of ideas for copy and visuals. However, they were thwarted in their endeavours by a number of problems.

Firstly, advertising industry self-policing regulations prohibited the use of certain words and images (for example, the notion of 'safety', plus a visual of someone asleep while wearing contact lenses), and insisted on the inclusion in all advertising of a warning that the *Ikon Breath O$_2$* lens was a medical product that should be purchased through a medical specialist. This constriction meant that the creative team could not use the idea of 'continuous wear' because, even though so certified by Japan's Ministry of Health, opticians and doctors were generally of the opinion that *Ikon Breath O$_2$* lenses were bound to affect individual wearers in different ways. NFC was terrified of antagonizing the medical world which would often be recommending its product, so the product manager concerned refused to permit the use of any word or visual connected with 'continuous wear'. Thus, to the account team's collective dismay, the product's end benefit to consumers could not be effectively advertised.

Secondly, precisely because *Ikon Breath O₂* lenses had to be recommended by medical specialists, NFC's advertising campaign needed to address the latter as well as young women users. In other words, the campaign's tone and manner had to appeal to two totally different segments of the market, while at the same time satisfying those employed in the client company. This caused the creative team immense difficulties, especially because – thirdly – the product manager of NFC's contact lens manufacturing division was convinced that the high differential coefficient set *Ikon Breath O₂* lenses apart from all other contact lenses on the market and would appeal to members of the medical profession. So he insisted on emphasizing what he saw as the unique technological qualities of the product. In other words, not only did he relegate young women who were expected to buy the product to secondary importance; he also ignored the marketing team's recommendation that user benefit be stressed. Instead, for a long time he insisted on the creative team's focusing on product benefit, even though the DK factor was only a marginal and temporary advantage to NFC.

As a result of these two sets of disagreements, the copywriter came up with two different key ideas. The first was based on the product's characteristics, and thus supported the manufacturer's (but went against his own marketing team's) product benefit point of view, with the phrase 'corneal physiology' (*kakumaku seiri*). The second also stressed a feature of the product, but managed to emphasize the user benefits that young women could gain from wearing lenses that were both 'hard' and 'soft' (*yawaraka*).

The former headline was the only way to break brand parity and give *Ikon Breath O₂* a temporary distinction from all other lenses on the market (the product manager liked the distinction; the marketing team disliked the temporary nature of that distinction). At this stage in the negotiations, the account executive in charge felt obliged to tow an obsequious line, but needed to appease his marketing team and ensure that the creative team came up with something else if at all possible, since corneal physiology gave *Ikon Breath O₂* lenses only a temporary advantage. As a result, the copywriter introduced the word 'serious' (*majime*) into discussions – on the grounds that NFC was a 'serious' (*majime*) manufacturer (it was, after all, a well-known and respected Japanese corporation) which had developed a product that, by a process of assimilation, could also be regarded as 'serious'. Moreover, by a further rubbing-off process, as the marketing team agreed, such 'seriousness' could be attributed to users who decided to buy and wear *Ikon Breath O$_2$* lenses. In this way, the distinction between product benefit *and* user benefit might be overcome.

The copywriter's final idea was the one that broke the deadlock (and it was at certain moments an extremely tense deadlock) between the account team as a whole and members of NFC's contact lens manufacturing division. After a series of meetings in which copywriter and designer desperately tried to convince the client that the idea of softness and hardness was not a product characteristic, but an *image* designed to support the benefits to consumers wearing *Ikon Breath O$_2$* lenses, the product manager accepted the account team's proposals in principle, provided that 'serious' was used as a back-up selling point. 'Soft hard' (*yawaraka hard*) was adopted as the key headline phrase for the campaign as a whole.

It can be seen that the marketing team's analysis of how NFC should successfully enter the contact lens market encountered two stumbling blocks during the early stages of preparation for the advertising campaign. The first was within the account team itself, where the copywriter in particular tended to opt for the manufacturer's approach by emphasizing the product benefit of *Ikon Breath O$_2$*. The second was when the Agency's account team had to persuade the client to accept its analysis and campaign proposal. But the next major problem facing the account team was how to convert this linguistic rendering of its market analysis into visual terms. What sort of visual image would adequately fulfil the marketing aims of the campaign *and* make the campaign as a whole – including television commercial and promotional materials – readily recognizable to the targeted audience? It was almost immediately accepted by the account team that the safest way to achieve this important aim was to use a celebrity or personality (*talent* in Japanese) to endorse the product. Here there was little argument, because it is generally recognized in the advertising industry that celebrity endorsement is an excellent and readily appreciated linkage device in multimedia campaigns of the kind requested by NFC. Moreover, since television commercials in Japan are more often than not only 15 seconds long and therefore cannot include any detailed product information, personalities have proved to be attention grabbers in an image-dominated medium and to have a useful, short-term effect on sales because of their popularity in other parts of the entertainment industry. At the same time, not all personalities come across equally well in the rather differing media of television and magazines or newspapers, so that the account team felt obliged to look for someone who was more than a mere pop idol and who could act.

It was here that those concerned encountered the most difficulty. The presence of a famous personality was crucial since s/he would be able to attract public attention to a new product and hopefully draw people into retail outlets to buy *Ikon Breath O₂* lenses. It was agreed right from the start that the personality should be a young Japanese woman, in the same age group as the targeted audience. (After all, a 'blue eyed foreigner' endorsing *Ikon Breath O₂* contact lenses would hardly be appropriate for brown-eyed Japanese.) Just who this woman should be, however, proved problematic. Tennis players (who could indulge in both 'hard' activities and 'soft' romance) were discarded early on because the professional season was already well under way at the time that the campaign was being prepared. Classical musicians, while romantic and thus 'soft', were not seen to be 'hard' enough, while the idea of using a Japanese 'talent', Miyazawa Rie (*every*one on the account team's favourite at the time), was reluctantly rejected because, even though photographs of her in the nude were at the time causing a minor sensation among Japanese men interested in *soft* porn, she was rather inappropriate for a medical product like a contact lens which was aimed at young women.

Any personality chosen had to show certain distinct qualities. One of these was a 'presence' (*sonzaikan*) that would attract people's attention on the page or screen. Another was 'topicality' (*wadaisei*) that stemmed from her professional activities. A third was 'future potential' (*nobisei*), meaning that the celebrity had not yet peaked in her career, but would attract further widespread media attention and so, it was hoped, indirectly promote *Ikon Breath O₂* lenses and NFC. Most importantly, however, she had to suit the product.

In the early stages of the campaign's preparations, the creative team found itself in a slight quandary. It wanted to choose a celebrity whose personality fitted the 'soft-hard' and 'serious' ideas and who would then anchor a particular image to *Ikon Breath O₂* lenses, although it proved difficult to find someone who would fit the product and appeal to *all* those concerned. Eventually, the woman chosen was an actress, Sekine Miho, who epitomized the kind of modern woman that the creative team was seeking, but who was also about to star in a national television (NHK) drama series that autumn – a series in which she played a starring role as a 'soft', romantic character. Although popularity in itself can act as a straightjacket when it comes to celebrity endorsement of a product, in this case it was judged – correctly, it transpired – that Sekine had enough 'depth' (*fukasa*) to bring a special image to *Ikon Breath O₂* lenses.

Once the celebrity had been decided on, the creative team was able to fix the tone and manner, expression and style of the advertising campaign as a whole. Sekine was a 'high-class' (or 'one rank up' in Japanese-English parlance) celebrity who matched NFC's image of itself as a 'high-class' (*ichiryū*) company and who was made to reflect that sense of eliteness in deportment and clothing. At the same time, NFC was a 'serious' manufacturer and wanted a serious, rather than frivolous, personality who could then be photographed in soft-focus, serious poses to suit the serious medical product being advertised. This seriousness was expressed further by means of very slightly tinted black and white photographs which, to the art director's eye (but, not initially, that of the product manager) made Sekine look even 'softer' in appearance and so match the campaign's headline of *yawaraka* hard. This softness was further reinforced by the heart-shaped lens cut at the bottom of every print ad, and on the front of the brochure, which the art director made green rather than blue – partly to differentiate the *Ikon Breath O$_2$* campaign from all other contact lens campaigns run at that time, and partly to appeal to the fad for 'ecological' colours then current among young women in particular.

This case study shows that there is an extremely complex relationship linking marketing and creative aspects of any advertising campaign. In this case, market research showed that *Ikon Breath O$_2$* lenses were special because of the safety that derived from their technical quality, but that consumers themselves were not interested in technical matters since their major concern was with comfort. Hence the need to focus the advertising campaign on user benefit. Yet the client insisted on stressing product benefit – a stance made more difficult for the creative team because it could not legally use the only real consumer benefit available to it (continuous wear), and so had to find something that would appeal to both manufacturer and direct and indirect 'consumers' of the lens in question. In the end, the ideas of 'soft hard' and 'serious' were adopted as compromise positions for both client and agency, as well as for creative and marketing teams.

Advertising, marketing and ethnography

What does this ethnography of marketing practices in a Japanese advertising agency tell us in relation to the three involved disciplines of anthropology, advertising and marketing?

Firstly, there is the sheer richness of the ethnographic data and observations acquired over an extended period of fieldwork in an organization such as the one described here. Sociological analysis of this material reveals a number of interesting organizational features in the Agency and in the industry in which it operates in Japan – features that were directly relevant to the way in which marketing is practised there. For example, the way in which sums of money – or accounts – are distributed affects ongoing relations *between* major players (clients, media and agencies) in the industry. Some of these relations are institutional, others interpersonal. As shown in the case study described here, apparently 'objective' marketing analyses and strategies can be upset by 'subjective' interpersonal relationships upon which so much business organization in general depends. But the distribution of accounts also affects relations *within* an advertising agency. The sheer number of accounts handled by an agency in Japan, where the split- rather than competitive-account system prevails, encourages competitiveness and co-operation among employees, as well as the development of a shared knowledge of marketing issues taken up by the Agency.

The fact that such co-operation and shared knowledge are also seen to be characteristic of Japanese institutions in general suggests that a particular *economic* mechanism may be adopted precisely because it coincides with *cultural* ends. This becomes more than a mere possibility when we find that the split-account system also contributes to an agency's financial stability and the maintenance of a 'permanent' employment system characteristic of (part of) the Japanese corporate system as a whole (cf. Moeran, 2000).

Secondly, the – at times incongruous – relation between economic, artistic and personal objectives found in interaction among members of an account team, as well as between the account team and the client for which it is working, suggests that advertising may be characterized, at least in part, as a 'creative industry'. As such it has a number of common 'properties' (Caves, 2000: 2–10). For a start, as in the film, music, fashion, publishing and other similar industries, demand is uncertain and nobody knows whether a particular product (in this case an advertisement) will in fact 'work' when placed before a consumer. This is why a corporate executive can famously exclaim that he knows that half his money is wasted on advertising, although he doesn't know which half. Market research can be used, of course, to find out about this 'experience good', but still success is unpredictable – whether we are talking about an advertising campaign, art auction, or Hollywood film. This is the *nobody knows* property.

Another common feature is that advertising requires all kinds of different expertise. An account team needs an AE to liaise with the client, a marketing team to conduct the necessary consumer research and analyse the results, a creative team to put marketing messages into linguistic and visual images. But, because advertisements must all attain a certain level of proficiency and conformance, every step along the way to the completion of a campaign must contain all the necessary elements doing their necessary job. An account team cannot function without a marketing analyst or copywriter. This is known as the *motley crew* property.

Then there is the fact that consumers typically compare creative products (this film with that, these paintings with those), which may be quite similar in character, but not identical. As a result, they cannot generally agree which is 'better' as a whole and there may consequently be buyers for all these similar products. This is what permits advertising to flourish in the first place. How often have we heard people arguing the points for and against a particular advertising campaign (that may appeal to men, for example, but infuriate women for its perceived sexism)? This Richard Caves calls the *infinite variety* property.

Cultural products also differ in the quality of skills they display. Some copywriters or television directors are clearly more imaginative than others, some account executives obviously better than others at interacting with clients. Thus, creative industries tend to negotiate a ranking of actors, directors, screenwriters, designers, models, photographers, solo pianists, orchestras, conductors, and so on. This ranking of talent tends to pervade a lot of the conversations taking place among those concerned in the film, fashion or music worlds and gives rise to what is called the *A list/B list* property. In the world of Japanese advertising, the ranking of individuals does not directly lead to different payments for specific work done by those placed in the A list or B list, in the way that it does in – say – the film industry. But it does do so indirectly, since those who are successful at their job are promoted, and promotions bring with them financial advantages. There is also an obvious ranking of corporations (Dentsu, Hakuhodo, Asatsu among agencies) which fits in with a culturally accepted and encouraged 'status gradation of industry' (Clark, 1979).

Finally, creative activities often involve complex teams (the *motley crew* property) who have to co-ordinate their activities temporally. An advertising campaign must be ready by a certain date, and all those with input must be there when needed during the production process. This means that those who can meet a certain production schedule (actors or cameramen in the film industry, for instance) are likely to get the nod over those who are not sure, even though the latter may be preferred candidates for the activity in question. Advertising relies on close temporal co-ordination in the production of a campaign and the prompt realization of revenues (through media placement) to make it economically profitable. This is the *time flies* property, which we have also seen upheld in the allocation of accounts to different members of the Agency's various divisions.

What does this ethnographic analysis tell us about marketing in general? For a start, there is a paradox. The fact that the advertising industry shares with creative industries such as the art, fashion, film, music and publishing worlds, a number of fluid properties that affect its economic outcome, suggests that this kind of marketing practice cannot be treated in the way that its practitioners constantly espouse. In other words, marketing people may aim to be positivist, science-like (rather than scientific, as such), and rationalist in their ad campaigns, but there are factors that prevent this. They may aspire – and to some degree are able – to measure and predict on the basis of observer categories, but this is mainly because they know that this is the simplest way to sell a campaign to a client. Marketers in the Japanese advertising agency also tended to make clear-cut categories that would be easily understood by their colleagues in other divisions in the Agency. These categories broke down the consumer world into a series of binary oppositions (between individual and group, modern and traditional, idealist and materialist, and so on [cf. Lien, 1997: 202–8]), which were then represented in matrix or quadripartite structures. (The Agency's Purchase Decision Model, for example, was structured in terms of think/feel and high/low involvement axes.) In this respect, their work could be said to exhibit a basic form of structuralism. One of these oppositions was that made between product benefit and user benefit (with its variant, end benefit). As this case study has shown, this is a distinction that lies at the marketing heart of all advertising. It needs to be teased out, if we are successfully to decode particular advertisements in a manner that goes beyond the purely semiotic interpretations of Barthes (1977), Williamson (1978), Goffman (1979) and others. What we need is an applied 'social semiotics' (Hodge and Kress, 1988).

In this respect, it can be seen that marketers' positivist, science-like approach is pursued primarily as a means of communication, rather than as a means of understanding. One of the factors anchoring marketing to the kind of structured thinking characteristic of modernist disciplines, perhaps, is that the creation of meaning in commodities is inextricably bound up with the establishment of a sense of difference between one object and all others of its class. After all, three major tasks of advertising are: to *stand out* from the surrounding competition in order to attract people's attention; to *communicate* (both rationally and emotionally) what it is intended to communicate; and to *predispose people to buy* or keep on buying what is advertised. The sole preoccupation of those engaged in the *Ikon Breath O₂* campaign was to create what they referred to as the 'parity break': to set NFC's contact lenses apart from all other contact lenses on sale in Japan, and from all other products on the market. At the same time, the idea of parity break extended to the style in which the campaign was to be presented (tinted monochrome photo, green logo, and so on). In this respect, the structure of meaning in advertising is akin to that found in the syntagmatic and paradigmatic axes of structural linguistics, where particular choices of words and phrases are influenced by the overall structure and availability of meanings in the language in which a speaker is communicating. That the work of Lévi-Strauss should be known to most marketers, therefore, is hardly surprising (see, for example, Levy, 1981). Marketing practice *is* in many respects an application of the principles of structural anthropology to the selling of products (cf. Douglas and Isherwood, 1979).

Those working in marketing and consumer research take it as given that there is one-way flow of activity stemming from the manufacturer and targeted at the end consumer. In fact, however, the case study presented here shows that advertising – as well as the marketing that an advertising agency conducts on behalf of a client – always addresses three different audiences. One of these is, of course, the group of targeted consumers (even though they are somewhat removed from the direct experience of marketers in their work). In this particular case, to complicate the issue further, there were two groups of consumers, since the campaign had to address both young women and middle-aged male opticians. Another audience is the client. As we have seen, the assumed or proven (dis)likes of both consumers and advertising client affect the final meaning of the products advertised, and the client in particular had to be satisfied with the Agency's campaign approach before consumer 'needs' could be addressed. At the same time, a third audience consists of the different members of the account team within the Agency itself, since each of the three separate parties involved in account servicing, marketing and creative work need to be satisfied by the arguments of the other two.

In this respect, perhaps, we should note that marketing people have spent a great deal of time over many decades making use of insights developed in learning behaviour, personality theory and psychoanalysis, which they then apply to individual consumers. In the process, however, they have tended to overlook the forms of social organization of which these individuals are a part (cf. de Groot, 1980: 44). Yet it is precisely the ways in which individual consumers interact that is crucial to an understanding of consumption and thus of how marketing should address its targeted audience: how networks function, for example, reveals a lot about the vital role of word-of-mouth in marketing successes and failures; how status groups operate and on what grounds can tell marketers a lot about the motivations and practices of their targeted audience. Anthropologists should be able to help by providing sociological analyses of these and other mechanisms which have relevance to the marketing endeavour. In particular, their extensive work on ritual and symbolism could be of use in foreign, 'third world' markets. Which brings us to the issue of 'culture'. If there is one word that has come to dominate business discourse since the mid-1980s, it is culture. Much of the discussion of culture has taken place in management studies and has been concerned with the advantages of developing organizational or corporate cultures. Much of it, too, stems from Japan – in the sense that American managers and academics seized on 'culture' as the explanation for Japan's economic success (and, at the time, American economic failure) and tried to apply what they saw as positive in Japanese business culture to their own organizations (cf. Salaman, 1997). Within the academic discipline of marketing, too, *all* international, as well as many introductory, marketing texts devote at least one chapter to the importance of understanding the cultural dimensions of marketing (Costa and Bamossy, 1995: viii). Given the issue of globalization, this is hardly surprising. What is surprising, however, is that – even though, as anthropologists, we might expect suddenly to be crowned kings of the cultural castle – in fact marketing academics pay scant attention to such disturbing ideas that capitalism – especially the Anglo-American form of 'free market' capitalism – might be no more than a cultural system (Sahlins, 1976), preferring instead to stick with the less taxing structural functionalism of such worthies in our discipline as Geert Hofstede (1980).[10] As Malcolm Chapman and Peter Buckley (1997: 234) wryly observe in a slightly different context, we need perhaps to spend some time entirely outside anthropology to realize that our carefully constructed cultural castles are for the most part unknown to those who use culture for practical business, marketing and organizational ends.

Finally, most products are made to be sold (even though, ideally, they should fit consumers' needs so perfectly that the selling is immediate and painless). As a result, different manufacturers have in mind different kinds of sales strategies, target audiences, and marketing methods that have somehow to be translated into persuasive linguistic and visual images – not only in advertising, but also in packaging and product design. For the most part, *producers* of the commodities in question find themselves obliged to call on the specialized services of copywriters and art designers who are seen to be more in tune with the *consumers* than are they themselves. This is how advertising agencies market themselves.

But within any agency, the creation of advertising involves an ever-present tension between sales and marketing people, on the one hand, and creative staff, on the other (the *motley crew* property); between the not necessarily compatible demands for the dissemination of product and other market information, on the one hand, and those for linguistic and visual images that will attract consumers' attention and push them into retail outlets to make purchases, on the other. This is not always taken into account by those currently writing about advertising. More interestingly, perhaps, the opposition that is perceived to exist between data and statistical analysis, on the one hand, and the creation of images, on the other, parallels that seen to pertain between a social science like economics or marketing and a more humanities-like discipline such as anthropology. Perhaps the role for marketing ethnography is to bridge this great divide.

Notes

1. Brown (1995: 37–9) suggests that the most useful perspective is that which sees marketing as exchange. This brings 'postmodern' marketing as a discipline paradoxically close to traditional economic anthropology in its focus.
2. The Agency's marketing activities have been reorganized since my fieldwork, because of both internal expansion and the acquisition of another large advertising agency. A major innovation has been the establishment of a Research Division and an impressive development of media-related statistical data, plus computer-generated quantitative analyses to assist account planners in their work.
3. Note that, unlike the Marketing department in Viking foods discussed by Lien (1997: 64), this description of the Agency's Marketing Department is structured in terms of units rather than individuals (managers) (cf. also Dore, 1973).
4. As in the film industry, the repeated gathering of different talents for different advertising campaigns in the Agency was rare (cf. Caves, 2000: 96–100).
5. The Media Planners do not usually participate in these early meetings since their main task is to provide information about suitable media, and slots therein, in which the finished campaign may be placed.
6. A similar point is made by Lien (1997: 111) in her study of Viking Foods.
7. Focus groups usually consist of about half a dozen people who represent by age, gender, socioeconomic grouping and so on the type of target audience

being addressed, and who have agreed to talk about (their attitudes towards) a particular product or product range – usually in exchange for some gift or money. Interviews are carried out in a small meeting room (that may have a one-way mirror to enable outside observation) and tend to last between one and two hours.

8. This is a typical suspicion affecting 'creative' and 'humdrum' personnel in so-called 'creative industries' (Caves, 2000: 4).

9. On this occasion, because the advertising budget was comparatively small, the media buyer was not brought in until later stages in the campaign's preparations. The AE in charge of the NFC account interacted individually with the media buyer and presented the latter's suggestions to the account team as a whole.

10. Or, as one anthropologist colleague recently asked, 'Geertz who?'

References

Arnould, Eric. 1995. 'West African marketing channels: environmental duress, relationship management, and implications for Western marketing'. In J. Sherry, Jr (ed.), *Contemporary Marketing and Consumer Behavior*. Thousand Oaks, CA: Sage, 109–68.

Barthes, Roland. 1977. *Image, Music, Text*. London: Fontana.

Brown, Stephen. 1995. *Postmodern Marketing*. London: Routledge.

Carrier, James, ed. 1997. *Meanings of the Market*. Oxford: Berg.

Carruthers, Bruce, and Sarah Babb. 2000. *Economy/Society: Markets, Meanings and Social Structure*. Thousand Oaks, CA: Pine Forge Press.

Caves, Richard. 2000. *Creative Industries: Contracts Between Art and Commerce*. Cambridge, MA: Harvard University Press.

Chapman, Malcolm, and Peter Buckley. 1997. 'Markets, transaction costs, economists and anthropologists'. In J. Carrier (ed.), *Meanings of the Market*. Oxford: Berg, 225–50.

Clark, Rodney. 1979. *The Japanese Company*. New Haven: Yale University Press.

Costa, Janeen, and Gary Bamossy, eds. 1995. *Marketing in a Multicultural World*. Thousand Oaks, CA: Sage.

De Groot, Gerald. 1980. *The Persuaders Exposed: Advertising and Marketing. The Derivative Arts*. London: Associated Business Press.

Dore, Ronald. 1973. *British Factory/Japanese Factory*. Berkeley and Los Angeles: University of California Press.

Douglas, Mary. 1973. *Natural Symbols*. Harmondsworth: Penguin Books.

Douglas, Mary, and Baron Isherwood. 1979. *The World of Goods: Towards an Anthropology of Consumption*. New York: Basic Books.

Goffman, Erving. 1979. *Gender Advertisements*. New York: Harper & Row.

Hodge, Robert, and Gunther Kress. 1988. *Social Semiotics*. Cambridge: Polity.

Hofstede, Geert. 1980. *Culture's Consequences: International Differences in Work-Related Values*. London: Sage.

Kaitaki, Jack. 1987. 'Celebrity advertising: a review and synthesis'. *International Journal of Advertising* 6: 93–105.

Kotler, Philip. 1986. *Principles of Marketing*. Englewood Cliffs, NJ: Prentice-Hall.

Lévi-Strauss, Claude. 1966. *The Savage Mind*. London: George Weidenfeld & Nicolson.

Lévi-Strauss, Claude. 1969. *Totemism.* Harmondsworth: Penguin Books.
Levy, Sidney. 1981. 'Interpreting consumer mythology: a structural approach to consumer behavior'. *Journal of Marketing* 45: 49–61.
Lien, Marianne. 1997. *Marketing and Modernity.* Oxford: Berg.
McCracken, Grant. 1989. 'Who is the celebrity endorser? Cultural foundations of the endorsement process'. *Journal of Consumer Research* 16: 310–21.
Malefyt, Timothy, and Brian Moeran, eds. 2003. *Advertising Cultures.* Oxford: Berg.
Moeran, Brian. 1996. *A Japanese Advertising Agency: An Anthropology of Media and Markets.* London: Curzon.
Moeran, Brian. 2000. 'The split account system and Japan's advertising industry'. *International Journal of Advertising* 19: 185–200.
Parry, John, and Maurice Bloch, eds. 1989. *Money and the Morality of Exchange.* Cambridge: Cambridge University Press.
Sahlins, Marshall. 1976. *Culture and Practical Reason.* Chicago: University of Chicago Press.
Salaman, Graeme. 1997. 'Culturing production'. In P. du Gay (ed.), *Production of Culture/Cultures of Production.* London: Sage/Open University, 235–84.
Sherry, John, Jr. 1995. 'Marketing and consumer behavior. Into the field'. In J. Sherry Jr. (ed.), *Contemporary Marketing and Consumer Behavior.* Thousand Oaks, CA: Sage, 3–44.
Watson, C. W., ed. 1999. *Being There: Fieldwork in Anthropology.* London: Pluto.
Wells, William, John Burnett and Sandra Moriarty. 2000. *Advertising Principles & Practice,* fifth edition. Saddle River, NJ: Prentice-Hall.
Williamson, Judith. 1978. *Decoding Advertisements: Ideology and Meaning in Advertising.* London: Marion Boyars.

3
The Virtual Consumer: Constructions of Uncertainty in Marketing Discourse

Marianne Elisabeth Lien

Marketing and uncertainty: a cultural approach

Why are marketing professionals so obsessed with future scenarios? Why do product managers buy reports that they never read? What is the cultural basis of uncertainty in the marketing profession? The marketing profession is ripe with paradoxes that are not explained by economic theory alone. In this chapter I explore some of these. Based on ethnographic research in a marketing department, and on subsequent discussions with practitioners in the marketing profession, I draw attention to the interface of marketing knowledge and marketing practice, as it unfolds in the day-to-day 'business' of constructing food products and food adverts.

There is a long history in the social sciences of a division between culture on the one hand, and markets on the other. This also involves a division of labour through what appeared, until recently, to be a tacit agreement between economics and anthropology that economists deal with disembedded transactions and rational calculations while anthropologists deal with people and culture. This division served for many years to set the agenda within the sub-discipline of economic anthropology where the focus, traditionally, has been upon non-market transactions and small-scale systems of distribution, rather than the complexities of modern markets. In other words, economic anthropology dealt with economies that were explicitly different from economies described in the field of economics, representing thus the Other, either within or external to the researchers' own societies (informal economies, non-market economies). This implied, for many years, an extraordinary lack of attention among anthropologists with regard to 'ordinary' business transactions, or to industrial or post-industrial economies of the capitalist, modern world.

This division of labour reflects a more general dichotomy in western societies between what Parry and Bloch (1989) refer to as 'market' on the one hand and 'morality' on the other, or between commodity exchange and gift exchange.[1] Parry and Bloch's recognition of this much-referred dichotomy as a western cultural construct, rather than as a universal phenomenon, has been significant in opening up for a field of inquiry that applies a cultural approach to markets and to capitalism (see, for instance, Dilley, 1992; Abolafia, 1996; Carrier, 1997; Lien, 1997; Miller, 1997; Callon, 1998). Such approaches have shown that what we commonly refer to as 'the market' is not only highly variable, but is also subject to a wide range of interpretations. Thus, far from being attributed with a fairly stable set of meanings, the market is a contested, flexible, and highly abstract concept, seemingly self-evident and elusive at the same time. Michel Callon (1998) argues that rather than denouncing *Homo Economicus* as pure fiction, the myth of economics, we need to explore the diversified forms through which this entity may be expressed. He maintains that just as 'so-called traditional societies are populated – sometimes even over-populated – with calculative agencies... so-called modern societies are endowed with as many non-calculative agencies as calculative ones' (1998: 39–40).

However, for Callon, calculation takes on a meaning which involves much more than the simple and utilitarian 'cost–benefit' approach attributed to *Homo Economicus*. Callon introduces an analytical framework from studies of science and technology (SST) in which economic processes may be treated as 'just another kind of socio-technical-discursive arrangement, like cars or nuclear physics' (Barry and Slater, 2002: 180).

This merging between SST and sociology or anthropology of economic processes represents a radical move, with implications beyond the scope of the present discussion. Yet, Callon's insistence that calculation is both a technical and an ethical practice 'depending on a set of technical devices and discursive idioms that make calculation possible' (Barry and Slater, 2002: 181) is relevant as a starting point for the present analysis. According to Callon, to the extent that *Homo Economicus* may be said to exist, he is not to be found in the 'natural state' so often referred to in economic textbooks, but rather: 'He is formatted, framed and equipped with prostheses which help him in his calculations and which are, for the most part, produced by economics' (Callon, 1998: 51). This opens up new horizons for economic anthropology, where the objective may be not so much that of '*giving the soul back to a de-humanized agent*' but rather to '*explore the diversity of calculative agencies' forms and distributions*' (Callon, 1998: 51).

Marketing is a field of knowledge which is both ambitiously academic and intensely applied, and which operates precisely at the interface between economic theory and economic practice. Quoting Callon once more, it is a 'set of tools and practices taken from practitioners and reconfigured by 'academic' marketing specialists' (1998: 27) which then, after numerous transformations, is mediated back to practitioners as a standardized prescription of how things ought to be done. Marketing thus represents (along with accounting) a profound mediator between the economics and economies – or between disciplinary knowledge and day-to-day practice. Much like the concept of *hybrids* as discussed by Latour (1993), Callon sees marketing not only as a mediator between the two, but also as an agent actively promoting the construction and constitution of each of them. Callon's approach to marketing and economics serves to remind us of the need to pay attention to interrelations between knowledge or beliefs and everyday practice. I contend that this ethnographic credo is of no less importance as the topic of study grows increasingly complex, abstract or virtual, as in the case of market relations and global economies (Carrier and Miller, 1998).

In this chapter, I will explore the interface of marketing knowledge and marketing practice, focusing specifically on the ways in which marketing mediates and reconfigures notions of time, change, consumption and consumers. I will discuss specific interpretations of the market, and their implications for the ways in which marketing practitioners conceive of their own knowledge, their position vis-à-vis consumers and their ability to make sound marketing decisions. The argument is developed on the basis of eight months of fieldwork conducted in the marketing department of a Norwegian food manufacturer (see Lien, 1997, for a comprehensive account), and was first presented at a European Conference for Advertising Agencies in Bergen in 2000. The presentation sparked a prolonged media debate in Norway and repeated presentations for audiences in the marketing profession. This chapter incorporates reflections that draw upon comments from such discussions. Although the argument springs from studies of the food production and consumption in Norway, the implications are much broader and are relevant across a wide range of fields and cultural contexts.

All cultural communities share some assumptions that are rarely questioned, often referred to in the social sciences as 'doxa'. The task of an anthropologist is to uncover such doxic assumptions, and to trace their origin and their implications. This may be useful, not only as an academic exercise, but also as a key to self-reflection for those who

belong to the marketing profession. Put very simply, a person's understanding of the world has important consequences for her interpretations
of new situations, and for what she sees as relevant knowledge. In this
chapter, I argue that the way in which the marketing profession
conceptualizes markets and consumers may in fact some times *prevent*
them from gaining certain types of knowledge that they actually
require. Based on this argument, I will then ask how it may be that
a discipline which prides itself on helping practitioners to make sound
marketing decisions may in fact develop conceptual tools that serve to
undermine a type of insight that marketing practitioners need, and
even seek. This question involves an ethnographic analysis of the
interface between marketing as a discipline and marketing as practice,
or, following the terminology of Callon (1998), between economics and
economies.

The core of the argument may be summarized as follows. Firstly,
contemporary marketing is characterized by a relentless search for
knowledge about markets and consumers. Masses of information are
continuously produced to meet this search for knowledge (Lien, 1997).
A key observation is that such information, however different it may
appear, tends to share a particular bias in the sense that it is structured
by a focus on the future and on change. Repeated references to novelties,
news, the future and anticipated change serve to constitute what I will
refer to as a *bias of temporality* in marketing discourse. Secondly, marketing
research on consumption tends to portray consumers as if they were
strangers, acting unexpectedly, in ways that are difficult to understand
or foresee. This image of the consumer as unpredictable and unknown,
reinforced in part by consulting agencies, serves to constitute an image
of a *consumer as someone you don't know*, another bias in marketing
discourse. I will maintain that these two conceptual paradigms serve as
basic organizing principles in much of what is going on in the business
of marketing and advertising, or what we may refer to as the commoditization of marketing knowledge. Together they contribute to what
I have previously described as a *feeling of uncertainty* among marketing
practitioners, and which is another characterizing feature of the marketing
profession (Lien, 1997; see also Applbaum, 1999; Shenhav, 1994). The
term uncertainty does not refer to insecurity or a low self-esteem on
a personal level. Rather, it indicates what I refer to a collective sense of
uncertainty, or the shared awareness in the profession (expressed particularly strongly among product managers) that one simply 'does not
know' and that this lack of knowledge is somehow problematic, or
could make a difference in the near future. This feeling of uncertainty is

crucial to understanding the striking gap between, on the one hand, the massive amount of resources that is spent on buying information, and, on the other hand, the fact that so little of this information appears to be really analysed or taken into account in day-to-day practice or decision-making (Lien, 1997). In the following two sections, I shall elaborate each of these conceptual paradigms, starting with the *bias of temporality*.

The bias of temporality

As an outsider to the marketing profession in the 1990s, I was amazed to observe how much time and effort was being spent among the practitioners in speculating about something that in fact did not yet exist, such as 'the twenty-first century consumer', or 'agencies in 2010'. Getting access to the latest news, and particularly to future scenarios, was frequently explained as the main reason for spending time at seminars and conferences (Lien, 1997). Consultants launching such events are generally well aware of this and tend, through their marketing efforts, to frame events as unique opportunities for preparing for the future. A similar tendency is evident in bestselling books on management, creativity and leadership throughout the past decade.[2] This tendency is particularly salient in the field of new computer technologies, where speed, change and visions of the future are the focus of attention (Willim, 2003), but the tendency is also evident in a range of other fields.

Why is the future so important these days? And why are business people so obsessed with prophecies that claim to actually *predict* the future? The ability to prepare for the future is, in many ways, a universal necessity and part of the historical background for the successful expansion of humankind. But the cultural solutions do not necessarily involve such massive consumption of prophecies. For most people, knowledge of the past and the present would seem sufficient. This is not because nothing ever changes, but, rather, because any period of change will always contain an element of continuity. Some marketing professionals have argued that marketing is different, because in marketing, and particularly with regard to food habits, the changes are so much greater and so much more unpredictable than in most other areas, and probably also than in most other historical periods. Sociologists and anthropologists studying food and consumption in Scandinavia in the last quarter of the twentieth century argue, on the other hand, that this has been a relatively stable period. It has been a prosperous period, particularly in Norway, and there have been marked changes with regard to women's participation in the workforce and with regard to appropriation of information technology. But in spite of rising incomes and in spite of an increasing availability of imported foods, eating habits have remained relatively stable (Bugge and Døving, 2000). By and large, the 1990s is not a decade that will be seen as one of dramatic change as far as food consumption is concerned. It appears, in other words, that what characterizes the marketing profession in this field is a focus on change, rather than change itself.

Clearly, the significance of change at any given time is relative, and about as hard to predict as the fall of the Berlin Wall, or the terrorist attack on the Twin Towers. What is interesting, therefore, is not so much who is right and who is wrong, but rather how a notion of change is sustained in discourse and day-to-day practices, how it is played out in different areas, and how a preoccupation with the future may structure and facilitate certain decisions at the expense of others. I do not claim that nothing changes, but rather that changes are less profound than they may seem, simply because the continuities, which are always there, are *systematically overlooked*. Let me give an example.

In 1985, a consultancy agency called Carelius/Eckbo was contracted by the Norwegian food industry to produce a strategic plan for the next ten years. The report is a genuine and well-founded attempt to predict what would happen in the Norwegian food market from 1985 to 1995. Reading the report more than 15 years later, it is hardly surprising to note that many of the predictions never happened. The report is radical, because it predicts dramatic changes in many parts of the food sector, but at the same time it appears old fashioned, in the sense that it bears the unignorable mark of the 1980s. A few examples illustrate the point (Carelius/Eckbo, 1985). According to the report, irradiation might soon be allowed for a lot of products, such as chicken (p. 150), and could solve the problems of salmonella once and for all. As we know now, irradiation has not been a major method of food preservation in Scandinavia to date, and salmonella remains a significant problem. Furthermore, according to the report, microwave ovens would soon appear on every kitchen counter, and even in miniature format, 'to be plugged in anywhere, like an electrical razor' (p. 136). This way, people could bring their microwave around, and the market for ready-made frozen food (TV dinners) would increase tremendously. In 1996, 63 per cent of the Norwegian population owned a microwave oven (Sandlie, 1999), but their use has hardly revolutionized Norwegian eating habits, which still rely largely on the use of regular ovens. Finally, according to the report, snacks would gradually replace ordinary meals: Lunch would become a snack meal, while a family dinner would become a rare event (p. 75). This represents perhaps the gravest misinterpretation of Norwegian eating habits, and one of the most recurring myths of the popular press, partly due to extensive references to North American trends and to trend research commentators (Lien, 1999). A recent review of all available statistics on Norwegian eating habits concludes that in spite of such predictions, eating patterns in Norway remain stable and the dinner remains a significant family meal (Bugge and Døving, 2000). There are other predictions in the report that never came true, but also some that are right, such as a predicted increase in the use of pasta (p. 139), pizza (p. 82) and poultry (p. 127), and an interest in Mexican and Oriental foods. Interestingly, the single food item that increased most dramatically during this period, low-fat milk, is hardly mentioned at all in the report.[3]

The report cited above is a sober and careful presentation of future trends, and more radical examples are easily found. Nevertheless, it exemplifies the tendency in such consultancy reports to emphasize change at the expense of continuity. Norwegians eat pork chops, carrots, bread, skimmed milk and potatoes – items considered by both trend researchers and the public to be staple, everyday items. Although food habits research concludes that eating patterns are relatively stable (Bugge and Døving, 2000; Lodberg-Holm and Mørk, 2001),[4] there is hardly any mention of stability in the report. Instead, the significance of things that were seen as novelties or recent inventions around 1985 (such as irradiation and microwave ovens) is overemphasized and predicted to have enormous consequences for the future. This exercise is repeated in the case of practically every novelty, in spite of the fact that, as most marketing professionals are well aware, a great part of the innovations that find their way to the market disappear within a period of five years. The report is but one example of a more general tendency in marketing discourse in which a preoccupation with change remains a key feature, while signs of stability are systematically overlooked.

Temporal practices are never neutral; rather, they are entangled in structures of production and exchange which are culturally and historically specific. Numerous scholars have tried to capture related experiences of change and speed as symptomatic features of the current historical epoch. Anthony Giddens has referred to this era as one of *high modernity* (Giddens, 1991), while Zygmunt Bauman captures a feeling of fluidity through the term *liquid modernity* (Bauman, 2000). David Harvey links the general 'speed-up' and time–space compression to the recent move in capitalism towards *flexible accumulation*, (Harvey, 1990: 285), a phenomenon which according to Arjun Appadurai brings *the aesthetic of ephemerality* as its civilizing counterpart (Appadurai, 1996: 85). Across all of these conceptualizations is a realization that the anticipation of progress has become endemic, that new inventions have become routinized to the extent that all we know for sure is that 'nothing remains stable'. However, the description of such a bias of temporality across a broad range of related fields, does not, in itself, explain its profound expressions in the field of marketing discourse. Instead, we need to ask more specifically: what are the mechanisms through which marketing professionals have come to embrace this language of temporality?

Part of the explanation may be found in the marketing discipline's 'raison d'être' as a mediator between economic theory and economic practice, or between knowledge and practice. Unlike more established academic disciplines, from its very beginnings in the US in the early decades of the twentieth century marketing has been based on collecting, ordering and distributing practical knowledge to its practitioners. Frank Cochoy (1998) describes the establishment of marketing as a process in which the extreme marginality of its early pioneers (in relation to classical economics and to the business world) became, paradoxically, their source of strength. Through a process by which information from the business sphere was tediously collected, ordered, and standardized within a conceptual frame that served to express much of what practitioners already knew – but at a different level of abstraction – pioneers in marketing carved out a field of their own (Cochoy, 1998). Through the use of standardized concepts, common arenas and disciplinary gate-keepers, the marketing pioneers gradually succeeded in establishing a discipline that was systematic, cumulative and universal in its claims. Operating thus at the interface between economic theory and the business world, the marketing profession represents a Latourian hybrid, engaging simultaneously in bringing together and in setting apart. Business practice that had previously been carried out pragmatically, and without an overarching theoretical rationale, gradually became the subject of an abstract order, which, in itself, remained unattainable and distant to the business practitioner, except through the appropriation of a semi-academic marketing discourse. The history of marketing is therefore, as Cochoy maintains, also the history of 'the progressive separation of marketing knowledge from market practices' (Cochoy, 1998: 198). A discipline that is founded upon the simultaneous separation and mediation between knowledge and practice is bound to lead a precarious existence. If it becomes too closely involved with purely academic issues, it will lose its value to practitioners. Conversely, if it becomes too involved in the day-to-day challenges of business life, it will be unable to maintain the level of abstraction that makes the discipline (appear) indispensable as a transmitter of knowledge. As Cochoy demonstrates, the history of marketing is a history of men and women who have successfully embraced this challenge. The challenge, however, is not over yet.

The bias of temporality, so central to the marketing profession around the turn of the millennium, may be understood against this background. In order to secure a basis of funding, marketing must be seen as useful by contemporary practitioners. Stirring a sense of urgency, risk or fear of lagging behind, marketing consultants succeed in attracting the attention of advertisers and suppliers. Operating in a market characterized in part by flexible accumulation, they are all painfully aware that shifts and changes do happen, even if their own field of business has been stable so far (as in the case of food habits). Claiming privileged knowledge of the future may be interpreted as one strategy by which the marketing profession latches on to this tendency, and transforms it to a novel business niche. More precisely, by describing future scenarios within their clients' field as entirely different from the present, marketing professionals indirectly suggest that this future is a 'territory' for those privileged few who know the way; that is for those who are able to adapt in time. In this way, they stir a feeling of risk, uncertainty and urgency,[5] but because they also provide the 'map' to the future, risk may be alleviated by careful planning. In this way, the emphasis on change becomes part of a more complex relation of mutual dependency between marketing practitioners and their consultants, one in which the bias of temporality proves itself indispensable to consultancy business. The most obvious example of this would be the trend-analyst, for whom success is based upon a widespread anticipation of change in the general public, and who necessarily share an interest in maintaining a bias of temporality.

While trend-analysts and certain market research agencies clearly contribute in constituting images of rapid change, the significance of such institutions *alone* can hardly account for the bias of temporality within the marketing profession. After all, if the future scenarios did not strike a chord in the audience of marketing practitioners, they would be unlikely to sell. Why are the marketing practitioners, and especially those operating in relatively stable fields of business, so receptive to future scenarios? What is it about marketing that makes it such fertile ground for what Appadurai (1996) calls the aesthetics of ephemerality? One of the central concepts in the field of marketing is that of the market. I shall argue that what I have referred to above as the bias of temporality is, in fact, deeply integrated in the most common usages of the market concept.

Market metaphors

Metaphors serve as mediators of knowledge (Lakoff and Johnson, 1980). Perceiving one phenomenon in terms of another represents an important mechanism by which new phenomena are understood, and new associations and connections may be recognized. Often, metaphors help us to make sense of abstract concepts by referring to something more familiar. In this way, metaphors help us to make the connections between knowledge and practice. By providing a set of images in terms of which we think about reality, metaphors also contribute in shaping that reality to us. Metaphors may thus become self-fulfilling. This is particularly relevant in fields such as marketing, which mediate between abstract knowledge and day-to-day practice. Following Fernandez (1974), we may argue that a metaphoric assertion evokes a dominant state of mind which involves as specific set of *performative consequences*, as it privileges certain principles with regard to what is interpreted as appropriate action. Each metaphoric structure thus serves simultaneously as a model *of* the world, and as a model *for* appropriate action.

Studying metaphors in marketing discourse, I have looked especially at the concept of the market. Instead of applying an arbitrary definition of the market, I considered the way in which the term was used among marketing practitioners, product managers and marketing managers in the marketing department of a major food manufacturer in Norway (Lien, 1997). Among the different terms used during meetings, in print, and as part of informal conversation, the term 'market' (in Norwegian: *marked*) was among those most frequently referred to. Along with a few other key concepts such as 'product' and 'consumer', the term market represents one of the most significant terms of reference in the realm of business. Through analysis of various types of discourse in the marketing department, I discovered four metaphoric structures which, together, may account for nearly all instances in which the term 'market' is applied.[6] Among these, two are particularly important in relation to a bias of temporality, and in the following I will discuss these only (but see Lien, 1997, for a complete account).

The market as an environment of natural selection

Market discourse often involves metaphors, terms and images that draw upon the realm of nature and biology. This relates to notions of the market as an abstract entity, and to single elements of the market, such as products. For instance, the notion of the lifecycle is prominent. Products are described as having a 'life of their own', they are 'born' they are 'babies' and they eventually 'die'. Products must be improved in order to 'stay alive'; and when a product is taken off the market, it is sometimes justified by the comment that 'it does not have the right to live'. Numerous models depicting products' life cycles reflect this way of conceptualizing the market.[7] Adaptation is emphasized, and the image often evokes the Darwinian approach to evolution as a process of natural selection, or the notion of 'survival of the fittest'. According to this perspective, the market – as the natural environment – becomes the final judge, the final arena for determining the fate of the product. This metaphor is often applied when referring to a product's failure or success, and thus serves as an analytical tool.

The market as a flux of transformation

The notion of the market as a flux of transformation is closely related to the metaphor above, but rather than emphasizing changeability as an attribute of products, changeability is referred to as a characteristic of the market itself. The market is described as highly dynamic, constantly changing and thus unpredictable. This image is often evoked in relation to the practitioners themselves, their worries and concerns. For instance, marketing managers often refer to the need to 'feel the pulse of the market' or 'pick up signals from the market', and to respond to these in order to ensure that products will succeed. Adaptation is crucial here, as in the case above, but in order to adapt one must also know the changes in the market. Information thus becomes highly valued, and it follows from this particular metaphoric structure that information must be not only updated, but focused on the future in order to be useful. This metaphor is particularly important for under-standing the bias of temporality. In the day-to-day practice among product managers, this metaphoric structure appeared to be the one most frequently applied, and also the most dominant in creating a script for appropriate action. A direct continuity may thus be established between the metaphors of the market as a flux of transformation, day-to-day marketing practice and what I have referred to above as a bias of temporality.

Metaphors are never right or wrong, true or false, but rather ways of emphasizing certain aspects of a phenomenon at the expense of others. But once they are put to use, metaphors tend to take on a life of their own, they shape the way we think about the world, they justify our actions, and they inform our expectations with regard to the behaviour of others. If every product manager believes that products must be changed in order to adapt to a changeable market, that market will soon materialize, regardless of whether the description was right in the first place.

To summarize, I maintain that an emphasis on change tends to dominate marketing discourse at the expense of continuity, and that it serves to reproduce a bias of temporality within the marketing profession. A bias of temporality contributes to a feeling of uncertainty among its practitioners. This is because the more we celebrate information about the future, the less we will tend to value knowledge about the past and the present. As knowledge tends to be based on experience, the bias of temporality thus makes a product manager's own experience seem less relevant, simply because it is necessarily located in the past.

The virtual consumer

Let me turn now to a second conceptual paradigm within marketing discourse; *the idea that the consumer is someone you don't know*. The notion of the consumer is a modern one. According to Raymond Williams (1983), it did not become part of our everyday vocabulary until the 1950s, but since then it has gradually and almost totally eclipsed the term customer. This shift in vocabulary from customer to consumer reflects a final step in a historical process of separation of the field of production from the field of consumption. A customer is someone you meet, a customer is part of an ongoing business relationship, while a consumer is an abstract figure in an abstract market (Williams, 1983: 79). The shift from the term customer to the term consumer thus represents a shift in terms of level of abstraction, or, following the terminology of Callon, a change of framing.

During the early phases of capitalism, trade was mainly local, and happened without the intervention of shops (Carrier, 1994). Gradually, intermediary traders took over, and the *distance* between producer and consumer increased, along a spatial, a temporal as well as a social dimension. Today, as trade and production are increasingly transnational phenomena, a product's place of origin is often hard to determine. This applies not only to combined products, which may be created on the basis of ingredients from a wide variety of places, but also to more simple products. For instance, a smoked salmon may originally have been hatched and reared in France, then moved to a marine farm in Iceland in order to grow to the point of harvest, whereupon it has been transferred to Denmark in order to be smoked, packed and distributed.[8] During this process, the fish may have been subject to the legal ownership of a wide range of companies whose ownership structures defy most attempts of defining their locality. Consequently, from the consumer's point of view, the issue of a product's origin is increasingly complex and difficult to ascertain.

Similarly, from the producers' point of view, consumers represent an abstract aggregate of transactions taking place in a number of shops far from the company premises, and sometimes in places that are not yet known. Consequently, the idea of a continuous and regular relationship to a 'customer' is increasingly inappropriate to circumstances in the real world. The task becomes one of calculation and of measurements, one of transforming a vast number of purchases in an infinite time and space to calculable facts that may be distinguished, measured and compared. Through such processes of disentanglement, economics (market research) serves its role of formatting the market in a way that makes it appear intelligible to practitioners (Callon, 1998). Through such calculations, for example, the sales figures for the south-eastern region of Norway for April this year may be compared with the sales figures for April in the previous year. By means of sophisticated trans-formations, sales figures are matched to key characteristics of consumers involved, enabling the marketing practitioner to 'know' with some degree of certainty, the sociological characteristics of the people that operate at the other end of the transaction chain. Sometimes, such processes of disentangling lead to a final re-entangling, often referred to as consumer segmentation, in which the results are presented through narratives of imaginary consumers, depicted in great detail as, for example, 'single mother, with two children, working for the public sector, with a preference for ethnic foods and New Age literature' (see also Lien, 1993). In this way, the disentangled virtual consumer becomes a person of flesh and blood, one you can imagine as the woman living next door. Consumer segmentation is produced for a great majority of brand products in the market, even for ordinary, everyday products that appear not to be associated with any particular fads or lifestyle trends. Such processes of disentangling and re-entangling leave us with a notion of consumers that confirms a stereotype image whose most important attribute is that it helps us to think about consumption. 'Virtual consumers' (the results of re-entangling) serve in this way as a device that helps us think about phenomena that appear otherwise (as a result of disentangling processes) too complex to grasp.

While sophisticated surveys of consumers allegedly facilitate a sense of familiarity with increasingly distant consumers, 'real' consumers remain literally out of sight. During my fieldwork in the marketing department of a Norwegian food manufacturer, I was struck by the contrast between the *total absence of consumers* on the one hand (no consumer ever passes through the entrance to the marketing department), and the *relentless gathering of information about consumers* on the other. Face-to-face encounters between food manufacturers and food consumers were in fact extremely rare. This was rarely seen as a problem, but aptly captured by a print on the bulletin board of one of my informants, which read 'A Consumer is Someone Who Does Not Work in Marketing'. Yet the more detached and analytic interest in consumers was paramount, and part of the reason why they accepted an anthropologist in the corridors. Some of my informants would claim that much more time and money ought to be spent on gathering information about consumers. Others would claim that the data available was not utilized sufficiently, but all would agree that *their knowledge of consumers was incomplete*. This notion of not knowing all there is to know provides fertile ground for anyone who wishes to stir feelings of uncertainty within the marketing profession.

Occupying the role of an outsider, I sometimes asked marketing professionals responsible for the design and marketing of food products whether they might consider employing a housewife, a woman who would possess a type of competence in feeding the family that few of the young men who were aspiring product managers seemed to possess. But my suggestion was not taken seriously. Firmly based in an era of modernity, the marketing managers were not prepared to challenge the basic foundation of their professional career: the fundamental division in modern societies between our personal, private experiences and our professional lives. To do so would have been to challenge the legitimacy of the marketing profession itself, and particularly the efforts of the pseudoscientific laboratories set up to measure the preferences of 'consumers', as part of its efforts of commodifying knowledge of every-day life.

Consequently, those who enter a marketing department enter as professionals, rather than as private consumers. Experiences from last night's supper are hardly legitimate as a basis for marketing decisions. Knowledge of consumers is always knowledge, as the bulletin print indicates, about 'someone else who doesn't work in marketing'. This peculiar construction of consumers represents an instance of what James Carrier and Daniel Miller (1998) have referred to as 'virtualism'. According to Carrier, abstraction leads some people to adopt an abstract economic world view in which the 'concepts and models of economic abstraction...are taken to be the fundamental reality that underlies and shapes the world' (1998: 2). This becomes 'virtualism' when 'people take this virtual reality to be not just a parsimonious description of what is really happening, but prescriptive of what the world ought to be; that is, they seek to make the world conform to their virtual vision' (Carrier, 1998: 2).

While, according to Miller, neo-classical economists 'make no claim to represent flesh-and-blood consumers' (1998: 200), I will argue that this is precisely what the marketing profession will do. Unlike their more academically oriented colleagues in neo-classical economics, practitioners in the marketing profession are expected to present the 'world as it is', and they do so with convincing dedication. Equipped with fragments of state-of-the-art sociology (Giddens, Bourdieu) and with 'real-life' photographs of 'real people' to represent the typical 'prototype' of various segments of consumer cartography, they portray an image of the world of consumers which is both familiar and intriguing. Elements of resemblance are carefully balanced by strategies of distancing, creating a blend of consumer 'types' that is both familiar and strange. Most importantly, perhaps, the images of consumers thus portrayed serve the purpose of confirming the role of marketing research as a necessary intermediary for anyone who wishes to understand 'the consumer'. In a manner that resembles the commoditization of future scenarios (bias of temporality, see above), the marketing profession invokes an image of consumers as unknown territory, but one to which the marketing profession may provide a map. In this way, risk is temporarily alleviated and the mutual dependency between marketing practitioners and their consultants is further confirmed.

Do consumers really exist?

I have suggested that the 'virtual consumer' is an abstract construct which has emerged as a result of a historical development from early capitalism to high modernity which involves two fundamental features: (1) the historical separation of production from consumption (physically as well as socially); and (2) the split between the private and the professional in the social organization of work. Once these divisions were well established, constructing *representations of* consumers by means of increasingly sophisticated methods of calculations became a real possibility. Widening divisions between acts of production and acts of consumption called for experts of translation, and the niche commonly referred to as market research or consumer research was born. This is the background for the emergence of what I have referred to as the 'virtual consumer'.

However, the term 'virtual consumer' is slightly misleading, in the sense that it assumes the existence of something that is not 'virtual' – a consumer that is somehow real. But do consumers really exist? When I presented the argument above to various audiences in the marketing and advertising professions, I sometimes invited all consumers in the audience to please raise their hand. The result was consistent across all audiences: Complete silence and no hands raised. Usually, the atmosphere became tense, and some turned to laughter. Was I serious? What did I mean? Yet the point that I tried to make through this exercise hardly required any explanation: The term 'consumer' is not meaningful with regard to identification at a personal level. It does not offer any lasting source of identity. With the exception of the few minutes we pause to reply to market surveys, hardly any of us identify ourselves as consumers. To the extent that identity is seen, at least partly, as self-determined, *there are no consumers among us, only people that consume.*

The consumer that emerges from market research analyses is therefore the result of a conceptual transformation of a part-time activity (shopping, consumption) to an image of a person that is removed from her immediate social reality, stripped of most things that appear as significant in life: work, love, friends or family, and reconstructed as a coherent figure whose primary purpose is that of *representing* some typical acts of consumption. The term 'consumer' is, in other words, a part-time activity reconstructed as a person, and reclassified as 'hedonist', 'traditional', 'retro' or 'generation x', whatever term appears appropriate in the light of current fads of market research. Instead of understanding consumption as a practice deeply entangled in most other dimensions of life, consumption becomes short-hand for stereotyping of a person. A consumer, in other words, rests upon processes of disentangling that cut the links to practically everything that makes any of us a *person.* It is in this way one may argue that a consumer is, in fact, a result of virtualism, or a phantom narrated by market and consumer research.

Consumption is necessarily a part-time activity, and takes on meaning in relation to other life-projects. Once we focus on persons as coherent human beings, it turns out that consumption is *not* first and foremost about self-identity, lifestyle or fads of fashion. Consumption is first and foremost about relationships. This basic insight is convincingly demonstrated through Daniel Miller's ethnographic study of shopping in North London (Miller, 2001). The virtue of Miller's study is that it takes consumption to the context of intimate relationships, of household, and of communities – that is, contexts in which persons interact as complex human beings, and not as 'consumers'. Through its ability to materialize moral values relevant to the enactment of social relationships, consumption is about morality and about love. A second point that emerges from Miller's study, but also from other studies of consumption, is that acts of consumption are engrained in ordinary everyday life. For instance, a recent collection by Jukka Gronow and Alan Warde (2001) confirms that consumption has to do with practices that are to a large extent routinized, repetitive, ordinary, inconspicuous, pragmatic and collective. In this way, the authors emphasize experiences that tend to be shared, and that are unlikely to be subject to immediate and radical change.

Conclusion: how to 'get real'

I have argued that the bias of temporality and the virtual consumer are paradigms that nurture and sustain feelings of uncertainty, urgency and risk, even in markets primarily characterized by stability and shared, ordinary practices of consumption such as the food market. To some extent, these biases are integral to the commoditization of marketing expertise through consultancy transactions, and constitute a business on their own. However, the paradigms are more widely shared, and may be seen as key constituents of the continuous formatting of the economic practice by the economic (marketing) discipline.

As the emphasis on change and the processes of disentangling both enhance differentiation at the expense of continuity in marketing discourse, latent knowledge acquired by personal experience (through acts of consumption) are systematically devalued. Because such personal knowledge would potentially enhance competence, paradigms such as the bias of temporality and the virtual consumer tend to make practitioners in the trade *appear* less competent and less qualified to sell products than they actually are. In other words, human resources related to personal and professional experience are not often fully utilized as a basis for future decisions.

This is not an attempt to divert resources in marketing research in the direction of ethnographic studies of the kind that Daniel Miller has carried out. On the contrary, if any suggestion should emerge from this, it would be a plea to 'get real'[9], in the sense of adopting a sceptical stance with regard to the transformations that occur when phenomena are simply framed at increasingly complex levels of abstraction. Virtualism has provided us with 'markets' and 'consumers' that appear to us as entities with their own inherent logic, increasingly distant and out of reach. This has brought about a spiralling rise of investments in technical devices intended to decipher signs from such distant phenomena. However, consumption does not happen in isolation. To 'get real' would mean to realize that consumption happens right now, closer than we think, and that we do not even need to construct an image of 'consumers' to understand it.

Acknowledgements

Thanks to the editors and to participants at numerous seminars for useful comments and constructive discussions.

Notes

1. This dichotomy has a wide range of loosely related parallels, such as modern and traditional, public and private, *Gesellschaft* and *Gemeinschaft*, etc.
2. For instance, on the back of Rolf Jensen's bestseller *The Dream Society* (1999), prospective readers are told that 'A new era is coming, a new battle for the market has begun' (Jensen, 1999). Numerous other examples could be mentioned.
3. Annual surveys of consumer expenditures show that from 1983–85 to 1996–98, the consumption of low-fat milk increased from 8.1 kg per person per year to 55.1 kg per person per year, an increase by more than 600 per cent (Lodberg-Holm and Mørk, 2001). Low-fat milk was introduced on the Norwegian market in 1984.
4. Annual surveys of consumer expenditures in Norway show remarkably stable levels of consumption for a wide range of products. For instance, in the period between 1983–85 and 1996–98 the consumption of meat and meat products remained stable at 46 kg per person per year, the consumption of cream went from 5.6 to 5.3 kg per person per year, consumption of tea remained stable at 0.2 kg per person per year (Lodberg-Holm and Mørk, 2001). Other surveys show that *rutabaga*, a common tuber in Norway, remained stable for more than 40 years, from 1955 to 1995, at the level of 3.1 kg per person per year (Døving and Lien, 2000).
5. A similar feeling of risk and urgency is described in other fields as well in Scandinavia around the turn of the millennium, such as in computer technology (Willim, 2003) and in regional planning (Berg, Linde-Laursen and Löfgren, 2000).

6. These metaphorical structures are 'the market as territorial space', 'the market as a battlefield', 'the market as an environment of natural selection' and 'the market as a flux of transformation'.

7. Cf., for instance, the model developed by the Boston Consulting Group, a leading North American consultancy firm, frequently quoted in marketing textbooks (Kotler and Armstrong, 1987).

8. The example is based on recent debates in the salmon industry, cf. Intrafish: 'New labels: is Scottish salmon's identity at risk?' 6 May 2002 (www.intrafish.com).

9. I borrow this expression from Daniel Miller (2001), who – in the tradition of Hegel – uses the term 'real' to denote an activity (shopping, in his example) 'that actually realized the rationality inherent in it in terms of the historical moment within which we can encounter it' (Miller, 2001: 179). To 'get real' in this context would imply the realization of the intentions of business practice without the distractions and diversions that increasing levels of abstraction bring about. To 'get real' would imply a move away from virtualism.

References

Abolafia, Mitchel Y. 1996. *Making Markets: Opportunism and Restraint on Wall Street*. Cambridge, MA: Harvard University Press.

Appadurai, Arjun. 1996. *Modernity at Large*. Minneapolis: University of Minnesota Press.

Applbaum, Kalman. 1999. 'Survival of the biggest: business policy, managerial discourse and uncertainty in a global business alliance'. *Anthropological Quarterly* 72(4): 155–66.

Barry, Andrew and Don Slater. 2002. 'Introduction: the technical economy'. *Economy and Society* 3(2): 175–93.

Bauman, Zygmunt. 2000. *Liquid Modernity*. Cambridge: Polity Press.

Berg, Per Olof, Anders Linde-Laursen, and Orvar Löfgren. 2000. *Invoking a Transnational Metropolis: The Making of the Øresund Region*. Lund: Studentlitteratur, University of Lund.

Bugge, Annechen, and Runar Døving. 2000. *Det norske måltidsmønsteret – ideologi og praksis (Norwegian Eating Habits – Ideology and Practice)*. Report 2. Lysaker, Norway: National Institute for Consumer Research.

Carelius, Gunnar and Jan Kerr Eckbo. 1985. *10-års strategisk plan for visse deler av næringsmiddelindustrien 1985–1995. Delrapport I–III (10 year strategic plan for selected parts of the food industry, 1985–1995, Report I–III)*. Consultancy Report. Oslo, Norway: Carelius/Eckbo.

Callon, Michel, ed. 1998. *The Laws of the Market*. Oxford: Blackwell Publishers.

Carrier, James G. 1994. *Gifts and Commodities: Exchange and Western Capitalism since 1700*. London: Routledge.

Carrier, James G., ed. 1997. *Meanings of the Market: The Free Market in Western Culture*. Oxford: Berg.

Carrier, James G. 1998. 'Introduction'. In J. G. Carrier and D. Miller (eds), *Virtualism: A New Political Economy*. Oxford: Berg, 1–24.

Carrier, James G., and Daniel Miller, eds. 1998. *Virtualism: A New Political Economy*. Oxford: Berg.

Cochoy, Frank. 1998. 'Another discipline for the market economy: Marketing as a performative knowledge and know-how for capitalism'. In M. Callon (ed.), *The Laws of the Market*, Oxford: Blackwell, 194–221.

Dilley, Roy, ed. 1992. *Contesting Markets: Analyses of Ideology, Discourse and Practice.* Edinburgh: Edinburgh University Press.

Døving, Runar, and Marianne Lien. 2000. 'Myten om den perfekte kålrot' (The myth of the perfect rutabaga). *Norsk Antropologisk Tidsskrift (Norwegian Journal of Anthropology)* 11(2): 108–28.

Fernandez, James. 1974. 'Persuasions and performances; of the beast in every body and the metaphors in everyman'. In C. Geertz (ed.), *Myth, Symbol and Culture.* New York: Norton, 39–60.

Giddens, Anthony. 1991. *Modernity and Self-Identity.* Cambridge: Polity Press.

Gronow, Jukka, and Alan Warde, ed. 2001. *Ordinary Consumption.* London: Routledge.

Harvey, David. 1990. *The Condition of Postmodernity.* Oxford: Blackwell.

Jensen, Rolf. 1999. *The Dream Society: How the Coming Shift from Information to Imagination will Transform your Business.* New York: McGraw Hill.

Kotler, Philip, and Gary Armstrong. 1987. *Marketing: An Introduction.* Englewood Cliff, NJ: Prentice-Hall.

Lakoff, George, and Mark Johnson.1980. *Metaphors We Live By.* Chicago: The University of Chicago Press.

Latour, Bruno. 1993. *We Have Never Been Modern.* New York: Harvester.

Lien, Marianne. 1993. 'From deprived to frustrated; consumer segmentation in food and nutrition'. In U. Kjærnes et al. (eds), *Regulating Markets, Regulating People: On Food and Nutrition Policy.* Oslo: Novus Press, 153–71.

Lien, Marianne. 1997. *Marketing and Modernity.* Oxford: Berg.

Lien, Marianne. 1999. 'Hvorfor spiser djevelen Pizza?' (Why does the Devil eat Pizza?) *Samtiden* 1: 82–8.

Lodberg-Holm, Anne, and Eiliv Mørk. 2001. *Forbruksundersøkelsen 1996–98.* (*Consumer Expenditure Surveys 1996–98*). Oslo: Statistisk Sentralbyrå (Central Bureau of Statistics).

Miller, Daniel. 1997. *Capitalism: an Ethnographic Approach.* Oxford: Berg.

Miller, Daniel. 1998. 'Conclusion: a theory of virtualism'. In J. G. Carrier and D. Miller (eds), *Virtualism: a New Political Economy.* Oxford: Berg, 187–215.

Miller, Daniel. 2001. *The Dialectics of Shopping.* Chicago: University of Chicago Press.

Miller, Daniel. 2002. 'Turning Callon the right way up'. *Economy and Society* 3(2): 218–33.

Ortony, A., ed. 1979. *Metaphor and Thought.* Cambridge: Cambridge University Press.

Parry, Jonathan and Maurice Bloch, eds. 1989. *Money and the Morality of Exchange.* London: Routledge & Kegan Paul.

Sandlie, Hans-Christian. 1999. *Med teknologi skal hjemmet drives: en forbruksundersøkelse av hva nordmenn har i sine hjem* (A Consumer Survey of Technological Items in Norwegian Homes). Lysaker, Norway: National Institute for Consumer Research.

Shenhav, Yehouda. 1994. 'Manufacturing uncertainty and the uncertainty of manufacturing: managerial discourse and the rhetoric of organizational theory'. *Science in Context* 7(2): 276–96.

SSB 2001. *Forbruksundersøkelsen 1996–98* (*Consumer Survey 1996–98*). Oslo: Statistisk Sentralbyrå (National Bureau of Statistics).

Williams, Raymond. 1983. *Keywords*. London: Fontana Press.
Willim, Robert. 2003. 'Claiming the future: speed, business rhetoric and computer practice'. In C. Garsten and H. Wulff (eds), *New Technologies at Work: People, Screens and Social Virtuality*. Oxford: Berg, 119–45.

Part II

Conceptualizing Morality in the Marketplace

4

Market Missions: Negotiating Bottom Line and Social Responsibility

Christina Garsten

Introduction: corporate globalization backlash?

Markets, as mechanisms of value transaction, have begun to penetrate deeply into our everyday lives. With recent social change, such as the remodelling of welfare states and intensified globalization of trade, the spirit of market capitalism increasingly colours our ways of thinking about the dynamics of societies as well as the make-up of social relations. Economic rationality, based on the idea that everyone is out for themselves and solely interested in maximizing their own pleasure and minimizing their experience of pain (Fevre, 2000: 200), appears in a variety of guises.

Corporations, as key actors in the marketplace, have come to symbolize much of what markets and economic rationality are believed to be about – competition, pricing, as well as greediness, and a hungry spirit on a constant search for profit. Corporate power now extends beyond national borders, maximizing the advantages of operating both within and beyond national structures, while at the same time relying crucially on the legal, fiscal, environmental and human organization of the nation-state (Appadurai, 1996: 168).

The expanded presence of transnational corporations on the global scene also implies that these companies are in a position to exert much greater influence within many societies. Many command resources that are formidably large in relation to those at the disposal of different groups and organizations within a nation-state. Their impact can be wide-ranging, impinging not just on economic factors, but also on the environment and social and cultural patterns. With the gradual dismantling of national regulations and trade barriers, a related retreat from welfarism and corporatism, and the establishment of flexible and entrepreneurial corporations as the template for organizational design, disorganized capitalism has taken a strong grip on the world. Large-scale global economies leave us with a fragmented political authority with limited power to fashion markets (Palan, 2000).

Much of our thinking about markets and their actors has been informed by a split between the benevolent state on the one hand, and the profit-oriented market on the other. A commonly held view is that getting involved in wider societal issues risks taking a corporation's eye 'off the ball' but also means intruding on the arena of the nation-state. Milton Friedman's view (1970) that 'the business of business is business' and the sole social responsibility of a corporation is to maximize profits for its shareholders is indicative of this.

In recent years, we have seen the development of a slightly different set of ideas positioning a new role for corporations in the global economy. As a response to tougher and closer media coverage, an awareness of the risks accompanying global trade, and a growing grassroots' critique and political action, corporations have to respond to politically conscious consumers and other critical actors (see, for example, Micheletti, Chapter 6 in this volume). A growing number of corporations are engaging in what may be seen as a normative add-on to capitalism. The idea that business has a broader social responsibility or citizenship role has strengthened with the globalization of markets (see, for example, Addo, 1999; Andriof and McIntosh, 2001; Compa and Diamond, 1996; Sullivan, 2003). Evangelists of 'corporate religion' and 'corporate citizenship' suggest new ways to conceptualize the relation of things economic to things social. Corporate social responsibility, commonly referred to as CSR, has since the 1990s emerged as one of the priorities in the policy documents and yearly reports of corporations. Corporate actors are seeking to develop and integrate codes of conduct and guidelines into their corporate cultures and management systems (see, for example, Leipziger, 2003). In this way, business leaders respond to stakeholder pressure and aim to project a new image of business as not just profit-seeking, not just greedy or self-interested, but also socially responsible, morally conscious, and ethically minded.

Since the United Nations Secretary General challenged world business leaders to 'embrace and enact' the Global Compact initiative in 1999, a number of similar initiatives at various levels, and with different kinds of organizations as initiators, have entered the scene. Non-governmental organizations (NGOs), such as Amnesty International, the Clean Clothes Campaign, and Solidar, support the efforts of the UN to promote the basic principles of a market informed by human rights principles and codes of conduct. Consultancies, such as the Caring Company, specialize in counselling business leaders in social accountability. Business organizations, such as Business for Social Responsibility, and networks, such as CSR Europe, work to facilitate enterprises' building of a global market with 'a human face'.

Likewise, a number of new tools and professional roles for organizational actors have emerged. Social standards, policies, codes of conduct, and a number of assessment practices abound (cf. Brunsson, Jacobsson and assoc., 2000). Corporations undergo ethical certification and enter into partnerships with other organizations to manifest accountability to the state, to the wider public and to potential consumers. A host of new professional positions are developed for the pursuit of corporate social responsibility – 'corporate social responsibility manager', 'manager codes of conduct', 'ethical trading manager', and the like. In the immediate surroundings of business corporations, a number of organizations, such as Global Reporting Initiative and Social Accountability International, are following up on the implementation process through social reporting and verification systems. Needless to say, the field of corporate social responsibility has also become a favourite concern of the media, with a number of magazines targeting CSR issues around the world. What we see is the development and growth of a new policy area, with an intricate network of organizations, new forms of partnerships, and its own particular language to support it. In this policy web, relations and interconnections between the social on the one hand, and the economic on the other, between moralities and markets, are increasingly complex and constantly renegotiated.

In this chapter, I will explore the field of corporate social responsibility as one in which organizational actors discuss and negotiate the relation of 'things social' to 'things economic'. In discussions of corporate social responsibility, managers try out partially new ways of conceptualizing the enterprise mission, the meaning of profit, and what it means to be a 'global player'. They try out new ways of combining profit with social accountability. In the process, they negotiate bottom line reasoning with sustainable futures, markets and moralities. By tracking the use of keywords such as 'accountability', 'transparency' and 'partnership', and by identifying the discourses in which they play a part, as well as the new institutions, norms, and areas of expertise they bring into existence, we may gain some understanding of the cultural and organizational logics inherent in the process of change in which they emerge. I will look into some of the more dominant keywords of the market *lingua franca* that are used in the field and how corporate actors aim to re-position the corporation in society by using these keywords. Such keywords,

I suggest, may function as Trojan horses that bring market notions into discussions of social issues, as seemingly apolitical and neutral tools for fashioning the workings of global market processes.[1]

CSR conferences: arenas for pursuing the common good

Doing fieldwork in the area of corporate social responsibility invites a number of methodological challenges. To begin with, it is not easy to determine where the field starts and where it ends. The field seems to appear in a number of different localities, only to evaporate or diffuse again as easily at it emerged. It may appear in a countryside village outside of Stockholm, at the premises of the Swedish Ministry of Foreign Affairs, at the European Commission in Brussels, or in luxury hotels in Brussels or Miami, only to mention a few of the places I have visited in the field. The field of corporate social responsibility, it seems, is 'here, there, and everywhere' (cf. Hannerz, 2003).

For the anthropologist, this is as frustrating as it is positively challenging. The actors seem, at first, to be continuously new ones, giving the impression of a field that continuously renews itself, or keeps on adding new members and associates. Having attended a few conferences and meetings, though, one begins to realize that some actors tend to appear now and again, that the issues discussed are quite similar across contexts, and that there are, after all, some patterns in the field.

Some degree of continuity begins to appear as one lets go of the idea of locating the field in space, as it were, and instead sets out to 'follow the metaphor', the 'plot', or the 'story' (Marcus, 1995). The field of corporate social responsibility is to a great extent a discursive arena, replete with keywords, such as 'accountability', 'transparency', 'corporate citizenship', 'partnership', and the like. These keywords are used in a great number of organizational settings and types of activities, in policy documents, in yearly reports, in internal discussions, and, not least, at conferences. Such keywords have a mobilizing function, with the capacity to energize and to give direction to thoughts and actions. In this sense, they are 'attention direction devices' that direct attention to particular issues and facilitate coordination across time and space (cf. Power, 2003: 14).

Conferences, as temporary organizations of interests, may be seen as arenas for the enactment and pursuit of corporate social responsibility. To some degree, corporate social responsibility is about conferencing. This does not amount to any cynicism on my part; my point is simply to emphasize the importance of conference participation as a way of 'doing' corporate social responsibility. True, the potential impact is judged at local level, where issues of social responsibility are to be put to work; down the supply chain, in factories, sweatshops, in domestic units, and elsewhere. But much of the field of corporate social responsibility is about corporate leaders presenting their cases and their experiences, discussing with one another, debating with NGO and union representatives, and setting up new meetings. Conferences are arenas for the performance of corporate social responsibility talk; arenas where the discourse of CSR is created, negotiated, and elaborated upon. They are arenas for drawing lines of inclusion and exclusion; for the marking of identity between those who believe in CSR and others; and not least, for the creation of visions, action plans, and for making a difference. Conferences are thus also part of what makes up 'the local' in this widely dispersed and globalizing field. They are 'where the action is' (cf. Strathern, 1995).

One such conference, arranged by the *Ethical Corporation* magazine on the theme Labour Standards and Human Rights, was held in the splendid premises of the SAS Radisson Hotel in Brussels in the autumn of 2003. The conference drew together around 400 participants: representatives of large transnational companies as well as smaller ones, NGO and union representatives, civil servants, a number of researchers, and some journalists. While these different actors may well be at different ends of the table outside the conference venue, during the conference days they were engaged in joint discussions about how the field of corporate accountability might best be developed.

The official agendas of conferences are often complemented by more informal, but equally important ones, organized spontaneously. The very possibility of meeting informally with representatives of different kinds of organizations is a main attraction in attending arranged conferences. One of the conference delegates told me that she often goes to conferences in order to meet with other professionals engaged in the same business sector – outside the conference programme. This is, in her view, where the really interesting and worthwhile meetings take place. In the textile industry, for example, it is often the case that CSR professionals share many of the same kinds of problems. These may have to do with matters such as the supply chain, wage levels, and political unrest in the country where the supplier operates. Another reason for conferencing, she underlined, is that it offers valuable opportunities to socialize with other CSR professionals of the same nationality. Hence, Swedes tend to stick together or meet up, as do the Danes and the Dutch. 'We hardly have time to meet up at home, so we organize meetings in connection with conferences', she explained. Among the CSR 'insiders', some conferences are also better known than others for facilitating such extra-programme meetings. And they are not necessarily those that take place in the more attractive cities.

The people who are engaged in the corporate responsibility area may be said to constitute a particular 'tribe' of transnationalism (cf. Field, 1971; Hannerz, 1990: 243). As mentioned above, the upsurge in the demand for corporate social responsibility has resulted in the creation of new professional positions and roles in corporations, NGOs and state agencies. Their particular role in the organizations they represent, their knowledge and expertise in the area, their experiences and perspectives, and their capacity to mediate between the global and local, make this 'tribe' an important collectivity in the globalizing of markets. They may be looked upon as part of a specific form of 'discourse coalition', in which actors might perceive of their interests and positions as widely different, but are nevertheless attracted to a specific and common set of storylines, that is, the discursive elements that keep the coalition together (Hajer, 1995: 65). CSR conferences are arenas where the members of this discourse coalition get together, try out their positions, negotiate on the meanings of concepts and tools, and visualize ways ahead.

As stated by Carrier (1997: 47), 'The Market model is expressed in language, and languages model our experiences.'[2] The Market model is like a *lingua franca*, in the sense of being a creature of public discourse between groups defined by the different places they occupy in society. Different collective actors in society, such as corporations, NGOs, and public agencies, have their own specialized languages that express specific experiences, perspectives, and interests. The various arenas where corporate social responsibility takes shape are also arenas where the *lingua franca* of the Market model is developed and put to use. Let us now take a closer look at the particular language of CSR.

A community of words

The conference delegates at the *Ethical Corporation* conference in Brussels seemed very aware that they were part of a discursive coalition or community, where the members spoke the same language, and where they used the same words as signifiers. There were several mentions of the particular language of CSR during the conference. Moreover, there was a sense of awareness of the fact that skilful use of this language determines who is 'in' and who is 'out'. By way of short comments or humorous remarks, delegates would let the other participants understand that there is even a degree of redundancy in the use of keywords. One of the business leaders started his PowerPoint presentation by acknowledging that 'this is a community of words', and then went on to outline the basic principles underlying the work of his company in the area of CSR. Another conference delegate opened his presentation by apologizing for the redundancy in the terminology he was going to use: 'I will be talking the talk of corporate social responsibility'. This remark stirred a wave of laughter among the slightly embarrassed and amused audience, who would recognize themselves in his situation.

As is evident in the examples above, conferences are arenas where one may display one's connection to a community of words. By joking or playing with the appropriate vocabulary, one may give evidence to one's mastery of the language and membership of the community. As a particular type of language, the CSR *lingua franca* also serves an exclusionary function. This is why even people who may be sceptical about the inherent meanings of a concept or phrasing may choose to engage in the *lingua franca* in order to communicate with the other actors in the field. Although they may not agree with the business version of CSR, union and NGO activists often choose to employ the same terminology as the corporate people, and vice versa.

The power of the Market model depends to a great extent on the activation of the particular 'keywords' that are central to this language, and that may act as metaphors for change. Without engaging too deeply in the meanings of such keywords, I will describe briefly some of the more dominant ones. The point is not to provide a discursive content analysis, but to give an idea of the kinds of keywords that are used as signposts and markers of belonging in this particular discourse coalition.

Transparency

The call for 'transparency' is perhaps one of the more salient features of contemporary market language. Transparency appears as a powerful remedy to corporate scandals of various kinds, and serves to mark the one who utters the word as having nothing, or at least little, to hide. As Sanders (2003: 149) has so succinctly put it: 'The desire to unveil the hidden, to disclose the closed, to reveal the concealed – in short to make transparent that which is out of sight – is as central to economic processes as it is to political ones (Larsson and Lundberg, 1998)'. Transparency is intimately connected to the globalization of markets, both as a way to strengthen the dynamics of global capitalism, but also to reveal and control the everyday workings of local and global economies (Sanders, 2003: 148–9). Transparency is also central to the operations of transnational organizations, such as the United Nations, the European Union, the World Bank, the World Trade Organization and numerous non-governmental organizations (Clamers, 1997; Kopits and Craig, 1998; Kratz, 1999; Marceau and Pedersen, 1999). It is therefore hardly surprising that transparency is at the top of the agenda of many CSR conferences, some of which are even entirely devoted to the area. At the Business for Social Responsibility Conference in Miami in 2002, one of the participants, a male business leader in his early forties, claimed that: 'Transparency is about communication, about telling the full story in order to offset conspiracy theories among our customers. It is about opening up our books to show what we are doing, to build trust. Facts are friendly. Transparency is so much more than a single document.'

Another participant, a male NGO representative, underlined that business leaders have a responsibility to report to those who have legitimate interests: 'Stakeholders have a right to know. Transparency builds good relationships with stakeholders.' A third participant, a man who had set up his own CSR consultancy in the aftermath of an environmental crisis caused by the company at which he was employed, had his own view on transparency: 'Transparency is about telling what makes us uneasy. It goes beyond what you would want to know. Basically, we should demand from companies what we demand from our children – that they tell when they did wrong, that they are honest. Transparency is a personal thing.'

Accountability

The use of the term transparency often goes hand in hand with that of 'accountability'. Calls for greater transparency inevitably lead to considerations of the responsiveness of the organization to civil society, and therefore its accountability (Bendell and Lake, 2000: 229). Just like transparency, accountability is an offspring of the globalization of markets and the accompanying problematics of governance. And just as the trope of transparency extends beyond markets, to universities, state agencies, and international aid, so does that of accountability. In the field of CSR, accountability requires that the company acts responsibly and accounts for its actions or inactions in some form of report provided for its stakeholders (see, for example, Holland and Gibbon, 2001: 279). The idea of accountability hovers behind the vast array of standards, reporting initiatives and verification procedures that are put to work. These are then, to some extent, to be seen as part of the 'accountability toolkit'. But, with Bendell and Lake (2000: 229), we may ask: to what extent can a company owned by shareholders be accountable to employees, communities and the wider society, and what mechanism can ensure this? Where are the boundaries of accountability to be drawn?

There is no single and simple answer to these questions. Rather, answers tend to vary both among and between organizations. This was clearly demonstrated at the Business for Social Responsibility Conference in Miami. During one of the group discussions, the main topic was the issue of accountability with reference to international supply chain relations. The group consisted of approximately forty business representatives and a few consultants and researchers. The discussion started off rather tentatively, with participants cautiously sharing experiences and testing their views. The difficulties of drawing the lines of accountability were aired. Could an American company be accountable for working conditions at a subcontractor location in Sri Lanka? Is it really the responsibility of the employer to make sure that the workers on banana plantations in South America have appropriate housing conditions? And how does one go about checking up on subcontractors so that they adhere to the company code of conduct and the core conventions on labour rights? A sharing of experiences then followed, in which different views were expressed, but no single answer was agreed upon. The limits of accountability were left diffuse. What was at stake here was, among other issues, the extent to which a corporation can be held accountable for areas that do not directly involve its core activities, but that have to do with the larger context in which corporations operate, or with conditions further down the supply chain. As a backdrop for this issue, reflections were made on social as well as environmental risk scenarios, and the organizational complexity of global chains of production.

The concept of accountability has the capacity to draw together different actors and to spur actions, but is imbued with conflict and open to negotiation. While NGOs and state agencies tend to demand that accountability is stretched to include all areas of operation that are affected by the activities of a corporation, all the way down the supply chain, business leaders advocate a more limited area of accountability. A top manager at a Swedish business association made this clear at a recent seminar organized by the Swedish Ministry of Foreign Affairs: 'We must be clear about the fact that it is always the state who is to be held accountable if human rights and workers' rights are not observed in the country in which you are operating.'

While the ambiguity of accountability is kept more or less intact at conferences, it is in practice, at the local level, that the boundaries of accountability are put to the test and where its conflictual nature is revealed.

Dialogue

Now and then, conference convenors and business leaders in their presentations emphasize 'dialogue' as a necessary component of relationships between businesses, NGOs, trade unions and state agencies. In the context of engaging with stakeholders, dialogue refers to the conversation between a business and at least one of its stakeholders. It is believed that through dialogue it is possible to exchange experiences, views, information, and to acquire knowledge. Dialogue may in this way contribute to mutual learning. It is also a way to ease the conflict of interest between parties and to enhance confidence building. To engage in dialogue is generally not seen as involving any binding structure of interaction, but to be something quite informal, voluntary, and non-binding. It may also be the first step to the establishment of a partnership relation. The value of dialogue as a keyword is indicative of the weight with which an 'open, participatory approach to policy making' is stressed in CSR initiatives.

Partnership

In recent years, the notion of 'partnership' has evolved from a legalistic business concept into more common usage as a general inter-personal term and inter-organizational idea. It has become a powerful organizing principle for people and organizations throughout the world (see, for example, Murphy and Coleman, 2000: 208–9). 'The new era of partnership' has seen the rise of public – private partnerships, a closer collaboration between NGOs and trade unions, between NGOs and corporations, and a number of coalitions, networks, and alliances of various sorts. As noted by Murphy and Coleman (2000: 209), this keyword is a carrier of many hopes: 'The emergence of a global civil society based on partnership principles is now considered as one of the real hopes of democratising the global political economy (De Oliveira and Tandon, 1994; Korten, 1998).'

In the pursuit of corporate social responsibility, partnership provides a vehicle for joint activities that may favourably influence the perception of all parties. Forming partnerships with NGOs can be a way for corporations to gain credibility. At CSR conferences, the significance of choosing the 'right' partners, whether they are NGOs, local action groups, public officials, or other company representatives is often stressed. Partners are carefully selected. They need to be trusted, accountable and reliable. The success or failure of putting a code of conduct to work, and of doing profitable business is often dependent upon the choice of local partner, business leaders tend to say. They are quite keen to give examples of the process of choosing a partner, and the criteria that entered into this choice.

Despite the risks of working with partners who may have different priorities, the idea of partnership is generally an accepted and much-celebrated form of collaboration and governance. Inherent in the idea of partnership is also the notion that the relationship is a voluntary relationship between equal partners, and sometimes with a romantic overtone (as is evident in relations between individuals). It expresses a commonly held belief, especially among business leaders, that a voluntary approach to regulation of CSR is the favoured way forward.

People

Another keyword frequently used at CSR conferences is 'people'. In these contexts, 'people' refers to locals, employees or other stakeholders living and working in the geographical site at the end of the supply chain, where products are assembled or raw materials collected.

At the Business for Social Responsibility Conference in Miami, a company manager in the clothing industry in Guatemala gave a detailed account of the social and healthcare programmes they are running to improve the living conditions and health status of their employees. Having gone through the extensive presentations, illustrated by colourful slides with examples of housing improvements, medical clinics, and the like, he concluded that: 'We want to provide good values and good judgement... Really for us it's about community. We are in the people industry... We want our employees and their families to feel they are part of something bigger.' Others expressed similar concerns. 'It's very important to listen to the people', one company representative underlined, as he was describing the implementation of their corporate policy down the supply chain.

An understanding of the social context of production is generally considered essential for a successful social change programme, or for making sure human rights, workers' rights and social standards are respected and abided by. 'People' are brought into conferences by colourful slides and ample citations from 'the local context'. A number of voices from across the world are thus represented. And yet, they remain 'virtual people' in the sense of appearing as an anonymous crowd, referred to, but not socially present (cf. the notion of 'the virtual consumer', in Lien, Chapter 3 in this volume). The emphasis on people and community nevertheless serves to align business discursively with the calls for a more 'humane capitalism' and to make manifest and convincing the idea that successful business operations are also able to provide better social conditions for people across the world.

Thus, a standardized set of keywords provides the members of this transnational discourse coalition with a *lingua franca* that facilitates communication among parties who may represent different interests. The particular strength of this language and its associated keywords is that it has the capacity to flow across contexts, to disentangle itself from the particularities of local context and to re-entangle with new actors in new contexts and situations. Its very abstractness and visionary character facilitate its use across social contexts, across organizations, countries, and cultural boundaries of any sort. The keywords are free-floating signifiers, rarely rooted in any particular place, yet they direct attention in particular ways. Because of their flexible usage, their supposed neutrality, and not least their visionary appeal, they make up an attractive toolkit for the successful navigation of market actors in all parts of the world.

While some keywords appear with some frequency and continuity across space and time, the discourse of corporate social responsibility is not a stable landscape. Words like 'transparency' and 'accountability' will acquire a range of contingent meanings or existing meanings may be stretched in novel and unpredictable directions, when used by different actors with differing interests, and when introduced into new areas of operation (cf. Williams, 1976; see also Shore and Wright, 2000).[3]

Moreover, the Market model as a public language is far from a neutral vehicle for communication. Those who are exposed to this particular *lingua franca* are also shaped by it, and learn the ways of thinking and acting associated with it (Carrier, 1997: 49). The language may then work as a motivational force with the capacity to influence and mobilize people in certain ways. The power of this language to some degree explains the attraction of conferences and other venues where 'talk' is placed at the top of the agenda. Conferences are venues for people with different interests to mobilize other stakeholders to be positively tuned into their ideas, to evangelize and spread the word, so to speak.

Market discourses are, in other words, performative. They give direction for daily practice, and they prescribe and encourage certain types of behaviour, sometimes supported by various types of practices, such as those of evaluation, reward, and sanction.

Re-positioning the corporation

Studying how market keywords are used during conferences, meetings, in presentations and in documents, and as part of informal conversations, I was able to discern four metaphoric structures that represent different ways in which corporate actors position themselves in society. Whilst these images or metaphoric constructs are based on interviews and participant observations, they are not entirely *emic*[4] in character, but represent my own interpretations and extrapolations of the empirical material. These constructs may serve the purpose of illustrating different voices in the process of engaging with CSR, and how this engagement is perceived in organizational life.

The entrepreneurial corporation

For the majority of business leaders, corporate social responsibility is basically about business. A business manager told me emphatically that: 'Let's face it, the bottom line is still profit'. Several managers have expressed similar views. The big picture is that significant changes in the world, such as increased access to information, extensive media coverage, supply chains stretching across national boundaries, and a general awareness of global risk scenarios have changed the everyday context for business leaders. Issues that have earlier been looked upon as marginal to success are now at the forefront of business. The entrepreneurial corporation recognizes the importance of these management issues and plans accordingly, simply because the costs of failing to do so would be considerable, not least in terms of bad reputation and damage to the brand. Instead of sidelining critical issues into some marginal department, they are taken on because they can serve business profitably. The common view is that business should respond to stakeholder demands for accountability and transparency not because it is nice to do, but because it may strengthen the brand and enhance profitability in the long run. 'CSR is a long-term, and slightly risky, investment in the brand, it's actually an entrepreneurial activity', one business manager told me. Corporate social responsibility, then, does nothing to overturn Milton Friedman's dictum. In this view, the business of business is still business. This is where the market imperative is most evident. Engaging in social issues is seen as a way of actually strengthening market value – a way of being entrepreneurial.

The collaborative corporation

It is often stated, in conference presentations as well as in business literature (see, for example, Grayson and Hodges, 2002), that the contributions that business can make to a particular community are often best achieved by the corporation working with other businesses and/or with government and NGOs. Collaboration with community groups and government is understood as a way to gain credibility, not least if these organizations are seen as trustworthy. The collaborative corporation continually re-evaluates its relations with others – with suppliers, customers, employees, community groups, and government agencies. The need to establish new patterns of working together is stressed. Partnership is also seen as a way to move beyond dialogue, to mobilize a wider range of resources, enhance innovation, and increase access to different types of skill.

The collaborative corporation aims to engage in dialogue and partnership as ways to manage stakeholders' expectations, reduce risks, and develop new markets. Business leaders are generally aware of the fact that there are also risks to a collaborative approach: it requires transparency in processes and in decisions, accountability within the partnership, determining the rights and responsibilities of each partner, the criteria for participation, and so on – issues that may be difficult to agree upon (see also Holliday, Schmidheiny, and Watts, 2002: Chapter 6). As one business leader stressed in a conference presentation: 'It is very important to select your partners carefully, and this may take time. You need to know your partners very well.' The collaborative corporation is well aware of the value of recognizing reputational risks and the potentials of reducing these risks by way of opening up for dialogue and partnership.

The cosmopolitan corporation

Metaphorically speaking, some corporate leaders aim to project an image of themselves and their companies as cosmopolitans of sorts. Cosmopolitanism, as we know, may come in a variety of different forms and expressions (Hannerz, 1990). When talking about corporations and their leaders as cosmopolitans, what stands out is their stated willingness to mediate between different cultures; to act as bridgeheads into other, territorially based cultures; and to establish contact between cultures (Garsten, 2003; cf. Hannerz, 1990: 245). Needless to say, the kinds of experiences and images that are mediated by corporate actors are premised on market value. While they play a role in organizing world culture into some degree of coherence, they are also mapping a world of distinctions, created out of business segmentation and competitive advantage motives. The cosmopolitan corporation has a strong interest in the survival of certain kinds of cultural diversity, since the market to a great extent thrives on the exploitation of diversity.

But the type of cosmopolitanism expressed here is not so much a deep involvement or interest in the Other, as a built-up skill in manoeuvring between cultures in search of marketable images.[5] Nor do corporations always show such cultural sensitivity as one could hope for, as evinced for example in local grassroots protests. Nevertheless, in the cosmopolitan corporation, words such as 'diversity management', 'corporate citizenship', 'people', and 'local culture' are often heard. Marcus' (1998: 7) phrasing may serve to illustrate this positioning: 'the emphasis on organizational competitiveness is still there, but the discourse is inflated with concerns about values, corporate personhood, the relation of individuals to community – in general, those topics that might have been considered before as "soft" in relation to "means–ends" modifications of organizational practices with the bottom line of competitive enhancement always in sight'.

We may view this type of approach as a re-positioning of the corporation into a cosmopolitan in the world, with a degree of cultural sensitivity and cultural competence as part of its competitive advantage (Garsten, 2003).

The conscientious corporation

A fourth metaphor for the re-positioning of the corporation in the wider society is that of the conscientious corporation. This is where the call for ethics and morality is strongest, where morality testing of employees is seen as legitimate, and where transparency and accountability are endorsed as ways of 'flushing through' and 'cleansing'. Managers of conscientious corporations take the issue of CSR very seriously, and in their enthusiasm they take on the role of 'missionaries' or 'evangelists' of what they see as ways of contributing to a new and better world order.

Business leaders who give voice to this metaphor tend to give personalized accounts of their thoughts and actions in a problematic situation, the moral dilemmas involved, and the value of integrity. Such stories tend to turn into a sort of 'confessional tales', powerful in their personalized and authentic nature. Here the formation of 'an organizational conscience' would seem to be strongly related to individual reflexivity and the expression of individual voices (see also McMillan and Hyde, 2000). An American consultant, who left his employer in the aftermath of a corporate scandal to start up his own consultancy in the CSR area, told me: 'It all starts with the individual, it's an accumulated result of the actions of individuals'. Conscience as a collective property of organizations has started to gain some recognition among NGOs, where it is looked for and rewarded as examples of 'best practice' in CSR. As an example, Social Accountability International (SAI), a New York-based NGO that works to improve workplaces and combat sweatshops by developing and promoting socially responsible standards, has instigated The Corporate Conscience Awards (CCA). The CCA recognize progressive companies that respect the rights of workers and the community. They honour outstanding social and environmental performance and seek to encourage widespread adoption of award-winning responsible business practices. There are three award categories: 'Environmental and Community Positive Impact', 'Innovative Partnership', and 'SA8000 Responsible Workplace' (superior performance in implementing the SA8000 workplace standard). Any interested party may submit nominations for the awards, and the judgement is then made by a jury (see Social Accountability International, 2004).

While initiatives like the above may well be worthwhile tools in scrutinizing corporate behaviour, they also show that the area of corporate social responsibility itself is a promoter of many different kinds of markets, where the market for standards and reporting systems is complemented by a market for awards and distinctions.

These metaphoric structures represent different ways in which the role of the corporation in society is negotiated and positioned, slightly different uses of the Market *lingua franca*, and with some shifts in the emphasis made. The metaphoric construct may be said to work as a model, not only *of* the world (Fernandez, 1974; Geertz, 1973), but more importantly, *for* the world. For actors in the field of CSR, they serve as tools for ordering the world, defining the role of corporations within it, and as a device for the structuring of their own thoughts and actions.

Conclusion: the Trojan horses of the Market model

CSR conferences are arenas where the dilemmas of economic rationality and social accountability are discussed and negotiated. However, the basic principles of economic rationality are generally not questioned in any substantive way. On the contrary, CSR conferences tend to celebrate the superiority of capitalism and economic rationality and to emphasize that profitability and expansion of markets is the only way forward.

Anyone who has participated in a conference devoted to these issues should have been struck by the air of agreement and consensus that permeates it. It appears that at least the majority of participants have come, not primarily to defend their own rather unique adversarial interests, but to connect to, and join other parties in what may appear as a common vision and road ahead. What comes across clearly in arenas such as the *Ethical Corporation* conference, is that it is replete with actors who strive to make a difference, to 'do good'. The area of corporate social responsibility is a world where promising visions of the future are sketched out and where new kinds of market Utopia are crafted, by reacting against or extrapolating from certain features of the present. And in this process, conferences are important arenas for market actors to share their visions and build support for their agendas. As pointed out by Koselleck (1985), in the present context of globalization and its resulting crises, the modern world faces a challenge in aligning the experience of past and present. The visions of human capitalism contained within the corporate social responsibility discourse help its actors place themselves within a temporality organized by human thought and humane ends as much as by the contingencies of uncontrolled events. In Carrier's view, there is strong motivational structure embedded in the Market model. Somewhat paradoxically, while the Market is explicitly concerned with choice, and individual difference would seem particularly suited to be the liberating mechanism to usher in a multiplicity of voices, the market also becomes its own master narrative (Carrier, 1997: 50; Fukuyama, 1992). With reference to the area of corporate social responsibility, the keywords of market discourse may function as Trojan horses, containers of meaning that bring in particular market understandings and perspectives in such a sophisticated way that the recipients are often unaware of them being delivered.

To some extent, and paraphrasing Harper (2000: 47), the keywords as well as the standards, codes of conduct, and reporting procedures aimed at regulating global business are in the business of creating a particular moral order. The social and ethical turn in business is a case of 'moral transformation', in which data and practices that are by nature conflictual and political are transformed and come to exist in a moral field. In this transformed moral field, the standards, the codes of conduct and related tools are given a status beyond political contestation, being viewed as morally and ethically sound, and, hence, difficult to question in principle. Such transformations are likely to be salient in all organizations and institutional contexts that are subject to some kind of audit (Harper 2000: 51). From this perspective, 'audit society' is much less rational and much more political than we may think (cf. Power, 1997). This moral transformation, I suggest, reflects the negotiating of bottom line and universal ideals, market and non-market understandings, without fully exploring the implications of the combinatory exercise. The combin-ation is made possible by the very ambiguity inherent in the discourse of corporate social responsibility. This is where we may conceive of the language of CSR as consisting of a number of Trojan horses, capable of introducing hidden meanings into everyday actions and regulatory processes. These hidden meanings make it possible to leave the dynamics of global capitalism unchallenged, while removing the 'winner-takes-all' connotations. Also, the resistance that market discourses and their imperatives may otherwise provoke from actors is, as least partly and for some time, removed.

This should not blind us to the fact that the formation and transformation of discourse is a dynamic process characterized by negotiations, resistance and ultimately power struggle (Garsten and Jacobsson, 2004). Generalized discourses, such as those of corporate social responsibility, are at some point translated into local contexts, where existing practices, traditions, and institutionalized ways of seeing things and doing things transform and reformulate ideas and keywords in specific ways. The members of this transnational culture – the corporate managers, the NGO activists, the union representatives, and others – create their own understandings of the keywords. In this sense, practice speaks back to discourse. It is largely in the practice of implementation, monitoring and verification of CSR processes that the different interests, interpretations and positions are revealed, and only rarely in arenas such as CSR conferences.

The performative power of the discourse of CSR becomes all the more evident as assumptions and, not least, its language are appropriated and spread by national or international organizations of unquestioned legitimacy. As stated by Carrier (1997: 53), 'the Market model, or any candidate for the status of public language, is likely to become powerful when it is adopted by institutions that are central to public debate, particularly governments'. The discursive transformations that take place as the United Nations, the European Commission, or the Swedish Ministry of Foreign Affairs engage in the area of CSR are thus of great social and political importance. They may involve neither a complete acceptance, nor a complete turnover of basic assumptions, but a gradual shift in understanding and framing, involving gradual changes in the ways people, communities and corporations are to be understood, as well as changes in assumptions regarding agency and responsibility and the type of knowledge and policy actions that are valued.[6] Such transformations, then, signify changes in culture and ideology and give way to shifts in the nature of economy and polity. And they contribute to the shifting allocation of responsibilities and capacities among collective actors in society.

Notes

1. The chapter builds on a combination of multi-sited, mobile fieldwork in a number of different arenas, such as conference venues, meetings, seminars, and the like, where the fashioning of socially responsible markets is discussed. As part of the research process, interviews with corporate leaders in different positions in large companies in Sweden, and with representatives of non-governmental organizations and consultancies were also conducted, and documents analyzed. The research project started in 1998 and is still ongoing. I am grateful to Raoul Galli, Mita Bhattacharyya and Annika Malmsten for their assistance in the project, not least by conducting interviews and gathering background data. I wish to thank the Bank of Sweden Tercentenary Foundation and the Swedish Research Council for funding this project.

2. The Market model, as a conception of the world, has been discussed at great length by Carrier (1997). Suffice it to say here that it draws attention to the basic assumptions underlying the Market, such as the assumption that the world consists only of free, rational, and self-reliant individuals, of buyers and sellers, subject to no constraints other than those they accept voluntarily (Carrier, 1997: 1–58).

3. Analogously, the word 'flexibility' was released from its traditional moorings, inflated in importance, and now, like a free-floating signifier, hovers over virtually every field of modern working life (Garsten, 1999; Garsten and Turtinen, 2000; Martin, 1994).

4. An 'emic' account is generally conceived of as one being close to the experienced social reality and to the accounts of informants.

5. Elsewhere (Garsten, 2003), I have suggested that the culturally sensitive firm may be seen as something of a 'dilettante cosmopolitan' (cf. Hannerz, 1992: 253).

6. Concerns regarding the politicization of business are also being raised from economists, business managers and others, who maintain that business should stick to business, and nothing else. For example, Henderson (2002) argues that if the worldwide ideological trends of CSR continue, more and more businesses and corporations will be under pressure to follow these types of management policies, with harmful consequences for society as a whole.

References

Addo, Michael K., ed. 1999. *Human Rights Standards and the Responsibility of Transnational Corporations*. The Hague: Kluwer Law International.

Andriof, Jörg, and Malcolm McIntosh, eds. 2001. *Perspectives on Corporate Citizenship*. Sheffield: Greenleaf Publishing.

Appadurai, Arjun. 1996. *Modernity at Large*. Minneapolis: University of Minnesota Press.

Bendell, Jem, and Rob Lake. 2000. 'New frontiers: emerging NGO activities to strengthen transparency and accountability in business'. In J. Bendell (ed.), *Terms for Endearment: Business, NGOs and Sustainable Development*. Sheffield: Greenleaf Publishing, 226–38.

Brunsson, Nils, Bengt Jacobsson, and associates. 2000. *A World of Standards*. Oxford: Oxford University Press.

Carrier, James G. 1997. 'Introduction'. In J. G. Carrier (ed.), *Meanings of the Market*. Oxford: Berg, 1–67.

Clamers, Malcolm, ed. 1997. *Developing Arms Transparency*. Bradford: Bradford University Press.

Compa, Lance A., and Stephen F. Diamond, eds. 1996. *Human Rights, Labour Rights, and International Trade*. Philadelphia: University of Pennsylvania Press.

De Oliveira, Miguel Darcy, and Rajesh Tandon, eds. 1994. *Citizens Strengthening Global Civil Society*. Washington, DC: CIVICUS World Alliance for Citizen Participation.

Fernandez, James. 1974. 'Persuasions and performances: of the beast in every body and the metaphors in everyman'. In C. Geertz (ed.), *Myth, Symbol and Culture*. New York: Norton, 39–60.

Fevre, Ralph W. 2000. *The Demoralization of Western Culture: Social Theory and the Dilemmas of Modern Living*. London: Continuum.

Field, James A. Jr. 1971. 'Transnationalism and the new tribe'. *International Organization* 25: 353–62.

Friedman, Milton. 1970. 'The social responsibility of business is to increase its profits'. *New York Times Magazine* 32–3 (13 September).

Fukuyama, Francis. 1992. *The End of History and the Last Man*. New York: The Free Press.

Garsten, Christina. 1999. 'Betwixt and between: temporary employees as liminal subjects in flexible organizations'. *Organization Studies* 20(4): 601–17.

Garsten, Christina. 2003. 'The cosmopolitan organization: an essay on corporate accountability'. *Global Networks* 3(3): 355–70.

Garsten, Christina, and Kerstin Jacobsson. 2004. 'Conclusion: discursive transformations and the nature of modern power'. In C. Garsten and K. Jacobsson (eds), *Learning to be Employable: New Agendas on Work, Employability and Learning in a Globalizing World*. Basingstoke: Palgrave Macmillan, 274–89.

Garsten, Christina, and Jan Turtinen. 2000. '"Angels" and "chameleons": the cultural construction of the flexible temporary employee in Sweden and the UK'. In Bo Stråth (eds), *After Full Employment: European Discourses on Work and Flexibility*. Brussels: Peter Lang, 161–206.

Geertz, Clifford. 1973. *The Interpretation of Cultures*. New York: Basic Books.

Grayson, David, and Adrian Hodges. 2002. *Everybody's Business: Managing Risks and Opportunities in Today's Global Society*. New York: DK Publishing, Inc.

Hajer, Maarten A. 1995. *The Politics of Environmental Discourse: Ecological Modernization and the Policy Process*. Oxford: Oxford University Press.

Hannerz, Ulf. 1990. 'Cosmopolitans and locals in world culture'. In M. Featherstone (ed.), *Global Culture: Nationalism, Globalization and Modernity*. London: Sage, 34–56.

Hannerz, Ulf. 1992. *Cultural Complexity*. New York: Columbia University Press.

Hannerz, Ulf. 2003. 'Being there...and there...and there! Reflections on multi-site ethnography'. *Ethnography* 4: 229–44.

Harper, Richard. 2000. 'The social organization of the IMF's mission work: an examination of international auditing'. In M. Strathern (ed.), *Audit Cultures*. London: Routledge, 21–53.

Henderson, David. 2002. *Misguided Virtue: False Notions of Corporate Social Responsibility*. London: Institute of Economic Affairs.

Holland, Leigh, and Jane Gibbon. 2001. 'Processes in social and ethical account-ability: external reporting mechanisms'. In J. Andriof and M. Molntosh (eds), *Perspectives on Corporate Citizenship*. Sheffield: Greenleaf Publishing, 278–95.

Holliday, Charles O. Jr, Stephan Schmidheiny, and Philip Watts. 2002. *Walking the Talk: The Business Case for Sustainable Development*. Sheffield: Greenleaf Publishing.

Kopits, George, and Jon Craig. 1998. *Transparency in Government Operations*. Washington, DC: International Monetary Fund.

Korten, David C. 1998. *Globalizing Civil Society: Reclaiming our Right to Power*. New York: Seven Stories Press.

Koselleck, Reinhart. 1985. *Futures Past: On the Semantics of Historical Time*. Cambridge, MA: MIT Press.

Kratz, Catherine. 1999. 'Transparency and the European Union'. *Cultural Values* 3(4): 387–92.

Larsson, Mats, and David Lundberg. 1998. *The Transparent Market*. London: Macmillan.

Leipziger, Deborah. 2003. *The Corporate Responsibility Code Book*. Sheffield: Greenleaf Publishing.

Marceau, Gabrielle, and Peter N. Pedersen. 1999. 'Is the WTO open and transpar-ent? A discussion of the relationship of the WTO with non-governmental organisations and civil society's claims for more transparency and public par-ticipation'. *Journal of World Trade* 33(1): 5–49.

Marcus, George E. 1995. 'Ethnography in/of the world system: The emergence of multi-sited ethnography'. *Annual Review of Anthropology* 24: 95–117.

Marcus, George E., ed. 1998. 'Introduction'. In *Corporate Futures: The Diffusion of the Culturally Sensitive Firm*. Chicago: University of Chicago Press, 1–13.

Martin, Emily. 1994. *Flexible Bodies: Tracking Immunity in American Culture – From the Days of Polio to the Age of AIDS*. Boston, MA: Beacon Press.

McMillan, Jill J., and Michael J. Hyde. 'Technological innovation and change: a case study in the formation of organizational conscience'. *Quarterly Journal of Speech* 86 (February 2000): 19–47.

Murphy, David F., and Gill Coleman. 2000. 'Thinking partners: business, NGOs and the partnership concept'. In J. Bendell (ed.), *Terms for Endearment: Business, NGOs and Sustainable Development*. Sheffield: Greenleaf Publishing, 207–15.

Palan, Ronen. 2000. 'New trends in global political economy'. In R. Palan (ed.), *Global Political Economy: Contemporary Theories*. London: Routledge, 1–18.

Power, Michael. 1997. *The Audit Society: Rituals of Verification*. Oxford: Oxford University Press.

Power, Michael. 2003. *The Invention of Operational Risk*. ESRC Centre for Analysis and Risk and Regulation: Discussion paper no. 16.

Sanders, Todd. 2003. 'Invisible hands and visible goods: revealed and concealed economies in millennial Tanzania'. In H. G. West and T. Sanders (eds), *Transpar-ency and Conspiracy: Ethnographies of Suspicion in the New World Order*. Durham: Duke University Press, 149–74.

Shore, Cris, and Susan Wright. 2000. 'Coercive accountability: the rise of audit culture in higher education'. In M. Strathern (ed.), *Audit Cultures: Anthro-pological Studies in Accountability, Ethics and the Academy*. London: Routledge, 57–89.

Social Accountability International (SAI). 2004. Online, http://www.cepaa.org/ (accessed February 29, 2004).

Strathern, Marilyn. 1995. 'The nice thing about culture is that everyone has it'. In M. Strathern (ed.), *Shifting Contexts*. London: Routledge, 153–76.

Sullivan, Rory, ed. 2003. *Business and Human Rights: Dilemmas and Solutions*. Sheffield: Greenleaf Publishing.

Williams, Raymond. 1976. *Keywords*. London: Fontana.

5

Between the Individual and the Community: Market and Morals in Venezuelan Economic Life

Miguel Montoya

Introduction

Every society must face the task of demarcating its economic space in a way that can provide for individual ambitions, while ensuring the survival and welfare of the community at large. This delineation of economic rights and responsibilities, the socially necessary, the possible, and the impossible, generally involves continuous confrontation and exchange between the state, different social sectors, and market actors. The content of the dialogue that takes place naturally has much to do with the society's specific situation in geography and history, and thereby, its particular culture.

This chapter is a reflection on recent economic discourse in Venezuela, a country rich in natural resources, that left behind an agricultural past at the beginning of the 1900s to become one of the world's leading petroleum exporters.[1] The rapid modernization and urbanization brought about by the mining economy had a substantial effect on the cultural life of the nation, but has not enabled most of its people to prosper. According to estimates nearly half of the population lives on two dollars a day or less.[2] Corruption, unemployment and crime are constant problems.

Here, I will focus on the period since the end of the 1990s, when popularly elected president Hugo Chávez undertook to reorient the nation's political and economic life, ostensibly to provide a greater measure of democracy and a better standard of living for the majority of Venezuelans. A large part of his initial agenda involved the national project of writing a new constitution to put an end to what he and his supporters judged to be forty years of corruption that had bankrupted the nation and brought most Venezuelans into economic misery. Chávez calls this rewriting of the constitution and the economic changes now in progress the *'revolución bolivariana'* (bolivarian revolution), a 'democratic revolutionary process', or *'la revolución bonita'* (the beautiful revolution). He says that it is a process in which the country's poor, who had previously had no influence in government, are finally able to make their voices heard. Chávez' rhetoric, nationalist and deeply moral, is laden with quotations from the Bible and from Latin America's *'Libertador'* and political theorist, Simón Bolívar. His political speech often returns to the concept of sovereignty, and that *el pueblo*, or 'the people', are sovereign, and their decisions must be respected, as must those of one nation *vis-à-vis* another. There is no examination, however, of who does, and who does not, make up the body politic of *el pueblo*.

I will argue that Chávez' appeal and rhetoric can in part be understood by reflecting on the rural, agricultural background and values of the majority of his supporters. His frequent public repudiation of the market as a partner in development is, in part, a consequence of how 'market' historically has been staged in Venezuela, but it is also a reflection of rurally based conceptions of economic life. By briefly presenting Venezuela's contemporary economic history, basing the analysis partly on Gudeman and Rivera's (1990) distinctions between the house economy and the corporate economy, I hope to show how rural 'house' values and practices permeate the daily life of the poor and resonate in Chávez' political discussions of economic life. I will then turn to a discussion of the public discourse about the relationships between the political, the economic, and the moral that took place when Hugo Chávez assumed power, and how this discourse might best be understood.

At the heart of the analysis is a distrust of the role of the market in society, and, by extension, over the possibilities held out by the global market. At a time when most countries are opening their economic borders, Chávez is doing the opposite, seeking to make the nation more self-sufficient, and repeatedly protesting that he is not for 'savage neo-liberalism'. I will examine the nature of this friction, suggesting that it is grounded in a cultural conflict between local and global identities, where trust in the market to supply basic needs is an important element.

Trade blocks and emerging markets

Throughout the world, the nature of trade is changing. In Europe, efforts to establish an economic community have been of political and economic importance for many years. The European Union is still growing, and is likely to do so for some time with the gradual integration of a multitude of Eastern European states. In the Americas, there is the Andean Pact, the *Mercado Común del Sur* (MERCOSUR), and the North American Free Trade Agreement (NAFTA), all formed to facilitate trade and incorporate the regions, nations and economies into one market. The negotiations currently underway on the Free Trade Area of the Americas (FTAA) are intended to create a free trade area spanning from Alaska to Cape Horn by 2005.[3] On the other side of the globe, the Asian countries have also united in different trade agreements: the Association of Southeast Asian Nations (ASEAN), and Asia–Pacific Economic Cooperation (APEC). Most of the countries being integrated into these economic blocks are developing countries, and many of them are labelled 'emerging markets'.

The growth of the concept of the emerging market can be seen as part of a shift in the conception of the economic potential of developing countries, and of the role of markets in economic growth. Much economic development aid worldwide has been focused on the provision of the infrastructure thought to be necessary for growth, such as transportation, improved communication systems, and cheap and abundant energy (Montoya, 1996). Investments have also frequently been made in improving farming technology and the competitiveness of local industries. But the financial markets that provide the capital for local investment in developing countries were mostly overlooked until 1986 when, as Mobius (1996) indicates, the International Finance Corporation (IFC) began to promote capital market expansion in these countries, hoping to thereby create a financial infrastructure conducive to economic growth.[4]

Communications technology has made the worldwide market a reality for some enterprises in developing countries that have previously been peripheral to world trade, and has also made them more attractive to investors. In the late 1980s and 1990s, the emerging markets were promoted as holding some of the best investment opportunities for those seeking rapid capital growth. Changing political and economic constellations and policies, and the concomitant globalization and liberalization of trade, are reflected in trade agreements. The accelerating rise of a global economy also ties people together through travel and work migration, such as that discussed by Sassen (1996, 1998), globally dispersed workplaces (Cravey, 1998; Garsten, 1994; Kamal and Hoffman, 1999; Ong, 1994), and savings invested in international capital markets via, for example, pension and mutual funds.[5] There is a gradual change in the way people conceive of the world and their place in it. We seem to be undergoing an economic transformation where markets are a new common denominator, incorporating more and more nations and peoples through such loosely related mechanisms as companies' search for profitability, labour migration, financial actors' pursuit of return on capital, and the many opportunities offered by telecommunications and the Internet.

The re-designation of developing countries as 'emerging markets' reflects both a shift in the character of world trade in the last decade of the millennium, and an attempt to define particular countries' economic situation, or role within the global economy. But these countries have different problems, potentials, and views of the market and the future, which stem from their resources, their economic histories, and their cultures. Each society must both provide for individual rights and guarantee the welfare of the larger community, and they do this in a variety of ways, designating different responsibilities to citizen and state.

Societies, like individuals, can be either inward-looking or outward-looking in their social and economic relationships with the wider world. Eric Wolf (1957) recognized this in his early work in Latin America, noting how rural communities that had experienced production for export, and benefited from it, tended to have a more open, receptive attitude toward the wider world than communities that had been excluded from such experiences. Similar orientations can still be relevant as societies around the globe become increasingly integrated into world-wide trade. In this chapter I am interested in particular, historically rooted ways of conceptualizing market activity and economic endeavour, and how they play out in Venezuelan political and economic life. I would like to suggest that although Venezuela is a modernized, energy-exporting country with a democratic, bureaucratic state system and is integrated into world markets through its exports and very considerable imports and strong economic ties with the US and Europe, in important respects its economic life is bound up with economic values that date from its history as an agricultural economy.

The house and the corporation

Aristotle was the first to make the distinction between acquisition for use and acquisition for sale, condemning the latter as something unnatural, that only lead to acquisition itself becoming a primary and endless goal. His thought profoundly influenced thinkers that followed him, from Aquinas and the Scholastics to Marx. Gudeman and Rivera (1990) further explore this distinction, linking it to two ways of conceptualizing and ordering economic activity, which they term the house and the corporation. The house is the smallest unit of the community, usually a family group, and represents the collective, where each member contributes according to individual capacity for the good of the whole. In this realm, all resources – material and labour – must be carefully hoarded and deployed to ensure survival. The corporation, on the other hand, stands for the corps; for individual endeavours, and is associated with trade. It moves out into the world, seeking trading partners and opportunities for gain.

Using data from Latin America, Gudeman and Rivera discuss the practices of monetized and non-monetized economies: two ways of managing resources, one of which concentrates on market exchange, and the other which maintains itself by avoiding trade as much as possible. Based on their observations of small-scale farmers in the Colombian countryside, they note how the largely non-monetized 'house economies' of the marginal rural households of Latin America have little possibility of competing in the marketplace, and try to manage their resources to avoid market exchange by producing for their own use, and using thrift, recycling, and ingenuity. When the house goes to the market, it goes only to buy what it cannot produce itself, and buys as little as possible. The 'corporation', on the other hand, operates within the market and does the opposite, buying to sell, and then buying and selling again, living off the profit margin. Gudeman and Rivera regard the 'house' and 'corporation' as deeply rooted, intertwined models for conceptualizing and managing economic life and understanding transactions; two ways of using resources that have been with us for a long time, giving rise to economic strategies which are intermingled in our modern economies. In the following I will summarize the main points of the economic history of Venezuela, and describe how the emergence of the oil economy affected Venezuelan society. This will act as a backdrop to the later discussion of how Chávez' presidency has been received.

Country and city, management and mismanagement

Lacking the mineral wealth that attracted Spanish colonists, Venezuela has had a rural economy throughout most of its history, and has been dependent on a series of major export products that were produced in different regions. In the early colonial period of the 1600s and 1700s, when the interior began to be settled, economic activities focused on the extensive cattle ranches established in the plains of Guárico and Barinas states, something that Rangel (1981: 21–2) attributes to the lack of labour which made a plantation economy impossible. Other factors were undoubtedly the suitability of the land and the cattle-ranching tradition of the New World settlers, many of whom came from Andalusia (Hennessey, 1978: 29; Bishko, 1952, 1963). Cattle hides and dried meat, then, were the major exports until replaced by cocoa, cultivated with slave labour, primarily in the coastal regions. Encouraged by the rising interest of Europeans for tropical crops, cocoa became the major Venezuelan export by the early 1700s, and Rangel (1981: 29–40) notes that it was the income from the cocoa plantations that made possible the rise of an oligarchy that would eventually declare itself independent of the Spanish Crown. Many of the cocoa plantations were destroyed during the struggle for independence from Spain, however (Roseberry, 1983: 71), and coffee, already under cultivation, eventually became the next export crop, with the major focus of production in the Andean region. Coffee cultivation was expanded and intensified by the peasantry that took refuge in the Andes from the Venezuelan Wars of Federation that raged in the *llanos*, or plains region, in the latter half of the 1800s (Cardoso, 1965). The boom in coffee production lasted until the definitive fall of prices with the worldwide depression of 1929. As the coffee economy declined, Venezuela focused on continuing to explore and exploit its rich oil deposits, which had begun to fill the national coffers starting in the early 1920s (Naím and Francés, 1995: 172). Today the country is highly dependent on the income generated by the oil industry.

The nation's conversion into a major petroleum producer led to an increasing a focus on urban areas. With the inflow of oil revenues, the country set about modernizing its infrastructure and providing public services such as housing, education and medicine. The public sector grew significantly with the many new jobs appearing in the state service sector, but a lack of corresponding investment in the agricultural sector contributed to Venezuela's rapid transformation from a rural to an urban nation. While in 1936 the percentage of the population in urban areas stood at 30 per cent, by 1950, the figure had risen to 54 per cent. In 1971 the figure had reached 75 per cent (Suárez, 1978), and by 1990, 90.5 per cent of the population was considered to be urban (ECLA, 1995). Statistics from the World Bank Group indicate that in 2002, 87 per cent of the population was urban, compared with an average of 76 per cent in Latin America and the Caribbean as a whole.[6]

Some rural – urban migrants, or their offspring, found work in the expanding public sector or in private businesses; others started small businesses of their own. But many more, however, ended up in the shantytowns of the cities, and are self-employed in the informal economy.

As in most of Latin America, the rapid growth of the shantytowns brought about new forms of social organization, generally based on patterns of respect and reciprocity characteristic of rural life (Lomnitz, 1977; Roberts, 1978, 1995).

The agricultural economy, and the first decades of the new oil economy, were characterized by a series of political dictatorships, but the modernizing nation became a democracy in 1958, when General Marcos Pérez Jiménez was overthrown in a popular uprising. For 35 years thereafter, two parties – the Social Democrats and the Christian Democrats – alternated in power every five years, distributing jobs and contracts to their supporters when in power. With democracy, fiscal mismanagement and corruption in public life became political issues, and gained force in 1983, when the country's current economic crisis made its début with a large devaluation, in which the currency, the *bolívar*, lost half of its value overnight. An enormous shock to the public, the devaluation initiated a period of economic difficulties that the government tried to ameliorate through a variety of mechanisms – primarily subsidies. A preferential exchange rate programme quickly designed to facilitate imports led to further accusations of favoritism and corruption. Drawing on the earlier public discourse about corruption in government, new political parties (for example, *Causa R*) began to form, and made the fight against corruption in government institutions their main platform. Via the mass media a lively and bitter debate began over morals in political life, and over the economic policies that should guide the distribution of the decreasing economic base brought in by oil exports.

In 1989, President-elect Carlos Andrés Pérez took office and he negotiated with the International Monetary Fund (IMF) to find a way out of the economic crisis. He applied an austerity programme recommended by the IMF, which eliminated food and fuel subsidies, thereby bringing even greater hardship to the majority of Venezuelans.[7] When Pérez raised fuel prices in April of 1989, a popular uprising broke out in Caracas. Four days of looting were brutally put down by the security forces. Called '*El Caracazo*', this abrupt and unexpected breach of control by both citizens and the government left a deep impression on the community, and marked the collapse of the distributive 'democratic oil-revenue' state model. Institutions, parties, leaders, and ideological and party platforms increasingly lost credibility. Pérez was eventually forced from power on economic corruption charges, and replaced by an interim president. A coalition government made up of many small parties headed by former president Rafael Caldera won the following elections in 1993, ruling until the end of 1998, but was unable to implement unpopular, although necessary, economic measures.

The 1990s were marked by domestic political disturbances, rising inflation, negative domestic growth, and the collapse of 14 banks between 1994–95, which brought an emergency economic plan involving foreign-currency controls.[8] The Social Democrat and Christian Democratic parties' legitimacy were intensely questioned at this time, in part due to corrupt practices, but also because of their previous incapacity to solve the nation's economic problems. Opinion polls from the time indicate that the main concerns of most people were their dissatisfaction with their personal economic situation, and government inefficiency and administrative corruption (Templeton, 1995: 79). A recurrent image in political discussions was that of the citizens of a very rich country living in dire poverty because of the corrupt and self-serving practices of their elected leaders.

Enter the Fifth Republic

In 1992, a paratrooper, *Comandante* Hugo Chávez, led a failed military coup attempt against Pérez' government. He and his fellow plotters were tried, convicted, and jailed. Chávez enjoyed substantial public support, however, and after spending two years in jail he was pardoned and formed his own political party, the *Movimiento Quinta República* (MVR), or Fifth Republican Movement.[9] His movement gradually gained the support of other small leftist parties, and won the 1998 election by a landslide vote, soundly defeating the traditional parties that had alternated in power for so long. The name of the new party was also its main platform. Their goal was to form a new republic by writing a new constitution via an elected constituent assembly, a process that began and ended in 1999, with the re-election of Hugo Chávez under the new constitution for a term of six years.

Many MVR supporters justified their party's success and the need for a new constitution by pointing at the state of the economy, the dismal poverty of over half the population, and the many corruption scandals brought to public attention during past years. Their standpoint was that it was time to clean up the government, and that with Venezuela's vast riches in natural resources, there would be plenty for everyone, if it were honestly and effectively administrated. Much of Chávez' immediate rhetoric and action as incoming president focused on alleviating the worst poverty and on saving money – petroleum prices were at a low point when he took office. Shortly after election, for example, he greatly reduced the number of bodyguards on the government payroll, sold off most of the aircraft used by high-ranking members of government, and spoke of turning the presidential summer residence into a home for street children, and part of the official residence, *La Casona*, into a soup kitchen for needy elderly. He also announced a series of programs, such as the *Plan Bolívar 2000*, that brought the military out of the barracks to work alongside volunteers from the population to alleviate pressing social problems, for example, by repairing roads, opening popular markets, cleaning up poor neighborhoods, and painting and repairing schools (El Universal, 1999a, 1999b and 1999c).

Such measures, however, were not directed towards the reactivation of the economy. Once Chávez took power, economists and financial leaders began to call for immediate government measures to pull the country out of its economic crisis. There was a strong feeling among scholars, economists, industrialists, bankers, investors, and others involved with the financial market that Venezuela should enter fully into a market economy and the process of economic globalization. They demanded political and economic guarantees that would encourage foreign investors to become active in the country – particularly in the areas of tourism, mining, and agriculture. Some pointed out that the national currency was being kept artificially high for political reasons, and favoured a devaluation to make national products attractive. A number also advocated the privatization of state companies, including a part of PDVSA (Petróleos de Venezuela, Sociedad Anónima), the state oil company, maintaining that this would create better efficiency and greater revenues for the state. The idea was to open up the country to investment and to competition, with the aim of making Venezuelan companies competitive both locally and globally. Market forces would work to create wealth; and there was a conviction that there existed particular economic sectors in which the country did have a competitive advantage and could be very successful.

The government discourse, however, was – and remains – more social and political than economic. It favours increased taxation to make those who earn more also pay more, strict authority over government ministries to prevent corruption, cuts in administrative spending, and subsidies for national industries. It has controlled the prices of basic foodstuffs, particularly meat, and in 2003, implemented foreign currency exchange controls in an effort to prevent capital flight. It is sceptical of privatization, feeling that the state should retain power over its property. Venezuela is a very rich country, this discourse continuously points out, with its petroleum, iron ore, gold, and fertile soils: Venezuelans should feel proud. As citizens of such a well-endowed country, there is no reason why they should be poor. It is corruption, laziness and mismanagement that are to blame, and what is needed is a moral awakening. This line of reasoning tends to be echoed from administration to administration, and as Coronil (1997: 67) points out, the idea that they are the citizens of a wealthy country and are entitled to a part of that wealth has become a part of the image that Venezuelans have of themselves. One can frequently hear people, including those who work from dawn well into the night, speak of the riches of their country – and add how unfortunate it is that, as a people, 'we Venezuelans' do not like to work, but prefer to spend the day in a hammock under the palms.

The economic projects that the Chávez government eventually announced in 1999 focused on increasing the production of selected agricultural products such as rice, sugar, and palm oil, and on encouraging the fishing industry. The general idea was to make the country more self-sufficient, to aim for export, and to channel more resources and opportunities to the poorest citizens. The largest portion of governmental policies concentrated on redistributing income, and used the social advances made in Cuba as a model, providing improved and free education (Bolivarian schools, based on a Cuban model), health care (with Cuban doctors serving the poorest shantytown neighbourhoods) and subsidized open-air markets run by the military.

House and corporation in modern life

This conception of a national economy as being primarily a matter of the management and distribution of resources can be seen as an outgrowth of the 'house' view of the economy, where resources are finite, and must be well managed for prosperity. Aristotle, for example, made a similar, if wider, definition of management, when he wrote that the leader of a nation could be compared to the head of a household, and should run a nation in the same thrifty and prudent way in which the manager of an estate managed his resources, making sure they could provide for his charges.

I would like to suggest that in contemporary Venezuela these two points of view, those of the government and of the opposition, are reflections of values stemming from economic practices, those of the house and of the corporation discussed by Gudeman and Rivera. One could say that much of Chávez' and his party's rhetoric and practices echo those of the house: thrift, maintaining control over resources, improving management, and living within one's means. They are goals that have a strong resonance among his supporters, many of whom are poor, of recent rural origin, and who have never fully entered into a more corporate economy. Like the peasants Gudeman and Rivera write about, their experiences with the market have been more negative than positive; it has not given them what they consider to be a fair deal, which enables them to meet their needs. The nation is ostensibly rich, but they are poor. The fight against corruption is as much a struggle for the affirmation of the importance of husbandry and parsimony as it is a struggle for social justice.

As Chávez protested against the luxury of the presidential buildings, prerogatives, and staff, the use of which he inherited as the incoming president, he sent a dual rhetorical message to his supporters, showing his own belief in the importance of frugality and his capacity as an administrator, as well as highlighting the wastefulness of previous governments. His emphasis on taxation, and the importance of citizens paying their taxes, indicated the need for a more just distribution of resources: finally, those who earned high salaries would contribute fairly to the national coffers, as would industrialists and tradesmen. Indeed, during Chávez' first years in office, his tax inspectors temporarily shut down and fined a wide variety of companies accused of tax fraud. In the same vein, his opposition to privatization as an economic strategy signaled another 'house' value, that of the importance of maintaining control of one's resources, one's economic base. The house struggles to keep as much of its resources as possible 'within the doors' (Gudeman and Rivera, 1990) rather than risk losing them in trade.

Such messages make good sense to the disenfranchised people who are Chávez' supporters. It is generally held that his most fervent, core supporters come from the shantytown neighbourhoods, or *barrios*, surrounding Caracas and other cities. The lack of adequate housing at reasonable prices in the nation as a whole sometimes obliges even middle-class people to live in or on the outskirts of a *barrio*. But on the whole, it is the *barrio* dwellers who are integrated into modern economic life in the least favourable positions and lack a steady income, usually earning their livelihood doing temporary manual labour, by working in domestic service or in the commercial service sector, or as street peddlers. The values passed on from their rural heritage are very salient in providing them with survival strategies and processes. They are obliged to practice thrift and parsimony, and depend heavily on kin and friendship networks of reciprocity and exchange in order to stretch their incomes enough to survive. Chávez, who also comes from a rural background, knows how to communicate with this audience. When he broadcasts his weekly television programme on Sunday mornings, sitting informally clad with a cup of coffee before the cameras and recounting his version of the events of the week, he is playing directly to them; and he underscores his awareness of the importance of this arena by frequently choosing it to announce new measures, social programmes and policies, which in earlier administrations were publicized before a formal audience. This is one way of maintaining the image of the republic's president as benefactor, and merging it with the images of father and charismatic leader.[10]

The early 1900s in Venezuela witnessed an historical figure with whose economic thought Chávez' economic policies might be paralleled. Juan Vicente Gómez, whose military dictatorship lasted from 1908 to 1935, was also from rural origins. During his rule, he privately accumulated hundreds of cattle ranches, *haciendas*, throughout the country, many of which he gave as gifts to his numerous illegitimate children. In this respect he is an exemplary metaphor for the rural 'house economy' in two ways: the primary aim of 'the house' is to be able to reproduce itself, and its primary base is land, or access to land. In his reproductive capability and his hunger for land, Gómez can be said to incarnate the head of a successful 'house'. Although he was a brutal dictator who tolerated no opposition, he is publicly admired today for paying off the entire national debt in 1930; an act that he presented as a tribute to national revolutionary hero Simón Bolívar on the 100th anniversary of his death (Maza Zavala, 1997). Oil income began to flow into Venezuela during Gómez' reign, and it was this income that ultimately made debt repayment possible – but its use for this end meant a corresponding lack of investment in the needs of citizens.

It is frequently said that Gómez was a down-to-earth leader who managed Venezuela like a *hacienda*, doing what he knew how to do, and leaving what he did not understand to others. He shunned the elite society of the time, and moved the national capital from Caracas, the largest city, to the (then) small town of Maracay. He refused honorary doctorates and other awards, and is mocked for being a simple, but crafty man. If one looks carefully at the record, one can note that Gómez was the one to finally unite the country, by ruthlessly eliminating competing *caudillos* (local warlords) around the country, thereby creating peace and security for citizens. He founded the national army, and restored the economic infrastructure for export that had been badly damaged during the wars of independence. Under his rule, or period of management, if you will, Venezuelan agricultural production and export expanded with increasing demand from Europe, and petroleum exports became the primary source of income, enabling him to finally pay off the national debt, which had been a huge burden to the country's economic development since independence. Although in some ways Gómez actually laid the bases for the institutions of a modern state, as Coronil (1997: 68) indicates, he has been widely regarded as a repressive and brutal antithesis of the modern state. In the public eye, he epitomizes the simple, but shrewd and wily peasant.

The market and sovereignty

Chávez and his administration want to take firm control over economic policy, and treat it as being separate from political life. This vision is more closed than open, and seeks to strengthen national identity and pride through the achievement of self-sufficiency and independence. It depends on the gains to be made through production and redistribution, rather than on those to be made through international trade. National sovereignty is an important issue for Chávez – as a nation, Venezuela must be allowed to make its policies without interference by other powers – and to an extent, one could say that the issue of self-determination is at the centre of the struggle over economic policies. While the majority of the many small parties that now make up the opposition to Chávez favour a solution that looks outwards towards the global market, viewing free trade as an important element in creating well-being for citizens, the administration's discourse continuously criticizes and rejects the movement towards wide trade integration and the formation, for example, of the Free Trade Area of the Americas (FTAA), although Chávez has signed the agreement, if with 'reservations'. His rejection of international trade as insidious and exploitative is a discourse that one recalls from the 1960s and 1970s, and it is hardly in tune with the economic changes underway in the world, as Giusti (2004) points out; the effects of globalization are complex, and processes of inclusion and exclusion crisscross regions and nations in unpredictable ways. The global financial system now ties nations together through processes in which communities gain power, or are powerless, as they compete in a global arena. It is increasingly difficult to attract new jobs and competencies without opening up to the global economy, which, in turn, brings with it the necessity of reaching compromises and thereby giving up a measure of control over economic life. At the heart of the conflict lies a disagreement over the possibilities held out by the global market, and, by extension, of the role the market should play in society.

The Venezuelan opposition – including economists, scholars, members of the financial and business community, politicians, and much of the middle class – are well versed in their knowledge of the efficiency of the market and the benefits of international trade.[11] While the administration's view of the economy is tied to a particular, locally based, and rural view of the market, those who favour a more complete entry into a global economy view opportunities in a world of transactions as theoretically unbounded, and profit possibilities as limitless, although they also point out that Venezuela must negotiate shrewdly to gain as much benefit as possible from trade accords. They seek favourable access to markets, particularly that of the US, as do the other countries of Latin America. The Chávez government, on the other hand, has launched a new proposal to counter the FTAA, called the Bolivarian Alternative for Latin America (*Alternativa Bolivariana para América Latina, ALBA*), which would aim to create funds to correct the economic disparities in the different countries of the region (Lares Martiz, 2004). It states that: 'Our principle is "as much market as possible, and as much state as necessary"' (Chávez Frías, 2004). In part, then, the conflict has to do with identity, whether one sees oneself as a citizen of an oil-producing nation that must live off the adept administration of this resource, or as a citizen of an oil-producing nation within a community of nations with other essential talents and useful products for trade.[12]

2004: A billion dollars for agricultural investment

While most citizens of today's capitalist societies regard the market and its processes as an inevitable part of human life, an efficient way of producing and distributing necessary goods and services, many Venezuelans take a different view. The state, they feel, should be responsible for assuring that its citizens can afford to acquire life's basics – food, housing, and a job – a belief made possible, in part, because of the inflow of petrodollars. In this context, the free market is considered to be a treacherous place where ordinary citizens have to put up with unfair prices and practices, and have little chance of acquiring all they need, a view which echoes those of rural people practising the economy of 'the house', and, indeed, the views of many former administrations, which, according to Naím and Francés (1995: 176), have generally regarded the market as politically destabilizing and/or economically unreliable. Chávez is not specifically anti-market, but by failing to provide the conditions within which the national market can operate effectively and by ignoring local market actors' needs and demands, his administration is effectively anti-market in practice. And while favouring trade blocs among economically equal countries within Latin America, the administration opposes the FTAA, which will include North America as well.

The political and economic convolutions that Venezuela has undergone since the beginning of Chávez' presidency are far too many and complex to recount here. Opposition to his administration has grown steadily, and a new civil society made up primarily of the middle class has developed in the country. After many mass actions and rallies to demonstrate their opposition, a failed coup attempt, and a two-month-long civil strike with severe consequences for the oil industry, numerous civil associations and small parties with different agendas are currently trying to make up a united front with the long-established political parties in order to see that a recall referendum ends Chávez' term in office by peaceful means. The toll of political turmoil on the economy has been significant. Many of the international companies that used Caracas as headquarters for their Latin American offices have moved elsewhere because of the lack of physical security, countless foreign companies have shut down production, and the overvaluation of the national currency has made local products uncompetitive, putting further numbers of workers out of jobs. A tolerance of frequent squatter invasions of both private and public property has resulted in public doubts about the government's commitment to the protection of private property.[13] Rising crime rates, the lack of economic opportunities, and fear of a 'Cubanization'[14] of the country has led the upper and middle class to convert their savings and assets into dollars, and capital flight has been immense, leading to the implementation of strict foreign exchange controls in 2003. Difficulties for the middle class have also meant increasing hardship for the lower classes. As small shops and businesses are forced to close or are liquidated by their owners, jobs, opportunities, services and purchasing power evaporate.

As noted above, Chávez comes from a rural background and ostensibly shares many of the values of his supporters regarding good management, thrift, and honesty. But as Quirós Corradi (2004) notes, democracy and management coincide in that their success is measured by a ruthless examination of the end results. In this examination, Chávez has not, in his five years in power, succeeded in bringing greater prosperity to the majority of the people in the country through policies of good management, thrift and honesty in government. His social programme, funded by the relatively high oil prices during his mandate, cost money, and have done little to improve the overall economic welfare of citizens.

The government is also under fire for subsidizing Cuba's energy bill: as of February, 2004, Cuba owed *Petróleos de Venezuela* (PDVSA) 750 million dollars for oil delivered in the three previous years, and little effort was being made to collect the debt (Barrionuevo and Córdoba, 2004). Highly criticized, Chávez faces an uncertain political future, and desperately needs funding for further investment in order to provide the results, or the public faith in future results, that can win him the referendum, or, should it not take place, re-election in 2006.

Chávez has chosen the issue of investment in the rural sector as his next arena for political battle. In this new political and economic scenario, the *Ministro de Planificación y Desarollo* (Minister of Planning and Development), Jorge Giordani, announced on *Aló, Presidente* (Hello, President; a weekly government radio program) that the *Banco Central de Venezuela* (BCV), the Venezuelan Central Bank, has a 'higher than ideal' international reserve of dollars – reputedly about six billion too much.[15] Of this sum, Chávez is demanding one billion dollars for investment in agricultural development. According to the head of the *Programa Agrícola Especial*, the Special Agricultural Programme, Arnoldo Márquez, the funds will be used to double or triple the normal production of cereals (maize and sorghum), vegetables, legumes, sugar cane, cotton, aloe vera, and oleaginous crops such as soya, thereby reaching national self-sufficiency in these crops (Rojas Jiménez, 2004).

This is an area in which Chávez can expect support, since investment of oil money in agricultural production is a familiar political goal, touted without great results by several preceding governments, and it has a resonance with the rural nexus of many city dwellers, who still have family in the countryside, may own a share in property there, and enjoy visiting rural kin on holidays. Increasing food production should also presumably lower costs, and guarantee food security. Thus, a defence of investment in agriculture and funding for grants or loans to farmers can be expected to win favour with an important segment of voters, as well as provide ample opportunity for populist rhetoric.

An analysis of the situation in the countryside shows that, so far, there has been a net decrease in agriculture in the five years since Chávez came to office, however. Only 1.6 per cent of the national budget is officially dedicated to agriculture and the programmes devised so far have been of an improvized nature. Quirós Corradi (2004) uses statistics provided by the *Alianza Agroalimentaria* (Agro Food Alliance) to show that the value of national agricultural production decreased by 5.1 per cent in 2001, 4.8 per cent in 2002, and a further 2.07 per cent in 2003. The amount of land utilized in agriculture decreased from 2.2 to 1.5 million hectares. Rural employment fell by 200.000 jobs, and the occupation of farms, threats, kidnappings and extortion increased in the rural sector, especially in frontier areas bordering Colombia. These statistics question the administration's true commitment to agricultural growth.

More salient, perhaps, is the fact that it is against Venezuelan law for the executive branch of government to demand and thereby receive money from the Venezuelan Central Bank. Economists agree that the influx of this money into the system would result in considerable inflation, and Gómez (2004) points out that if the goal is to foment sustainable agriculture, funds can be made available for farmers to take loans in commercial banks. Chávez and his supporters, however, present the 'release' of one billion dollars from the Central Bank as something that is owed to the *pueblo*. In an article in the Caracas morning paper *El Universal* on 18 January 2003, Manuel Caballero published and discusses a photograph of a Chavista demonstrator, reputedly a poor farmer from the state of Barinas, brandishing a machete on high during a political rally held in front of the Central Bank. Caballero points out how the monetary institution was established nearly 75 years ago through the support of both the government and the opposition, and was a national project, part of the modernization of the country. Pillaging it of a billion dollars by extraordinary methods would signal a retreat into Venezuela's pre-modern past, the 1800s, when the machete symbolized both work and violent death.

In the debate about the '*millardito*' one senses a shift in the manner in which Chávez employs economic rhetoric. Although on entering office he was seemed concerned with making savings and running an honest and efficient state, today he is focused on obtaining access to the economic resources with which to produce results that can keep him in power. He uses the economic arguments and symbolism that will appeal to the same constituency, but with a different goal. If there is a crisis in agriculture, which there is when Venezuela imports food and prices are high, and there is a billion dollars 'extra' in the national reserve, he reasons, then as president he should be able to take that money and employ it as he sees fit for the good of the country.

Because of the very superficial accountability mechanisms in place, Chávez' opponents doubt that the majority of the billion dollars will actually be invested in agricultural development. Rather, most of it will make its way into financing other social projects, and the media campaign that the administration will use to defend itself. They also question the wisdom of investing such large sums in agriculture. As anthropologist Patricia Márquez points out, Venezuela is today an urban nation, and it is highly unlikely that the masses of urban unemployed will be interested in, or have the skills necessary to participate in, an agricultural revival (Márquez, 2004).

Conclusion

In this brief presentation, then, I suggest that rather than viewing the struggle between the Chávistas and those who seek more liberal economic solutions solely in political terms, one might more fruitfully look at it in the light of competing conceptions of the way in which economies work. To trust or not to trust the market to supply one's needs? People's answers to this question are based on their past experiences and their practical knowledge of how economic life operates. Although Venezuela today is evidently a modern state with a market-based economy, its people, and the political and economic institutions they create, carry the values of a previous, agricultural, rurally oriented way of making a living. As Maza Zavala points out, although there is an inclination to fragment history, presenting it as a series of periods or epochs, it is in fact a steady current of intermixed events, one of which flows into another (1997: 199). In an essay on David Riesman's *The Lonely Crowd*, Wilfred McClay 1996: 437) quotes José Ortega y Gasset: 'the European man "has been 'democratic,' 'liberal,' 'absolutist,' 'feudal,'" and does "in some way continue being all these things; he does so in the form of having been them."' In using this quote, McClay wants to point out that people are far more complex products of history than they are usually given credit for being. This complexity reverberates through contemporary economic and political life.

In these days, which see repeated attempts to negotiate new patterns and conditions of trade, we strive, on the one hand, to create innovative commercial structures, but are hostage, on the other, to patterns of thought, a mindsets, that date from other economic conditions but still, to many, make good sense. In Venezuela the emergence of the oil economy and the rapid process of modernization have effectively integrated only a portion of the population into a market economy, and 'the market', for many others, still represents 'the enemy'. It may be a long time before such views of economic activity are transformed; before other truths are learned.

Chávez knows how to use the language opposing the market to his advantage, yet, on the other hand, he also speaks the language of the market. Faced by a lack of capital to develop the national oil company, which was battered by opposition-led strikes in December 2002–January 2003, he is now welcoming multinational companies to participate in the extraction of fossil fuels, seeking foreign investors to help expand oil production and develop the natural gas industry, and commentators say that his government treats investors preferentially (Forero, 2003). Thus Chávez puts on his red shirt and paratrooper's cap for mass rallies, introduces a series of *ad hoc* social programmes, and rails against oligarchs and US interventionism, while simultaneously wooing multinational business interests, thereby embodying the two faces of the nation-state. The opposition – or a part of it – is more likely to support a version of Phillip Bobbitt's (2004) 'market state', which favours voluntarism, deregulation, privatization, and job training rather than subsidies, and the use of incentives to induce voluntary compliance. At this point in time, it feels as if the market state is far from becoming part of Venezuelan reality.

Notes

1. I would like to thank the Bank of Sweden Tercentenary Foundation for the financial support to make the research for this chapter possible. An earlier version was presented at a session of the annual meeting of the American Anthropological Association in Chicago, USA, in November 1999.
2. According to statistics from the World Bank Group (http://wbln0018. worldbank.org, accessed on 28 February 2004), the number of Venezuelans living in poverty (on less than two dollars a day) rose from 12.2 per cent to 23.8 per cent between 1990 and 2000. Those living in extreme poverty (on less than one dollar a day) rose from 11.8 per cent to 23.5 per cent in the same period. The richest 20 per cent of the population obtain 53 per cent of all income; the poorest 20 per cent only three per cent of all income.
3. See 'Rediscovering the Americas', *The Economist*, 17 May 1997, p. 16.
4. The International Finance Corporation (IFC) is a subsidiary of the World Bank supported by over 160 member states. Its task is to promote the productivity and profitability of private companies in emerging markets through targeted investment assistance programmes. In recent years it has worked intensively to promote the development of capital markets that could finance projects in the emerging markets, and thus its input to the upswing in this rapidly growing sector has been substantial (Keppler and Lechner, 1997: 11).
5. In the spring of 1999 *The New York Times* ran a series of four articles about the global economy entitled 'Global contagion', which discusses how US workers are linked with workers in developing countries because of the international movement of capital through pension funds.
6. http://www.worldbank.org/data/, accessed on 28 February 2004.
7. This was Carlos Andrés Pérez' (CAP) second term. During his first term in office (1973–78) oil prices had hit an all-time international high, providing Venezuela with a bonanza, and he was thus recognized as a president whose mandate had brought great prosperity.
8. See García et al. (1997) for an excellent explanation of the banking crisis.

9. Chávez was pardoned by President Rafael Caldera, who was then the leader of the coalition government that succeeded Pérez' second term in office. In an earlier term as president of Venezuela (1968–73), when he had represented the Christian Democratic (COPEI) party that he had founded in 1946, Caldera successfully negotiated with the then very active Venezuelan guerrilla movement. Via an amnesty, he incorporated them into the formal political life of the country. His extension of a pardon to Chávez can thus be seen as the follow-up of a previously successful policy.

10. I have not been able to locate any analysis of the social groups that make up the mass of Chávez' core supporters. Based on field observation and the local and international media, however, I draw the conclusion that he is supported primarily by the armed forces, by public employees (who must demonstrate their loyalty), by the people who benefit directly from his new social programmes (poor *barrio* dwellers), by recent rural and urban squatters, and by urban street vendors, who have gained advantages under the current government.

11. While Chávez' political rhetoric tends to represent the country as consisting of two camps, the poor (his supporters) and the rich (the opposition), the political reality is certainly more complex. Political scientist Rigoberto Henriquez Vera points out that the democratic period after 1959 saw the rise of a broad middle class, the members of which make up the leadership potential in the country. See Alfredo Meza, 'Con el apoyo de los mercenarios no se hace una revolución' [A revolution can not be made with the support of mercenaries], in *El Nacional*, 22 February 2004, Section A7.

12. In this context it should be noted that oil-exporting Venezuela has a very different economy than the other countries of Latin America. Venezuela obtains 14.36 per cent of its GDP (gross domestic product) in trade with the US, compared to Argentina (3.8 per cent), and Brazil (4.51 per cent). Venezuela can subsidize an anti-market discourse with oil income, but Argentina and Brazil must more rationally seek markets for their products (see Lares Martiz, 2004).

13. See, for example, Rodríguez (2004) for a description of squatters in Caracas, and Rodríguez Pons (2000) about land invasions in Zulia and Bolívar states.

14. Chávez is a friend of Fidel Castro and an admirer of the Cuban revolution. He is adopting and implementing some of Castro's social policies in Venezuela, in many cases with the help of Cubans who come to participate in social projects in Venezuela.

15. Critics say that the idea of there being too much money in the national reserve is a legitimate concept, but this does not mean that one can simply take the money and spend it (Gómez, 2004). Domingo Maza Zavala, the director of the Central Bank, claims that the six billion dollar surplus (of a total of 22 billion dollars) is due to the inefficiency of the *Comisión de Administración de Divisas* (CADIVI), the administrative entity that is supposed to approve requests for foreign exchange funds under Venezuela's current foreign exchange controls (Rodríguez Pons, 2004). In other words, if this agency worked effectively in granting incoming applications for foreign exchange funds, there would be no 'surplus'.

References

Barrionuevo, Alexi and José de Córdoba. 2004. 'Venezuela y Cuba estrechan lazos y EEUU teme influencia anticomercial' [Venezuela and Cuba tighten bonds and the U.S.A. fears anti-commercial influence]. *The Wall Street Journal Americas*, 2 February, Section A12.

Bishko, C. J. 1952. 'The peninsular background of Latin American cattle ranching'. *Hispanic American Historical Review*, XXXII(4): 491–515.

Bishko, C. J. 1963. 'The Castilian as plainsman: the medieval ranching frontier in La Mancha and Extremadura. In A. R. Lewis and T. F. McGann (eds), *The New World Looks at its History*. Austin: University of Texas Press, 47–69.

Bobbitt, Phillip. 2004. 'Better than empire'. *Financial Times Weekend*, 13–14 March, W8–9.

Cardoso, Arturo. 1965. *Proceso de la historia de los Andes* [Historical Process of the Andes]. Caracas: Biblioteca de Autores y Temas Tachirenses.

Chávez Frías, Hugo. 2004. *De la Integración Neoliberal a la Alternativa Bolivariana para América Latina* [From Neoliberal Integration to the Bolivarian Alternative for Latin America]. Caracas.

Coronil, Fernando. 1997. *The Magical State: Nature, Money, and Modernity in Venezuela*. Chicago: University of Chicago Press.

Cravey, Althea. 1998. *Women and Work in Mexico's Maquiladoras*. Lanham, MD: Rowman and Littlefield.

Economic Commission for Latin America and the Caribbean (ECLAC). 1995. *Statistical Yearbook for Latin America and the Caribbean, 1994 Edition*. Santiago de Chile: United Nations. Economic Commission for Latin America and the Caribbean.

Forero, Juan. 2003. 'Venezuela tries to lure oil investors'. *The New York Times*, 19 December, W1.

Economist. 1997. 'Rediscovering the Americas'. 17 May, p.16.

García, Gustavo with Rafael Rodríguez and Silvia Salvato. 1997. *Lecciones de la crisis bancaria de Venezuela* [Lessons from the Venezuelan banking crisis]. Caracas: Ediciones IESA.

Garsten, Christina. 1994. *Apple World*. Stockholm Studies in Social Anthropology. Stockholm: Almqvist and Wiksell.

Giusti L., Luis E. 2004. '¿Aislamiento o integración?' [Isolation or Integration?] *El Nacional*, 25 January, Section A9.

Gómez, Emeterio. 2004. 'Qué es dinero inorgánico?' [What is inorganic money?] *El Universal*, 25 January, Section 1–13.

Gudeman, Stephen and Alberto Rivera. 1990. *Conversations in Colombia: The Domestic Economy in Life and Text*. London: Routledge & Kegan Paul.

Gudeman, Stephen. 2001. *The Anthropology of Economy*. Oxford: Blackwell Publishers.

Hennessey, Alistair. 1978. *The Frontier in Latin American History*. London: Edwin Arnold.

Kamal, Rachael and Anya Hoffman, eds. 1999. *The Maquiladora Reader: Cross-Border Organizing Since NAFTA*. Philadelphia, PA: American Friends Service Committee.

Keppler, Michael and Martin Lechner. 1997. *Emerging Markets: Research, Strategies and Benchmarks*. London: Irwin.

Kristof, Nicholas D., with Edward Wyatt. 1999. 'Who sank, or swam, in choppy currents of a world cash ocean'. *The New York Times*, 15 February 1999.

Lares Martiz, Valentina. 2004. 'Sobre este eje sólo giran las palabras' [Only words rotate around this center]. *Tal Cual*, 9 February, *Economía* 6–7.

Lomnitz, Larissa. 1977. *Networks and Marginality: Life in a Mexican Shantytown*. New York: Academic Press.

Márquez, Patricia. 2004. 'Del Mercedes al burro?' [From the Mercedes to the donkey?]. *El Nacional*, 14 January, Section A9.

Maza Zavala, Domingo Felipe. 1997. 'Una sola historia' [One History]. In Fundación de Los Trabajadores de Lagoven, (ed), *Historia Mínima de la Economía Venezolana*. Caracas: La Brújula, 199–217.

McClay, Wilfred M. 1996. 'The strange career of *The Lonely Crowd*'. In Thomas L. Haskell and Richard F. Teichgraeber III (eds), *The Culture of the Market. Historical Essays*. Cambridge: Cambridge University Press, 397–440.

Mobius, Mark J. 1996. *Mobius on Emerging Markets*. London: Pitman Publishing.

Montoya, Miguel. 1996. *Persistent Peasants: Smallholders, State Agencies and Involuntary Migration in Western Venezuela*. Stockholm Studies in Social Anthropology. Stockholm: Almqvist & Wiksell.

Naím, Moisés and Antonio Francés. 1995. 'The Venezuelan private sector: from courting the state to courting the market'. In Louis W. Goodman (ed.), *Lessons of the Venezuelan Experience*. Baltimore: Johns Hopkins University Press, 165–92.

Ong, Aihwa. 1994. *Spirits of Resistance and Capitalist Discipline: Factory Women in Malaysia*. SUNY Series of Anthropology of Work. New York: State University of New York Press.

Quirós Corradi, Alberto. 2004. 'Cuatro píldoras de un mismo frasco' [Four pills from the same bottle]. *El Nacional*, 1 February, Section A19.

Rangel, Domingo Alberto. [1969] 1981. *Capital y desarollo: la Venezuela agraria* [Capital and Development: Agrarian Venezuela]. Caracas: Universidad Central de Venezuela.

Roberts, Bryan. 1978. *Cities of Peasants: The Political Economy of Urbanization in the Third World*. London: Edwin Arnold.

Roberts, Bryan. 1995. *The Making of Citizens: Cities of Peasants Revisited*. London: Arnold; New York: Halsted.

Rodríguez, Gustavo. 2004. 'Los tomistas imponen su ley' [The squatters impose their law]. *El Universal*, 25 February, Section 2–20.

Rodríguez Pons, Corina. 2004. 'Maza Zavala: No existen las reservas internacionales excedentarias' [Maza Zavala: No surplus international reserves exist]. *El Nacional*, 29 January, Section A14.

Rodríguez Pons, Corina. 2000. 'Advierten sobre invasiones' [Warnings about invasions]. *El Universal*. 1 February, online, http://www.eluniversal.com/2000/02/01/01204GG.shtml.

Rojas Jiménez, Andrés. 2004. 'Gobierno prevé gastar el "millardito" antes de mayo' [The government expects to spend the billion before May]. *El Nacional*, 26 January, Section A16.

Roseberry, William. 1983. *Coffee and Capitalism in the Venezuelan Andes*. Austin, TX: University of Texas Press.

Sassen, Saskia. 1996. *Losing Control? Sovereignty in an Age of Globalization*. New York: Colombia University Press.

Sassen, Saskia. 1998. *Globalization and its Discontents: Essays on the New Mobility of People and Money*. New York: The New Press.

Suárez, María Mathilde. 1978. 'Cambios en la Economía Agraria en Poblaciones Rurales de los Andes Venezolanos' [Changes in the Agrarian Economy of Rural Populations in the Venezuelan Andes]. In *Actas du XLII Congrés International des Americanistes. Congrés du Centenaire, Paris, 2–9 Sept. 1976, Vol 1, 'Regiones et regionalisation en Amerique Latin'*. Paris: Publié avec le concours de la Fondation Singer-Polignac, 435–56.

Templeton, Andrew. 1995. 'The evolution of popular opinion'. In Louis W. Goodman (ed), *Lessons of the Venezuelan Experience*. Baltimore: Johns Hopkins University Press, 79–114.

El Universal. 1999a. 'Lateros e indigentes serán recogidos en Plan Cívico–Militar' [Beggars and indigents to be collected in Civic–Military Plan]. 22 February, online, http://archivo.eluniversal.com/1999/02/22/22416CC.shtml.

El Universal. 1999b. 'El Proyecto Bolívar 2000 depende de la comunidad' [The Bolívar 2000 depends on the community]. 26 February, online, http://archivo.eluniversal.com/1999/02/26/26401CC.shtml.

El Universal. 1999c. 'Proyecto Bolívar 2000' [The Project Bolívar 2000]. 8 March, online, http:/ /archivo.eluniversal.com/1999/03/08/OP19.shtml.

Wolf, Eric R. 1957. 'Closed corporate peasant communities in Mexico and Central Java'. *Southwestern Journal of Anthropology* 13: 1–18.

6

'Put Your Money Where Your Mouth Is!': The Market as an Arena for Politics[1]

Michele Micheletti

Introduction

'Put your money where your mouth is!' is old American slang. Although it is not quite clear how the metaphor originated, its meaning has never been in doubt. The expression is a challenge to anyone to back up their statements, opinions, or exaggerations with something tangible (Chapman, 1986: 345), which most frequently comes in the form of money. The metaphor can probably be dated to the late 1800s or early 1900s, at a time when market society became more widespread and money received a social and political value (Zelizer, 1997). Money has always been an important part of politics. Significant parts of civil society have historically concerned the political organization of money, and political parties have arranged themselves on ideological continuums on the basis of wealth and monetary distribution – with capital and labour forming polar opposites. Today, political scientists even consider economic contributions to networks, social movements, interest organizations, and political parties to be a form of political participation. The term 'pocketbook membership' defines this category of citizens who are only involved in political causes with their money. For years, we have brought money with us to our traditional forums for politics and citizen engagement.

The use of money to express values and opinions has deep historical roots, but an interesting shift is currently underway. Not only is money being brought into politics, but citizens are bringing politics to the market and confronting corporate actors in ways that would have been unimaginable in earlier years. New ways of using the market as an arena for politics are developing alongside the older methods used both nationally and internationally by social movements. We are witnessing the blooming of the phenomenon of political consumerism.

Properly defined, political consumerism is the use of the market for political purposes, to raise political issues, create responsibility-taking, control uncertainty, and solve common problems. Political consumers are people who use their consumer power to attempt to change objectionable institutional or market practices regarding issues of sustainability, justice, fairness, and non-economic issues that concern citizens' well-being. Political consumers act individually or collectively. Their market choices reflect an understanding of material products as embedded in a complex social and normative context which may be called the politics behind products (Micheletti, Follesdal and Stolle, 2003: xiv–xv).

This chapter explores the phenomenon of political consumerism. It begins with a discussion of the forms of political consumerism in practice today and shows how they reflect an understanding of material products as embedded in a complex social and normative context: the politics behind products. The cases used as illustrations in this section also show the important role played by women, marginalized groups, and young people as political consumers. The chapter then focuses on why consumer choice has evolved into political engagement by discussing what is prompting citizens to find new arenas for setting their political values and beliefs in motion. The next section addresses social science perspectives on the communicative value of money and the importance of consumption and consumer society, and lays the groundwork for the end of the chapter, which discusses the new terms and the new actor categories forged by the phenomenon of political consumerism.

Three basic forms of political consumerism

Political consumerism can take three different forms: negative, positive and public discursive. They represent different ways for citizens to use the market as an arena for politics. Negative political consumerism (boycotts) are the oldest form, having been used extensively by social movements as part of their protest repertoire. They are contentious in nature and represent a negative form because they encourage people to disengage from and protest against corporate actors. Positive political consumerism is a more recent form that tends to work together with rather than just against corporate actors. Examples of the latter are seals of approval labelling schemes and socially responsible investing (SRI) that encourage people to purchase 'good' products, producers, and services.

They are positive in orientation because they offer people positive consumer choices and do not consider business to be a political enemy, though this does not mean that they are uncritical of corporate behaviour. The third form does not involve the purchasing or non-purchasing of goods and services. Rather it concerns what, for lack of a better term, will be termed public discursive political consumerism, implying a variety of communicative efforts directed at business and the public at large about corporate policy and practice. Public discourse political consumerism can be just as contentious as boycotts or it can represent attempts to encourage dialogue with business and the general public about the corporate world.

The three forms of political consumerism defined above can be used separately or they may be used in different phases of struggles to improve the politics of products. People may simultaneously participate in all three forms in their actions against a particular product or producer. For example, they may target a product or producer in a boycott and use a labelling scheme to steer their choice of the same product category and thereby engage in positive political consumerism. At the same time, they may even use public discursive political consumerism to raise public consciousness about the politics of products and express displeasure about them directly to corporate actors. Boycotts are even called as a way to test whether the public is interested in corporate policy and practice and whether corporate actors are sensitive to public sentiment. They may, thus, be the first step in the process of establishing a labelling scheme. But this does not necessarily imply that the same citizens and consumer groups lie behind both negative and positive political consumerist actions. Some citizens refuse to purchase certain products even when boycotts have achieved their goals and have been called off by their organizers, as shown clearly after the first boycott of Nestlé for its marketing of breastmilk substitutes in the Third World (Friedman, 2003: 55). Other citizens may allow labelling schemes and other ethical pointers guide as many shopping choices as possible but remain uninvolved in boycotts and stay at home during protest demonstrations that express public outrage about particular business practices.

Negative political consumerism

Boycotts are the oldest form of political consumerism known today. For centuries and across the globe citizens have boycotted products and producers in order to express their dissatisfaction with business and politics. They have even targeted corporate actors and products to protest government policy, as shown by the boycott of South African goods, the more recent boycott of French export-sensitive products, and the current 'Divest in Israel Now' drive on American college campuses. Boycotts have been used in revolutionary and constitutional struggles, in protests for social justice, for civil and human rights, against environmental pollution and sweatshop working conditions, and by labour unions and other civil society associations. Some boycotts have a global profile, as illustrated by ongoing campaigns against Nestlé for its violation of the International Code of Marketing of Breastmilk Substitutes, Nike for labour abuses in offshore factories that manufacture its shoes and sporting goods, Microsoft for its anti-competitive practices, and Procter & Gamble for its animal testing policies (for a listing of and discussion about boycotts see Micheletti, 2003: 37–72, 82–9; Friedman, 1999).

Many boycotts are well known internationally. Some have had books written about them, have their own dedicated websites, and have even become part of folklore. Although not a recent one, the Montgomery Bus Boycott, staged in Alabama in the United States in 1955–56, shows how successful and effective boycotts work and why they become legends. Numerous books have been written about the boycott and its key participants, Rosa Parks and Martin Luther King (examples are Garrow, 1987; Stevenson, 1971; Crewe and Walsh, 2003; Burns, 1997; Dornfeld, 1995; Stein, 1993) and the Department of Sociology at University of Colorado at Boulder maintains a website on the boycott (see the Montgomery Bus Boycott page). This boycott also shows clearly the role that women and marginalized people often play in market-based political action.

Rosa Parks, a politically aware woman schooled in non-violent action, began the bus boycott. It was well supported by the African-American community and had Martin Luther King as its leader. It gave the anti-discrimination movement a new focus. Churches and women's groups were important actors. Traditionally the civil rights movement had relied on lawyers and court proceedings to desegregate America. The bus boycott showed that direct action and market-based action could be equally, or more, effective as litigation in the struggle for racial equality.

Moreover, it involved citizens at the grassroots level who assumed responsibility for their own and their group's well-being. The year-long boycott tested, empowered, and boosted African-American racial pride. It ended when the United States Supreme Court declared local laws requiring segregation on buses to be unconstitutional.

The Montgomery Bus Boycott has a secure place in American political history. It proved that collective market-based action could play a crucial role in breaking the cycle of racial history. Perhaps this at least partly explains the continued use of boycotts by African-Americans, other marginalized groups in the United States, as well as citizens in other countries. Survey research confirms the importance of boycotts for citizens in a variety of countries. World Value Survey data show that boycotting is on the rise as a potential, and increasingly implemented form of political engagement. The average for representative post-industrial societies was 5 per cent in the mid-1970s and 15 per cent in the mid-1990s (Norris, 2002: 198; see also Petersson et al., 1998: 55). Boycott increases have also been found in countries such as Mexico, South Korea, and South Africa (Inglehart, 1997: 313).

For citizens in some countries (for example, Nigeria) boycotting is one of the few safe ways for citizens to express dissatisfaction with foreign corporate presence and power. The Shell Oil Company is a frequent boycott target for Nigerian citizens. Survey results also highlight the importance of boycotts for young people. A recent Swedish study reports that almost 100 per cent of all young people between 16 and 29 years of age have actually participated or can consider participating in a boycott (Ungdomsstyrelsen, 2003: 171). Finally, boycotts are currently playing an important role in the contemporary movements critical of, or against, globalization. For instance, the organization Attac has been instrumental in the boycott of the World Bank for its debt and structural adjustment policies, as well as highly engaged in boycotts of multinational companies among others (as shown in an Internet search of Attac activities, November 2003).

Positive political consumerism

Positive political consumerism politicizes products by calling on buyers and sellers to purchase brands and support corporations that promote good environmental, working, and social conditions. They are 'beyond compliance' regulatory mechanisms (soft laws) because they encourage those involved to go further than required in governmental regulation ('command and control' hard laws) (Kollman and Prakash, 2001). Several positive political consumerist schemes are in operation today. Some of them, like socially responsible investing (SRI) institutions, offer people advice and the opportunity to place their money in stock companies and stock funds that reflect their political and ethical values. Examples of such institutions include Social Investment Forum, Ethical Junction, New Economic Foundation, and Council on Economic Priorities (see Micheletti, 2003: 104–7).

Many commentators view small investors' interest in the stock market and SRI as a new social movement and an innovative way to make a social and political statement (for example, Case, 1996). Socially responsible investing has long historical roots and became an important means of protest against the Vietnam War and corporate involvement in it for middle-class people who felt uncomfortable with street demonstrations (see Vogel, 1996, 2003). SRI is controversial. In certain quarters, its message of 'investing with your conscience' (cf. Miller, 1991) is offensive because it maintains that money and morality mix well and is, therefore, supportive of the capitalist system.

Another example, seals of approval product labelling schemes, also accepts capitalism and consumer society while attempting to mould them in a different direction. These schemes are characterized by a high degree of transparency, quality control, and accountability. They are run by governmental, quasi-governmental or non-governmental organizations and are institutions that develop criteria for assessing products on a variety of aspects. Assessment criteria are developed after discussion with the stakeholders (civil society associations, corporations, scientists, and policy makers). Companies submit their products for assessment and pay the assessment and certification fees. Products passing the tests are certified, which means that they can legally use the labelling scheme's logotype on the approved product for an agreed time period (for a discussion see Micheletti, 2003: 89–107).

Strong incentives encourage companies to seek certification. Consumers, employees, social movements, advocacy networks, governments, and even corporate actors may pressure them through boycotts, demonstrations, and contacts with company officials. Companies may decide that certification can get protesters off their back, as illustrated in the creation of forest certification schemes (Cashore et al., 2003: 191f.). Governments may include labelling as part of their procurement policy or decide, as in the case of paper provision in Sweden (Micheletti, 2003: 123ff.), to buy more environmentally friendly brands, implying that if companies want to compete for government contracts they need to certify their goods. Another incentive is characteristic of the market. If a company finds that its market competitors are certified it is more likely to seek certification for its products. Also, if a company is involved in export-sensitive markets in foreign countries whose people are aware of the politics of products, it is likely to want to certify its products. Two final incentives are the profit motive (money can be made from selling certified goods) and the image motive (certification pays off in goodwill) (Cashore et al., 2003; Jordan et al., 2003). Public legitimacy is the key goal for both the labelling schemes certifying goods and corporations seeking certification.

Examples of seals of approval labelling schemes are eco-labels, organic food labels, and fair trade labels. Fully-fledged eco-labels assess products (household chemicals, paper, transportation, white goods, office equipment, etc.) on the basis of a lifecycle evaluation (from production methods, to product use, and product waste management) and provide consumers with information about the environmental quality of products. About 30 such labels are today in operation on four continents (for example, German Blue Angel, EU-flower, US Green Seal, Nordic Swan, Japanese Eco Mark, and Swedish Good Environmental Choice) (Micheletti, 2003: 92–4, 111). Organic food labels ensure that food (fruit, vegetables, breads, meats, etc.) is produced by farmers who use renewable resources, conserve soil and water, and ensure that food is free of antibiotics, growth hormones, and commercial pesticides. A few schemes are the Australian Certified Organic, KRAV in Sweden, USDA Organic, and Organic Food Federation in the UK.

Finally, fair trade labels recognize the importance of consumers for improving the situation of producers and workers in developing countries. The kinds of goods that are labelled are cocoa, coffee, tea, honey, bananas, and textiles. Fair trade has grown in importance since the 1950s and has professionalized its operations, a development that is not seen by all supporters as advantageous because it means that fair trade is losing its social movement character and becoming interested in the profit motive (Rignell, 2002: 161–72). For these critics, money and morality do not mix well. The eco-labels, organic labels, and fair trade labels discussed here are, with few exceptions, nation-state based labels that are even part of a global political consumerist network in their field of specialization.

Forest Stewardship Certification (FSC) and Marine Stewardship Certification (MSC) are the latest institutions. They target our overuse of common pool resources caused by deforestation, over-fishing, corporate greed, and a lack of international governmental regulation. The term stewardship is central to this motion. It means actors' responsibility to manage their life properly with due regard to the rights of others, including other human beings and other living species. The schemes use a chain of custody certification, which for the FSC includes environmental, social, and sustainable forestry principles involved with harvesting timber and non-timber forest products, through to their transportation, processing, and the marketing of finished products (Cashore et al., 2003); and for the MSC, includes all parts of the supply chain, from fishing vessels to family dinner preferences (Peacey, n. d.). The FSC works closely with local communities and indigenous peoples in rainforests.

Some woodland owners consider its criteria to be too stringent and have established competing schemes. The Pan European Forest Certification takes into account the interests of small European woodland owners and co-ordinates national certification systems. The countervailing schemes want to create an international program for mutual recognition so they can develop a better international presence and compete more success-fully with the FSC (Micheletti, 2003:194; see also Bernstein and Cashore, 2000, 2001).

Public discursive political consumerism

This is the least-researched form of political consumerism. It appears to be the most recent form, and is quite attractive to young people. Discursive political consumer action can be contentious or can represent a co-operative strategy by attempting to engage in dialogue with busi-ness and the general public about corporate policy and practice. It can involve humour and spectacular events, as well as serious talks with business about the independent monitoring of production plants and the formulation and implementation of codes of conduct.

Discursive political consumerist action is used in particular by the fair trade movement. University students, labour activists, and people engaged in transnational advocacy networks for sustainable justice have been provoked by the global clothing industry's dealings in Third World countries (Mandel, 2000; Featherstone, 2000; Featherstone and USAS, 2002). Much of their outrage has focused on the Nike Corporation, a transnational corporation which is seen as a high-profile example of a company that cares more about its brand image than the human rights of its workers in the Third World (Ross, 1999; Fung, O'Rourke and Sabel, 2001; Klein, 2000).

An excellent example of discursive political consumerism in action is the now legendary Nike Email Exchange. As the exchange is accessible via Internet (Shey.net, no date; Peretti, 2001b) and in other volumes (see Peretti with Micheletti, 2003), only a short summary is offered here. A university student, Jonah Peretti, used a Nike online opportunity to order a pair of customized shoes with the word 'sweatshop' on them. His goal was to redirect Nike's publicity machine against itself in order to raise awareness about the working situation of Nike's overseas workers. Nike denied the request, but Peretti persisted to argue the validity of his proposed iD in an e-mail exchange with the Nike automated customer service with whom he initially placed his order: 'Your web site advertises that the NIKE iD program is "about freedom to choose and freedom to express who you are." I share Nike's love of freedom and personal expression. The site also says that "If you want it done right...build it yourself." I was thrilled to be able to build my own shoes, and my personal iD was offered as a small token of appreciation for the sweatshop workers poised to help me realize my vision. I hope that you will value my freedom of expression and reconsider your decision to reject my order' (Peretti with Micheletti 2003: 131).

Peretti forwarded the completed email exchange to a few friends, who sent it to other friends, who forwarded it to others. The exchange began to make a global impact. Over a three-month period, Peretti received 3,655 email inquiries about it; an estimated 11.4 million people received it shortly after it was made public (Macken, 2001), and the mass media picked it up. Stories appeared in different national newspapers, the NBC 'Today' show invited Peretti to discuss corporate social responsibility with a Nike representative, radio interviews followed, and Peretti was invited to speak at international and American political consumerist events and write an article for *The Nation* (Peretti, 2001b).

The Nike Email Exchange is an example of culture jamming, a contentious discursive strategy that turns corporate power against itself by co-opting, hacking, mocking, and re-contextualizing meanings. Other public discursive political consumerist actions demand serious replies from corporations to serious questions asked by political consumers about the politics of brand-name products, or engage consumers in discussions on the desirability and necessity of the production of sustainable goods. Still others create spectacular events through demonstrations and colourful parades and marches, by singing 'sweatshop' Christmas carols during the holiday season, by staging alternative fashion shows focusing on the work behind brand-name clothes rather than their stylish fit, and in 'sweatshop' Santa Claus visits to shopping malls at Christmas time. Shop owners in private shopping malls in certain countries have called the police to have the discursive political consumers cease their activities or be arrested.

Why political consumerism today?

Globalization is the general development that explains the sense of urgency felt by many people for political consumerism (Micheletti, forthcoming). It concerns both the globalization of problems (climate warming and 'social dumping', that is, forced low wages and benefits by corporations operating in developing countries), as well as the regulatory vacuums created by fast-moving economic globalization and slow-moving political globalization. Globalization has weakened the ability of states, institutions, and other actors traditionally viewed as being in charge of policy making to solve problems and to carry out their responsibilities for securing citizen well-being (Held and McGrew, 2000). This development has created, and continues to create policy vacuums and responsibility-floating (difficulty in pinpointing the institutions responsible for specific actions and problems) that lead to more serious problems regarding sustainability – problems that can be broadly defined as incurring environmental, economic, and social hardship. Economic globalization has opened up new opportunities for corporate business that cannot be effectively regulated by national environmental and labour market policy. At the same time, political globalization, or the creation of supranational governmental policy-making institutions, has been slow in developing. 'Globalization from below', as illustrated by political consumerist efforts and particularly labelling and certification schemes, is an attempt to create new steering mechanisms to deal with the negative side effects of economic globalization and the slow pace of political globalization.

If globalization is the problem identified by contemporary political consumerism, governance and post-modernization are the processes used by social scientists to explain the growing importance of political consumerism. The theory of governance questions the ability of the state (government) to solve the complex problems facing our more globalized world on its own. The solution of complex global problems, such as those targeted by political consumerism, requires co-ordinated efforts among states and other institutions and actors. Governmental policy failure may also be brought on by weaknesses in the national government itself, or the fact that compliance cannot be guaranteed by government regulatory efforts alone (Kooiman, 1993; Kollman and Prakash, 2001; Micheletti, 2003: 6f.). The governance perspective on policy making acknowledges the joint role of governmental, semi-governmental, non-governmental and private institutions as well as individual citizens in solving collective action problems and providing for the well-being of citizens (Peters and Savoie, 1995). This is also an acknowledgement of changes in the political landscape such as those illustrated by environ-mental deterioration and globalization. These changes call for new steering capacities offered by the governance approach to policy making. Policies and programs relevant for our common well-being (for instance, labelling schemes) can be formulated and implemented by institutions with new steering capacities outside the state. Policy takes on a new meaning, and a variety of actors are called upon to take responsibility for citizen well-being. Governance can also imply a more active role for citizens and, therefore, active participation and responsibility-taking by individual citizens and consumers for the implementation of policy measures aimed at improving common citizen well-being (cf. Beck, 1997; Beck and Beck-Gernsheim, 2001). As discussed in the previous section of this chapter, new actor categories are developing as a response to trends towards governance and the phenomenon of political consumerism.

Post-modernization, the other general theoretical explanation for the rise of political consumerism, is defined as basic change in the fundamental values of the citizens of industrialized and industrializing societies signaling '...a move away from the emphasis on economic efficiency, bureaucratic authority, and scientific rationality...toward a more human society with more room for individual autonomy, diversity, and self-expression' (Inglehart, 1997: 12). Post-modernization affects governments, citizens, and corporations. It highlights the increased individualization of society, political conflicts over values (post-materialism), and the focus on consumption over production as a potentially powerful steering mechanism for new regulatory politics. It erases the distinction between the private and public sphere and relocates 'politics' in all societal spheres, including consumer choices traditionally thought of as private in orientation, and ethical considerations about how individual citizens should be able to craft their own circumstances to be able to live a good life. Individualization and active citizenship, which stress the need for people to take a good look at the 'footprints' they leave behind in their behaviours and choices (cf. Rees, 1998; Micheletti, 2003: 2, 8, 30) and to assume more individual responsibility for solving problems, are integral parts of post-modernization. As discussed later, this leads to a new way of thinking about what we mean by citizenship.

Post-modernization has implications for corporate actors as well. A post-modernization of markets and companies is now taking place. The terms 'new age' company (Benjamin, 2001: viif.), 'promotionalism' (Knight and Greenberg, 2002), and 'corporate writing' (Boje, 2001) signal the transformation of industrial society companies that manufactured goods to postmodern ones that not only provide consumers with goods but also with 'good vibes' and a set of values and symbols to identity with. New age companies do not own factories in the country where they have their headquarters or in any other country. Instead, they contract out production to overseas factories not necessarily imbued with the values and symbols that are used to communicate the brand name in consumer society. Image-making and the association of corporate brand names with positive social values is the mission of pro-motionalism (Knight and Greenberg, 2002: 545), as illustrated by Nike's use of the word 'freedom' in the example of public discursive political consumerism discussed earlier. Promotionalism is crucial for buyer-driven commodity chains like those represented by the global garment industry and other consumer-society-oriented business enterprises. It helps corporations translate their public presence into economic success, continuity and good corporate identity (Knight and Greenberg, 2002). Corporate writing also promotes the image of business and helps it to deal with criticism and crisis. Writing is semiotically and interactively defined as a multitude and interconnection of media and includes corporate architecture, mission statements, annual reports, and websites, as well as the assessments of corporate policy and practice made by popular culture, academia, and social movements (cf. Boje, 2001).

Post-modern corporations are more careful about their corporate identities than their corporate physical infrastructures (factories, work-force, etc.), which they, in decreasing degrees, own and employ personally (Locke, 2003). Thus, avoiding blame and dispersing responsibility-taking to other actors and institutions is easy for them. However, as more time, effort, and resources are spent on image creation and maintenance than on the production process per se, post-modern corporations become highly dependent on publicity and, therefore, vulnerable to political consumerist campaigns of negative, positive, and discursive varieties.

Consumers as political actors: the controversial mix of money and morality

Political consumerism creates controversy. A common, sceptical view considers consumerism to be a new and threatening political ideology (Miles, 1998), counterproductive to citizenship (Pierre, 1995) and as conceding politics to economics by stripping politics of its ethical components (Mouffe, 1996: 22). Consumers are seen as narrow, self-interested, superficial economic actors without a sense of public responsibility and common good (Pierre, 1995: 64–7). Critics of consumer society and political consumerism point to the manipulative nature of capitalist society and the depraving effects of money, frequently seen as 'constantly enlarging, quantifying, and often corrupting all areas of life' (Zelizer, 1997: 12). Accordingly, promotional corporate communication and consumer society are corruptive because they are 'pie in the sky'. They sell us a false sense of compensation for our individual or collective psychological, social, and political failures or weaknesses (Grønmo and Lavik, 1988: 67; Ahrne, 1988; Miles, 1998: 20). The language of money is immoral, consumer society is ersatz good life, and political consumerism has nothing to contribute to global justice and sustainable development.

A different academic view maintains that the relationship between markets and politics, on the one hand, and consumption and citizenship, on the other, should be studied empirically as concerning preferences, identities, collective action, and spheres of justice. Economists study money as a means of communicating preferences regarding scarcity, a condition which is context-determinant and changing over time. Anthropologists approach money as a cultural transaction and structure (Douglas and Isherwood, 1978). Business schools now offer courses in business ethics and corporate social responsibility, both of which investigate just how well money and morality mix. The study of codes of conduct and management systems is important here. In interesting newer work, historians have probed the relationship between consumption, democracy, citizenship, and women's empowerment (Sklar, 1998; McGovern, 1998). More recently, sociologists have begun to theorize about shopping as a social experience and shopping malls as a public arena or sphere (Falk and Campbell, 1997). These are ideas that are restructuring the relationship between the public and the private, politics and markets, as well as consumers and citizens.

For these scholars, money is a tool, and tools, as Simmel has taught us, are social institutions 'through which the individual concentrates his activity and possessions in order to attain goals that he could not attain directly' (Simmel 1990: 210). Money is a very attractive and convincing tool. It is desirable because it is the means of acquiring values while being indifferent to the values themselves. Money is also blind or universal in the sense that it can be used by everyone – if they have it. It is a global language and, as shown by economic globalization, travels well. Money is an effective tool. It works fast and targets values precisely, thus the well-known saying 'money talks'. In this view, money can be an empowering and a liberating force (Simmel 1990: 222), and in the right hands and with the right guidance, it, as Marx noted long ago, is a radical leveller. It can help individuals gain independence from traditional groups and from individual work activities (Simmel 1990: 334–42) and it can work as a tool for political, social, and economic change.

Many contemporary scholars use Simmel's classic ideas as their point of departure for their post-modern theorizing about how money shapes subjective life, how subjective life affects how we use our money, and what this means for the history of ideas (cf. Sørensen, 2002). What they find is that the tool of money gives people self-expression by allowing them to purchase commodities that serve as markers of social rank, political identification, indicators of other shared collective identities, and signals of individuality. In some cases, self-expression through money does not promote political consumerism, as shown by the search for 'mass customized' clothes, which not only mirror our understandings of ourselves, but spur on niche marketing and causes problems for garment workers because it demands flexibility and small-scale, just-in-time production that presses overhead to keep prices down and runs counter to attempts to improve working conditions in the clothing industry through mechanization and standardization (Wark, 1999; Smith, 1999). In other cases, the self-expressing force of market transactions triggers consumers to use consumer society to put their money where their mouth is, as illustrated by the search for organic food and eco-labels by environmental activists and the use of labelling schemes and boycotts of trademarked clothes in the name of global social justice.

When fused with the concepts of governance and post-modernization, the concept of consumer society captures the role of money and consumption in constructing our everyday lives and underscores the fact that consumption is not just a by-product of production but an organizing relation in its own right. The implications of consumer society for political action, social life, and global relationships are now being investigated seriously in the social sciences. These studies show that markets matter and that consumerism is now a way of life (Livingston, 1998: 416). As discussed earlier, consumers, citizens, and even capitalists and corporate actors are moving from class society to consumer lifestyle society, and from industrial society to the post-modern society (Miles, 1998). Post-modern consumption also means that we buy products more for their sign-value than use-value, a development with enormous consequences for economic theories of consumption and studies of the corporate world, and a starting point for theorizing about the new actor categories that have developed along with the phenomenon of political consumerism.

Forging of new actor categories and responsibilities

The developments over the last few decades addressed in this chapter indicate that the relationship between consumers and citizens, and between politics and markets, have become increasingly intertwined. Global markets have become more important economically, socially, and politically. Consumption has increasingly become a matter of choice between a vast array of products and brands and, therefore, a problem of selection between values in global society (cf. Simmel, 1990: 31;

Princen, Maniates and Conca, 2002). People explore their character and develop their identities in the way they spend their money. Consumption, consumer behaviour, and consumer choice concern the allocation of values in society, and they are identity-forming processes. New citizenship theory in political science is beginning to recognize the plurality of political space, which gives weight to the claim that shopping, in certain instances, be considered an exercise of citizenship and that consumers can, in certain instances, have political agency (Trend, 1996; van Gunsteren, 1998; Delanty, 2000; see Micheletti, 2003: 15–18 for a discussion). Shopping helps form identities and allocates values in society. Political consumerism is an example of how citizens attempt to unite governance, post-modernization, and identity in a new, creative and potentially global democratic way.

Terms now used by scholars show clearly that political consumerism is forging new actor categories that combine both the public and the private spheres, consumer and citizen values, and forms of action. Sociologists and historians speak of consumer suffrage, consumer sovereignty, citizen-consumers, and even consumer republicanism. Consumer suffrage and sovereignty emphasize the 'freedom of choice' aspect of consumption – that is, individual liberalism. Consumer republicanism and citizen-consumers stress the importance of public virtue, public community, public ethics, and public morality in consumption and consumer choices (McGovern 1998: 57; Scammell, 2000; Micheletti, 2003: 15–24). The different terms also show how scholars vary in their interpretation of consumption from promotion of free will to promotion of the public good nationally and globally. Other terms indicate how scholars of the corporate world are wrestling with business ethics. It is common now to speak of corporate citizenship, private governments, and corporate social responsibility. Today we even mix money and morality, the marketplace and politics, and citizenship and consumption by using the terms 'socially responsible investing', 'ethical trade', 'ethical consumption', 'political consumerism', and 'fair trade'.

The role played by different actors is also being reformulated. Both consuming and producing goods can be interpreted as a governance strategy (a reaction to or solution for problems that government has with its regulatory policies and with improving our well-being). They can also be seen as part of the post-modern developments in which both individual and corporate identities are rethought. Working life is becoming less important as an organizing principle for political action, while private life and free time are gaining in significance, and leisure is emerging as a form of everyday involvement and engagement that forges new relationships between consumers and the forces of production nationally and globally (for an interesting article on the role of employees in this process see Fernstrom, 1986). The new cross-sphere terms are, actually, quite astounding. They forge new actor categories that cross the border between politics and economics and, therefore, use the market in new and innovative ways. The cross-sphere actor category of citizen-consumer assumes that consumers think publicly when they make consumer choices. Corporate social responsibility, private governments, and corporate citizenship proclaim that business corporations are political actors and, as such, need to follow public morals in their words and deeds. They need to apply the same values as democratic (public) institutions in their policies and practices (see Vogel, 1975: 17). Socially responsible investing and fair trade reflect an acknowledgement that money can be made morally and that making money morally makes a difference politically, socially, and economically. All the terms represent ideas that both recommend and reflect the collapse of the traditional spheres of activity and thought that have governed our lives for centuries (cf. Sørensen, 2002: 45–89). They challenge scholars to consider new centres of responsibility-taking and accountability in our more individualized and globalized world, and they argue that the new cross-sphere actors individually and collectively can make a difference.

Are these new actor categories and terms for actor policy and practice simply attractive in theory for scholars eager to make theoretical distinctions that put their names in the academic limelight? Can they be, and are they, put into practice? (cf. Morehouse, 1998: 51). My answer is that they should be taken seriously and investigated properly because they convincingly argue that consumption is a cohesive sphere that integrates politics and economics and collapses the public/private divide. They are put into practice in political consumerist networks whose activists believe that 'although the *structural* driver of our current system is capital accumulation and profit, the *transforming* driver may well lie elsewhere, namely in the sphere of consumption' (Zadek, 1998: 1). Even international governmental and non-governmental organizations take these new categories seriously, as do transnational corporations. The United Nations invests its goodwill in the Global Compact, which challenges 'business leaders to join an international initiative... that would bring companies together with UN agencies, labour and civil society... to advance responsible corporate citizenship so that business can be part of the solution to the challenges of globalization' (Global Compact, 2003). The Commission of the European Community invests in corporate social responsibility, produces white papers in the process of implementing it, and has created an award for excellence for corporate actors in its attempt to 'launch awareness-raising actions' in the areas of lifelong learning, diversity, and gender equality (European Commission, 2003). International non-governmental organizations like Amnesty are doing likewise. Its branches in many countries have established an Amnesty Business Club involving corporate actors in the belief that 'economic actors – be they companies or international financial institutions – are accountable for the human rights impact of their activities' (Amnesty International, 2003).

Finally, businesses are beginning to cross the line and mix moral concerns with their money matters by changing their management systems and developing codes of conduct. They are tripling their bottom line by including not only 'profit' as the value for assessing successful transactions but also the 'planet' (environmental concerns) and 'people' (social welfare). In this way they act as corporate citizens and focus on more than 'the economic value they add, but also on the environmental and social value they add – and destroy' (inKNOWvate, 2003). Political consumerism has, thus, prompted social scientists, consumers, governmental and non-governmental organizations, and corporate actors to take the market seriously as an arena for politics and 'putting your money where your mouth is'.

Note

1. This chapter was initially presented as a conference paper for the Nordic Political Science Association (NOPSA) meeting in Uppsala, Sweden in August 1999. In revised form, it now forms part of a research project, 'Political Consumption: Politics in a New Era and Arena', financed by the Swedish Research Council.

References

Ahrne, Göran. 1988. 'A labor theory of consumption'. In P. Otnes (ed.), *The Sociology of Consumption*. Oslo: Solum Forlag, 49–63.
Amnesty International. 2003. 'Economic globalization and human rights'. Online: amnesty.org/pages/ec-index-eng.
Beck, Ulrich. 1997. *The Reinvention of Politics. Rethinking Modernity in the Global Social Order*, translated by Mark Ritter. Oxford: Polity Press.
Beck, Ulrick, and Elisabeth Beck-Gernsheim. 2001. *Individualization*. London: Sage Publications.

Benjamin, Medea. 2001. 'Foreword'. In Archon Fung, Dara O'Rourke, and Charles Sabel (eds), *Can We Put An End to Sweatshops?* Boston, MA: Beacon Press, vii–xi.

Bernstein, Steven, and Benjamin Cashore. 2000. 'Globalization, four paths of internationalization and domestic policy change: the case of eco-forestry policy change in British Columbia, Canada'. *Canadian Journal of Political Science* 33(1): 67–99.

Bernstein, Steven, and Benjamin Cashore. 2001. 'The international–domestic nexus: the effects of international trade and environmental politics on the Canadian forest sector'. In M. Howlett (ed.), *Canadian Forest Policy: Regimes, Policy Dynamics and Institutional Adaptations*. Toronto: University of Toronto Press, 65–93.

Bloom, Paul N., and Ruth Belk Smith, eds. 1986. *The Future of Consumerism*. Lexington, MA: Lexington Books.

Boje, David M. 2001. 'Corporate writing in the web of postmodern culture and postindustrial capitalism'. *Management Communication Quarterly* 14(3): 507–16.

Burns, Stewart, ed. 1997. *Daybreak of Freedom: the Montgomery Bus Boycott*. Chapel Hill, NC: University of North Carolina Press.

Case, Samuel. 1996. *The Socially Responsible Guide to Smart Investing: Improve your Portfolio as You Improve the Environment*. Rockin, CA: Prima Publishing.

Cashore, Benjamin, Graeme Auld, and Deanna Newson. 2003. 'Legitimizing political consumerism: the case of forest certification in North America and Europe'. In Michele Micheletti, Andreas Follesdal, and Dietlind Stolle (eds), *Politics, Products, and Markets: Exploring Political Consumerism Past and Present*. New Brunswick: Transaction Publishers, 181–99.

Chapman, Robert L., ed. 1986. *New Dictionary of American Slang*. New York: Harper & Row.

Crewe, Sabrina, and Frank Walsh. 2003. *The Montgomery Bus Boycott*. Milwaukee, WI: Gareth Stevens Publishers.

Delanty, Gerald. 2000. *Citizenship in a Global Age: Society, Culture, Politics*. Buckingham: Open University Press.

Dornfeld, Margaret. 1995. *The Turning Tide, 1948–1956: From the Desegregation of the Armed Forces to the Montgomery Bus Boycott*. New York: Chelsea House Publishers.

Douglas, Mary, and Baron Isherwood. 1978. *The World of Goods*. London: Routledge.

European Commission. 2003. 'Corporate Social Responsibility: Anna Diamantopoulou announced winners of European Awards for Excellence in the Fields of Life Long Learning, Diversity and Gender Equality'. Online: http://www.health.fgov.be/WHI3/krant/krantarch2003/kranttekstmar3/030328m08eu.htm.

Falk, Pasi, and Colin Campbell, eds. 1997. *The Shopping Experience*. London: Sage Publications.

Featherstone, Liza. 2000. 'The student movement comes of age'. *The Nation*. October 16. http://www.thenation.com/index.mhtm

Featherstone, Lisa, and USAS (United Students Against Sweatshops). 2002. *Students Against Sweatshops*. London: Verso.

Fernstrom, Meredith M. 1986. 'Corporate public responsibility: a marketing opportunity?' In P. N. Bloom and R. B. Smith (eds), *The Future of Consumerism*. Lexington, MA: Lexington Books, 201–6.

Friedman, Monroe. 1999. *Consumer Boycotts: Effecting Change through the Marketplace and the Media*. New York: Routledge.

Friedman, Monroe. 2003. 'Using consumer boycotts to stimulate corporate policy changes: marketplace, media, and moral considerations'. In Michele Micheletti, Andreas Follesdal, and Dietlind Stolle (eds), *Politics, Products, and Markets. Exploring Political Consumerism Past and Present*. New Brunswick: Transaction Publishers, 45–62.

Fung, Archon, Dara O'Rourke, and Charles Sabel. 2001. *Can We Put An End to Sweatshops?* Boston: Beacon Press.

Garrow, David J. ed. 1987. *Montgomery Bus Boycott and the Women Who Started It.* Knoxville: University of Tennessee Press.

Global Compact. 2003. *What Is The Global Compact?* Online: unglobalcompact.org.

Grønmo, Sigmund and Randi Lavik. 1988. 'Shopping behavior and social interaction: An analysis of Norwegian time budget data'. In P. Otnes (ed.), *The Sociology of Consumption*. Oslo: Solum Forlag, 101–18.

Held, David, and Anthony McGrew, eds. 2000. *The Global Transformations Reader: An Introduction to the Globalization Debate*. Oxford: Polity Press.

Inglehart, Ronald. 1997. *Modernization and Postmodernization: Cultural, Economic, and Political Change in 43 Societies*. Princeton: Princeton University Press.

inKNOWvate. 2003. Triple Bottom Line. Online: http://www.inknowvate.com/inknowvate.

Jordan, Andrew, K. Rüdiger, W. Wurzel, Anthony R. Zito and Lars Brückner. 2003. 'Consumer responsibility-taking and eco labeling schemes in Europe'. In M. Micheletti, A. Follesdal, and D. Stolle (eds), *Politics, Products, and Markets: Exploring Political Consumerism Past and Present*. New Brunswick: Transaction Publishers, 161–80.

Klein, Naomi. 2000. *No Logo*. London: Flamingo.

Knight, Graham, and Josh Greenberg. 2002. 'Promotionalism and subpolitics. Nike and its labor critics'. *Management Communication Quarterly* 15(4): 541–70.

Kollman, Kelly and Aseem Prakash. 2001. 'Green by choice? Cross-national variation in firms' responses to EMS-based environmental regimes'. *World Politics* 53 (April): 399–430.

Kooiman, Jan. 1993. 'Governance and governability: using complexity, dynamics and diversity'. In J. Kooiman (ed.), *Modern Governance. New Government–Society Interactions*. London: Sage Publications, 35–48.

Livingston, James. 1998. 'Modern subjectivity and consumer culture'. In S. Strasser, C. McGovern and M. Judt (eds), *Getting and Spending: European and American Consumer Societies in the 20th Century*. Cambridge: Cambridge University Press, 413–29.

Locke, Richard M. 2003. *The Promise and Perils of Globalization: The Case of Nike*. Massachusetts: MIT Industrial Performance Center, Massachusetts Institute of Technology.

Macken, Deidre. 2001. 'The fin chain reaction'. *Australian Financial Review*. April 21 (online).

Mandel, Jay R. 2000. 'The student anti-sweatshop movement: limits and potential'. *Annals, AAPSS* 570 (July): 92–103.

McGovern, Charles. 1998. 'Consumption and citizenship in the United States, 1900–1940'. In S. Strasser, C. McGovern and M. Judt (eds), *Getting and Spending: European and American Consumer Societies in the 20th Century*. Cambridge: Cambridge University Press, 37–58.

Micheletti, Michele. 2003. *Political Virtue and Shopping: Individuals, Consumerism, and Collective Action*. New York: Palgrave.

Micheletti, Michele. Forthcoming. 'Le consumérisme politique: une nouvelle forme de gouvernance transnationale?'. *Sciences de la société* 62: 119–42.

Micheletti, Michele, Andreas Follesdal, and Dietlind Stolle, eds. 2003. *Politics, Products, and Markets: Exploring Political Consumerism Past and Present*. Rutgers, NJ: Transaction Publishers.

Miles, Steven. 1998. *Consumerism as a Way of Life*. London: Sage Publications.

Miller, Alan J. 1991. *Socially Responsible Investing: How to Invest with Your Conscience*. New York: New York Institute of Finance.

Montgomery Bus Boycott Web Site. Online: http://sobek.colorado.edu/~jonesem/montgomery.html.

Morehouse, Ward. 1998. 'Consumption, civil action and corporate power: lessons from the past, strategies for the future'. *Development: Journal of the Society for International Development* 41(1): 48–53.

Mouffe, Chantal. 1996. 'Radical democracy or liberal democracy'. In D. Trend (ed.), *Identity, Citizenship, and the State*. New York: Routledge, 19–26.

Norris, Pippa. 2002. *Democratic Phoenix: Reinventing Political Activism*. Cambridge: Cambridge University Press.

Otnes, Per, ed. 1988. *The Sociology of Consumption*. Oslo: Solum Forlag.

Peacey, Jonathan. No Date. 'The Marine Stewardship Council Fisheries Certification Program: Progress and Challenges'. Online: www.msc.org.

Peretti, Jonah. 2001a. 'My Nike media adventure'. *The Nation*, 9 April (online).

Peretti, Jonah. 2001b. 'Culture jamming, memes, social networks, and the emerging media ecology: the "Nike Sweatshop Email" as object-to-think-with'. http://xenia.media.mit.edu/~peretti/nike/

Peretti, Jonah with Michele Micheletti. 2003. 'The Nike sweatshop email: political consumerism, internet, and culture jamming'. In M. Micheletti, A. Follesdal, and D. Stolle (eds), *Politics, Products, and Markets. Exploring Political Consumerism Past and Present*. New Brunswick: Transaction Publishers, 127–44.

Peters, B. Guy, and Donald J. Savoie, eds. 1995. *Governance in a Changing Environment*. Montreal and Kingston: McGill-Queen's University Press.

Petersson, Olof et al. 1998. *Demokrati och medborgarskap* [Democracy and citizenship]. Stockholm: SNS förlag.

Pierre, Jon. 1995. 'The marketization of the state: citizens, consumers, and the emergence of the public market'. In B. G. Peters and D. J. Savoie (eds), *Governance in a Changing Environment*. Montreal and Kingston: McGill-Queen's University Press, 55–81.

Princen, Thomas, Michael Maniates, and Ken Conca, eds. 2002. *Confronting Consumption*. Massachusetts: The MIT Press.

Rees, William E. 1998. 'Reducing the ecological footprint of consumption'. In Laura Westra and Patricia H. Werhane (eds), *The Business of Consumption: Environmental Ethics and the Global Economy*. Lanham, MD: Rowman & Littlefield, 113–30.

Rignell, Hans. 2002. *Rättvis handel – Rörelse i rätt riktning? [Fair Trade – Movement in the Right Direction?]* Gothenburg, Sweden: Världsbutikerna för Rättvis Handel.

Ross, Andrew, ed. 1999. *No Sweat: Fashion, Free Trade, and the Rights of Garment Workers*. New York: Verso.

Scammell, Margareth. 2000. 'The Internet and civic engagements: the age of the citizen-consumer'. *Political Communication* 17: 351–5.

Shey.net, No date. 'The Life of an Internet Meme. A History of the Nike Emails'. Online: http://www.shey.net/niked.html

Simmel, Georg. 1990 [1907]. *The Philosophy of Money*, edited by David Frisby, translated by Tom Bottomore and David Frisby. London: Routledge.

Sklar, Kathryn Kish. 1998. 'The Consumers' White Label Campaign of the National Consumers' League 1898–1919'. In S. Strasser, C. McGovern, and M. Judt (eds), *Getting and Spending. European and American Consumer Societies in the 20th Century.* Cambridge: Cambridge University Press, 17–35.

Smith, Paul. 1999. 'Tommy Hilfiger in the age of mass customization'. In A. Ross (ed.), *No Sweat: Fashion, Free Trade, and the Rights of Garment Workers.* New York: Verso, 249–62.

Sørensen, Mads P. 2002. *Den politiske forbruger – en analyse af ideen og fænomenet* [*The political consumer – an analysis of the idea and phenomenon*]. Aarhus: Department of the History of Ideas, Aarhus University, Doctoral Dissertation.

Stein, Conrad R. 1993. *The Montgomery Bus Boycott*. Chicago: Children's Press.

Stevenson, Janet. 1971. *The Montgomery Bus Boycott, December, 1955: American Blacks Demand an End to Segregation.* New York: Watts.

Strasser, Susan, Charles McGovern, and Mattias Judt, eds. 1998. *Getting and Spending: European and American Consumer Societies in the 20th Century.* Cambridge: Cambridge University Press.

Trend, David, ed. 1996. *Identity, Citizenship, and the State.* New York: Routledge.

Ungdomsstyrelsen. 2003. *De kallar oss unga. Ungdomsstyrelsens attityd- och värdringstudie 2003* [They call us young. The Youth Council's Study of Attitudes and Values]. Stockholm: Ungdomsstyrelsen.

Van Gunsteren, Herman R. 1998. *A Theory of Citizenship: Organizing Plurality in Contemporary Democracies.* Bolder, CO: Westview Press.

Vogel, David. 1975. 'The corporation as government: challenges and dilemmas'. *Polity* 8: 5–37.

Vogel, David. 1996. *Kindred Strangers: The Uneasy Relationship between Politics and Business in America.* Princeton: Princeton University Press.

Vogel, David. 2003. 'Tracing the roots of the contemporary political consumerist movement: marketized political activism in the U.S. in the 1960s'. In M. Micheletti, A. Follesdal, and D. Stolle (eds), *Politics, Products, and Markets: Exploring Political Consumerism Past and Present.* New Brunswick: Transaction Publishers, 83–100.

Wark, McKenzie. 1999. 'Fashion as a Culture Industry'. In A. Ross (ed.), *No Sweat. Fashion, Free Trade, and the Rights of Garment Workers.* New York: Verso, 227–48.

Westra, Laura, and Patricia H. Werhane, eds. 1998. *The Business of Consumption: Environmental Ethics and the Global Economy.* Lanham, MD: Rowman & Littlefield.

Zadek, Simon. 1998. 'Consumer works!' *Journal of the Society for International Development* 41(1) (online).

Zelizer, Viviana A. 1997. *The Social Meaning of Money: Pin Money, Paychecks, Poor Relief, and Other Currencies.* Princeton, NJ: Princeton University Press.

Part III

Strategies and Legitimacies in Capital Flows

7
Modes of Knowing: The Fashioning of Financial Market Knowledge

Anna Hasselström

Introduction

When Ron was 17 years old he got a job at a brokerage house in London as a board boy – he ran errands for the senior brokers, delivered messages, kept buy and sell quotes updated on the white board, and so on. After a couple of years, his tasks slowly evolved into that of a broker. He was seated next to a more experienced broker, which gave him the opportunity to listen in on client conversations, and to watch all the other brokers going about their everyday business. He joined the others for drinks after work and when they took clients out. Eventually he also started broking small deals for small clients. Ten years later he had moved from broking to being a money market trader and had acquired the title 'head of the desk'.

Ron is from Essex, northeast of London. He has little formal education but says that he has had to become somewhat of an economist himself in order to form a view on the market – in order to interpret economic news. Knowing what to do, he says, has to do with a gut feeling he has, based on a 'feel for the market'.

In this chapter I discuss financial market knowledge as an aggregate of techniques used by financial brokers, traders, and analysts when manoeuvring in, and making sense of, the financial markets field (cf. Foucault, [1982] 1997).[1] Making sense of the market involves more than simply using the market. Through their everyday activities financial brokers, analysts and traders also perform or construct 'the market'. In this sense 'the market' is a model *for* as well as a model *of* reality (cf. Geertz, 1973).

Gaining financial market knowledge involves the acquisition of the skill to perform in particular ways in particular sociomaterial settings.

It is not a set of ready made, clear-cut knowledge structures for the broker, trader, or analyst to internalize. It is knowledge based on participation. It is a learning process – a way of engaging in the social world 'mediated by the differences of perspectives among the co-participants' (Lave and Wenger, 1991: 15).

Financial market *knowledge* is hence not only found in financial theory textbooks, but also diffused in the everyday relations and interactions between brokers, traders, analysts, clients, and technology, in what they do and do not, and in the overall political economy of the financial market field. It is knowledge that to a very large extent is learned on the job in the arenas of *trading, research, sales* and *entertaining*.[2]

The trading arena

The trading floors I have visited have all been very alike – whether in Stockholm, London, or New York. They are institutional hybrids in that they belong to often large organizations, such as investment banks, but are distinct from their central organizational activities. Trading floors are separated from the bank or company's other departments, access is restricted, and the governance structure and bonus wage system differ (Knorr Cetina and Bruegger, 2002a: 913). The actual trading floors are often open-spaced with rows and rows of desks, and the traders and brokers sit according to what financial instruments they trade or broke. The open layout and close proximity of others means that brokers, traders and analysts sitting on the trading floor are seen by, and can see others – all the time, which makes learning through participation and observation easier.

Traders and brokers are seated very close – in fact closer than what seems necessary in relation to everyday interactions. Certain paraphernalia are more or less standardized across floors, such as different time zones clocks, electronic indices boards, trading software, and real-time video and audio-links. This 'technology of practice' (Lave and Wenger, 1991: 101) of financial markets involves more than simply learning how to use them. The technology of practice also guides and disciplines brokers, traders and analysts. It affects what can and cannot be said and thought, and in what manner (cf. Knorr Cetina and Bruegger, 2002b; cf. Preda, 2002; cf. Shore and Wright, 1997; Zaloom, 2004).

Financial technology, such as certain software for trading, creates financial facts and problems by making them visible (Lépinay, n.d., Muniesa, 2000). In order to do that, and in order for users of techno-logy to use it in an unproblematic manner, the technology itself has to be partly 'invisible' or 'transparent', although it must still be visible 'in the form of extended access to information' (Lave and Wenger, 1991: 103). The invisibility aspect of information technologies allows us to focus on the visibility of the subject matter of the so-called market (cf. Muniesa, 2002).

On busy days many trading floors are noisy and stressful environments. The large open spaced floors offer almost no seclusion or privacy. Brokers and traders often used the word 'aggressive' to describe the work environment in financial markets. When I asked Maria, a Swedish sales trader in London, to elaborate what this meant she had great difficulty doing so. Eventually she said: 'Aggressive as in when your boss shouts: "you fucking idiot".' She also said that 'aggressive' includes the fact that everything is measured in figures and numbers: your work is constantly monitored and measured, and therefore you are always under evaluation. There is a constant pressure to perform – that is, to make lots of money. Apart from being a medium for exchange, money in the financial market also indicates who you are. As Abolafia (1996: 30) puts it, 'it is a measure of one's "winnings". It provides an identity that prevails over charisma, physical attractiveness, or sociability as the arbiter of success and power.'

The brokers and traders themselves often nurture the popular image of brokers and traders as hot-shot, aggressive, go-getters. There was a lot of swearing and yelling on the larger trading floors I visited in London and in New York – especially on busy days. At the English brokerage house where I spent most time, it was common to hear loud abuse along the lines of 'fucking cunt' or 'fucking idiot' flying through the air. Matt, a trader working for a large Japanese bank in London, gave another example: he was new at the desk and a trader from another desk approached him and wanted a price. Matt did not really know what to do and replied: 'I'll get back to you in two minutes', to which the trader responded: 'No, I want it now, you idiot!' Luckily, Matt explained, he had good desk colleagues that told the trader to 'fuck off'.

It is not only the relationship between colleagues that can be somewhat strained and unpleasant – the relationship between traders (clients) and brokers is also far from frictionless. The financial trading system is, in theory, based on opposing interests: both parties want to make as much money as possible out of the other party, which means that certain systemic tensions are built into the very structures of trading. Short-term gains have to be weighed against long-term exchange relationships with others (Abolafia, 1996). When talking about the relationship between brokers and traders one broker said: 'We hate them and they hate us. They all think we're wankers. They treat us like shit and we still have to go out with them.'

The newcomer will quickly learn that traits stereotypically associated with women are bad and should not be displayed, and be quickly disciplined into certain manners. This moulding into shape is aided by the fact that almost everything he says and does is visible for others – if he behaves in the wrong manner, that is, appears too soft, gives the wrong quote, or takes too long in giving a quote, the others around him will not hesitate to let him know by giving him nicknames, making up jokes about him, or telling stories about him in which he comes across as being stupid, ugly, smelly, a sissy etc. Through derogatory comments made in public, the newcomer is taught what is and is not acceptable to do and say.

But besides learning how to manoeuvre in the sociomaterial milieu described above, traders and brokers obviously also need to know how to actually trade and broke – that is, to give prices, buy and sell.

Quoting and trading: a few examples

Broking and trading are not always very straightforward. For example, sometimes a trader might not want to trade – if he, for instance, only has a limited amount of US dollars and wants to hold on to them. If a trader at a large bank asks a trader at a smaller bank to quote a price in dollars, it is difficult for the 'small' trader to say no, even if he himself wants to get hold of all the dollars he can. If the small trader was to say no, the large trader is likely to get annoyed and might turn somewhere else in the future with his business. There are, however, a number of strategies the small trader can use in order to avoid having to close a deal, and still not lose future business. One way is to quote a price a little higher than the market price, which will make the large trader turn to another bank to get a better deal. This strategy is, however, not free from risk: first, if this is done too obviously, the large trader will realize what is going on and get annoyed anyway. Second, if the small trader gives a high sell price, the buy price has to be high as well, as large spreads tend to annoy clients. If the large trader asks for a sell price, the small trader, who assumes the large trader does want to buy, but is unwilling to actually sell to him, quotes a high sell price hoping the trader will turn elsewhere. If the small trader is unlucky, the large trader might turn around and sell instead – the buy quote will then be higher than the market price, and the small trader cannot refuse to buy dollars at a higher price from the larger bank.

Another strategy to avoid closing a deal is to blame the credit limit, that is, the allowed exposure towards different banks. This is difficult, however, when dealing with large banks that have a good credit rating – once again, the trader runs the risk of being found out.

Being a trader thus means that you sometimes want to *avoid* doing a particular deal, whereas brokers, on the other hand, are more occupied in getting clients *to trade* all the time. Robert, an ex-broker from London, told me how he used to lower his voice and sound conspiratorial when talking to the client on the telephone about a certain deal. This, he argued, would make the client feel special and chosen, as though he was receiving a selective tip from Robert. Another possibility was to talk to the client on the phone about a deal and then suddenly pretend to angrily turn to an imaginary colleague and shout: 'No, don't! I've got a deal going here!' This would make the client on the other end think that another client wanted to do the same thing, and this would thereby 'push the client over the edge' so to speak, based on the idea that if others do it, it must be a good thing. Once again, these strategies are learned on the job by observing, imitating, and taking part in the work practices played out on and off the trading floor.

The research arena

The interesting thing about financial analysis is that despite the impressive mobilization of fact-gathering forces and statistical modelling procedures, neither fundamental nor technical analysis, nor any of their many combinations and variants, has succeeded in attaining the scientific validity which they systematically invoke. (Hertz, 1998: 17)

By 'research' I refer to economic and political 'information', 'knowledge' and 'facts' that are considered important by the traders and brokers themselves when making money, such as reports, statistics, articles, verbal accounts of past, present and future events, and different kinds of commercial financial media. These are distributed, more or less, through the same channels as the actual buying and selling of financial products, that is, via e-mail, the Internet, through face-to-face interaction, video links, speaker systems, telephones, Intranets and private news and trading networks such as Bloomberg, Reuters and Telerate.

Historically, the development of financial research and the scientific study of finance in the late nineteenth century can be seen as a moral imperative to separate speculators from mere gamblers and fraudsters. The process of recording and analyzing trading patterns, producing indices, and developing other kinds of financial research, was partly a political act that sought to legitimize, protect and enhance speculators' professional status, but it also changed the organization of financial markets (De Goede, 2001; cf. Thompson, 2000). For example, the 1867 invention of the ticker, a mechanical paper tape transmitting stock prices, made it possible for people to see small price fluctuations over days, it gave rise to technical charts and also to the profession of the stock analyst as an impartial distributor of information (Preda, 2002). Attitudes towards the value-adding character of research vary. Take Steve, a London sales trader, for example. He claims he is not driven by making money, but by the thought or knowledge that he knows more than anyone else (such as his colleagues and his clients). Steve works hard in trying to understand how the economy and the market work. Compared with other sales traders I met during fieldwork, Steve spent a considerable amount of time getting information and clarification from the in-house economists and analysts – he usually talked to them several times a day. Steve had thereby become fluent in the market language considered correct and valid among these economists and analysts.

Stewart (a proprietary trader also from London), on the other hand, seems to base his trading primarily on personal contacts: 'I don't read reports, because I know what the economists will say.' Despite this statement, he later admitted to reading the bullet points occasionally, but 'That is it. I want the information in one sentence. I don't need to know why something is in one way or another.' He says he does not care about written research, since the chances are that many others have seen it as well, and then the opportunity to make money is gone. But regardless of whether or not a broker or trader thinks he actually can learn something from research material, he must master this market language when justifying his decisions to others.

Large investment banks and brokerage houses usually have their own research departments. Economists and analysts who specialize in different geographical areas or financial products disseminate economic research through reports and newsletters. They may be reports on expected interest rate cuts in different countries, on the global economy in general, on a particular company's future earnings, and so on. Some research is only produced for the employees of the company, whereas other research products are distributed to clients as well. Economists and analysts often take an active part in the company morning meetings where future, and to some degree past events, are discussed. They also provide daily updates to traders via the in-house speaker system or via e-mail. Most of them also speak to clients during the day. In a nutshell, research departments essentially offer sales traders arguments, explanations, and investment ideas to use in their discussions with clients. They also supply their own traders with 'information' and 'facts', and the correct market talk. This market language provides brokers, traders, and analysts with a shared frame of reference or perspective (cf. Millo, n.d., a) in interpreting the world.

Evaluations and contradictions

Sometimes the analysts and economists are seated on the trading floor, but often they are seated on a different floor, or in a different city, or in a different country. Daniel works as an analyst for one of the larger British banks with a large trading floor in the City of London. He has a degree in economics and has worked for his current employer for 15 years. He is seated next to the proprietary traders on the trading floor. Daniel's reports are distributed to the bank's employees and their clients:

A: How do you decide what to write a report on?

D: I write about what I find interesting. I'm good at coming up with ideas, and then Stewart [the proprietary trader seated next to him] makes money out of them. I dig and sift through all kinds of written material; it is all about writing something that the big investors, such as Soros, like to read, and will actually pick up and read. This will bring in business.

A: But how do you know what to write?

D: It depends on what they talk about at the desk. What people talk about.

A: What about evaluation? Can your work be evaluated?

D: Oh yes, it is evaluated by the amount of business we get from a client.

A: Yes, but does someone actually sit down with your reports and compare with what happened?

D: No.

A: So you can never really tell whether a client chose your bank because of your reports or because of some other variable?

D: [a little annoyed] No, but it's the same for the traders. You can never tell if it's just luck.

Seated next to the proprietary traders, Daniel is in a position both to participate and to observe his desk mates and vice versa. Although they share certain work practices, they also enter into interaction with each other with different perspectives and horizons on life (cf. Hannerz, 1992). The production of financial market knowledge can therefore not be predicted. Events are constantly communicated, defined, interpreted, and negotiated between people in the same room or in another country. Knowing about financial markets becomes an activity in its own right, a way of being in the world (Lave and Wenger, 1991, cf. Zaloom, 2003).

Financial research offers technical-looking hands-on arguments and causal explanations, neatly presented and organized in tables, graphs, bullet points, bold print, mathematical models, etc., and accompanied by a company logotype. Analysts and economists make ample use of mathematical models when measuring the value or risk associated with a trade or investment. But these models do more than simply conveying a figure – they constitute the market by being 'tools of communication' (Hägglund, 2001). Certain models, such as models valuing shares and companies, and risk-assessing models in the options market (Millo, n.d., a), produce rules for evaluation and facts that can be discussed, agreed or disagreed upon, and measured. They discipline brokers, traders, and analysts into certain ways of thinking about, talking about, and acting on the world. By accepting certain models in fashion at a particular time and viewing them as valid, brokers, traders, and analysts from different walks of life, equipped with different sets of perspectives toward the world and the market, develop joint frames of reference (cf. Fligstein, 2001).

It is not necessary to know how the models work mathematically, as long as you learn how to talk about them in a correct manner (cf. Zaloom, 2003) – once again, this is learned on the job by taking part and observing others (although the technical appearances of models, as such, can obviously be learned through formal education). To master a certain degree of technical jargon and to be able to use complex theories when explaining causality are both important strategies in order to come across as being 'in the know' (Lowry, 1984).

Talking in abstract symbols, such as figures, is an important aspect of the increasing degree of abstraction and reductionism that characterizes financial markets, as well as many other spheres of contemporary life (cf. Norberg, 2001). Besides construing concepts, the acts of measuring can also have a neutralizing effect (Porter, 1995). Political and economic connections are glossed and transformed into different financial instruments, such as shares, options, and convertibles, which in turn are transformed into numbers and into authoritative 'financial facts' (cf. Bourdieu and Wacquant, 2001; Dilley, 1992; cf. Eriksen, 2001; cf. Norberg, 2001). Such facts are construed in the research arena, and this kind of knowledge is often referred to by sales traders in the sales arena.

The sales arena

Sales traders can be seen as peddlers in added value, trust, expert knowledge, and plausible explanations. They provide a personalized link (recognizable voices and faces) between the bank/brokerage house and the client (traders and fund managers). In this arena, information and knowledge are developed, collected, and distributed to clients in order to get them to trade.

Financial markets are thus characterized by constant communication between all kinds of actors. This communication is not only *about* the market, it *is* the market, the communication performs the market, in the sense that people keep track of what others do, and base their decisions on what others do, how they sound, what they say and do not say. Market fluctuations are interpreted by this 'market chatter' (Zaloom, 2004) between colleagues and counterparts. Constant communication guides them in their broking and trading activities, which in turn guide others, and so on. 'The Market', as an abstract, globally interconnected market following its own logic, hence constitutes, and is constituted by, the everyday performative workings of brokers, traders, and analysts.

Autumn 1998, 7.15 a.m., London, the City

Steve is late! He puts down his take-away coffee on his desk and starts shuffling papers around, trying to find a note pad. There it is! He then runs across the trading floor and sneaks into the auditorium where the other equity traders and sales traders are seated. Steve works with international equity sales at a large American investment bank. The morning meeting is already under way, and one of the in-house economists is busy talking about a management changeover in a European company that may affect the share price.

It is a small auditorium, seating roughly 80 people. A table with microphones is placed at the centre of the stage. The traders and sales traders listen, take notes, and ask the odd question. The economist finishes his briefing and Frankfurt is put through via the speaker-system. A sales trader from the German office gives her on-the-spot view. She talks for a few minutes, but according to Steve she doesn't 'add any value' – she does not really say anything new that Steve himself could not 'read off the screen', as he puts it. Here 'the screen' refers mainly to the financial news offered online by the large news agencies such as Reuters and Bloomberg. After that, other economists and traders take turns talking about the coming day's events.

7.30 a.m., London, the City

On his way out of the auditorium Steve picks up a bunch of photocopied papers lying at the exit. The papers contain abbreviated versions of what has just been said. He returns to his desk and starts calling clients. The idea is to 'add value'; to give the client information on what is going on in the market. Steve simply reads off his own short notes, but sounds as though he knows a lot more than he actually does. If he decides he has nothing new to say to his fund manager clients, he will not call them. Steve does not want to irritate them by taking up their time.

Later that morning, when checking his e-mail, Steve suddenly discovers a message from the in-house Latin America analyst. It had arrived earlier that day and he had somehow missed it. The e-mail was about a political decision in Brazil affecting IMF (International Monetary Fund) funding. This could be a possible problem for Steve's clients. After reading the e-mail, Steve rushes over to the analyst who had written it, and asks for more information about what the news might imply. He then calls two of his clients and tells them about this possible 'hot spot'. Both clients listen quietly when Steve explains what has happened in Brazil. When he finishes they ask him what this could mean, what the consequences might be and why it has happened. Steve, with his new-found knowledge of the topic, answers in a very authoritative and convincing manner, sounding very much 'in the know' of things. After hanging up, Steve walks around to some of the other sales traders and traders and tells them about the Brazil news.

12.30 p.m., London, the City

There is a lunch and investor/client meeting upstairs. Steve's bank has invited five Nordic companies together with possible investors to a day-long seminar. The company representatives take turns promoting their companies in order to attract investors. With PowerPoint presentations and lots of neatly printed handouts, they try to convince the present traders and sales traders that their particular company offers a lucrative future investment. Steve, who had brought me there, was not impressed and yawned openly several times during these presentations. After leaving the meeting early, Steve again complained: 'What a waste of time! It didn't add any value at all!' That is, the company representatives did not reveal any kind of information that Steve could pass on to his clients for them to 'trade on'. It was all old news.

Brokerage houses and investment banks often organize these kinds of conferences, bringing together potential clients (everything from a handful to several hundreds). This is mainly an attempt to attract investment capital – that is, the investment bank organizing the conference hopes to generate more business.

The afternoon turns out to be fairly quiet. Steve makes a few client calls before going out for a quick drink with me, the visiting anthropologist. It is his only free evening this week. Christmas is closing in, and there is a lot of client entertaining to do.

There is an in-built conflict between sales traders and traders. Both are supposed to make money for the bank they work for, but sales traders also have to be loyal, or at least appear loyal, towards their clients. Sales traders make money from commissions (either on a fixed base or as a percentage), while traders make money through trading. Obviously the trader wants to make a good spread between the buy and sell prices, whereas the sales trader wants to keep the client happy. That usually does not include wide spreads.

Enrique, from Spain, works for a large American investment bank in London at the high yield desk (junk bonds).[3] At one of their desk parties in a small club just off Oxford Street the analysts, sales traders, traders, secretaries, and back-office staff let their hair down. Enrique broke out in some sort of salsa-like routine and I complimented him: 'Enrique, you really know how to dance!' Without stopping he called out over his shoulder: 'Ah, I can bluff it. I'm a sales trader!'

The entertaining arena

Analysts, brokers, and traders are in constant contact with other brokers, traders and analysts; they have usually met their counterparts on several occasions and sometimes they have been doing business together for years. Although it differs depending on what market you are in, and what your personal opinion on entertaining is, face-to-face meetings, especially in the shape of entertaining, are very much part of global financial flows and financial markets.

The concept of entertaining as I use it refers to the different activities, besides trading, that traders and brokers do with their clients outside the official workplace. A lot of money and time is spent 'entertaining'. It can include going out for lunch, dinner or just drinks, going to strip clubs, football games, the theatre, horse races, and so on. Since investment banks and investment funds have counterparts (traders and investors), and use brokers from across the financial world, this also includes a lot of travelling to visit people. Brokers, traders, and analysts are routinely sent abroad, armed with the company credit card, to entertain clients or counterparts. December is *the* entertaining month of the year in London, New York, and Stockholm, and it is not unusual for a brokerage house or investment bank to throw big parties in their clients' and counterparts' countries, and have their own brokers or traders flown in for the occasion. Financial market newcomers usually start off these trips by accompanying more senior old-timers.

During my stay in London, a standard evening of entertaining usually started with a few drinks, followed by dinner and finishing off with a visit to a strip club to buy lap dances.[4] Besides some gossiping about colleagues getting hired or fired, there was usually very little job talk during these outings. One recurring theme during these outings was stories from 'the good old days' of broking and trading, and stories of spectacular parties they had been to that usually included anecdotes about strippers, sex, drugs, and how drunk everyone had been. Stories where someone had been publicly humiliated were often told with great animation.

Entertaining: added value and trust

A recurring explanation I encountered as to why entertaining as an activity exists, was that in many markets today the same price is given more or less to everyone, which means that you have to come up with something else, something extra to attract clients, such as various kinds of entertaining, or bits of information and knowledge.

Paul, the American bond analyst working in London, had a different view about the matter. When talking about what kinds of knowledge and activities matter in financial markets he said: 'I'll show you what really rules Wall Street.' He then took a paper and drew a large dollar sign: 'This is what it is all about. The really big ones, like Buffet[5] and those guys couldn't care less about being entertained. They just want to make money and don't care about that.' He then added: 'But there are loads of people in the market who do care.'

Despite his somewhat condescending attitude towards entertaining when discussing it with me at this time, he was, on another occasion, visibly chuffed when he told me how he had flown to Monte Carlo to see a couple of clients, and how he had been picked up at the airport by helicopter and taken straight into the city. He had met one client for lunch, then had the evening off, went to the casino, played a round of golf the next morning with another client, only to fly back to London in the evening. Such stories most likely boost his own feeling (and possibly those of his colleagues) of being a successful analyst, and also add to the popular image of what financial analysts do and who they are.

Entertaining is one way to create a seemingly more personal contact with clients and brokers. For example, Christos, a proprietary trader in London, said that personal relationships are important when deciding on the relevance of what, for instance, a broker might say. According to him, a good broker gives good prices quickly and adds value by dropping hints on what is going on in the market. When asked what he thought characterizes a good broker–client relationship, he answered without hesitation: 'trust'. I asked him to elaborate on what he meant by trust and he said: 'You learn whether you can trust someone or not by looking at someone's track record.' During our conversation he kept coming back to the importance of experience in knowing whether brokers 'bullshit' or not, and how to decide on the relevance of what they might tell him.

Christos, and many others, emphasized the importance of face-to-face meetings – he had himself met personally with most of his brokers, usually for dinner and drinks – and said that meeting face-to-face 'is the precondition for trust'. He also added that he would never trust anyone he did not like. To him, liking someone is another precondition that allows trust to develop. This kind of trust is, however, somewhat one-sided – for example, Christos never tells his broker exactly what he wants to do; whether he wants to buy or sell. When a trader contacts his broker to get a buy price, he often asks for both a buy and a sell price. He does this when he does not want his broker to know his position, suspecting that the broker might 'leak' to other traders or brokers, and thereby turn the market against him. This is a way to let the broker know that he is not trusted. The trader can also let the broker know what his intentions are, and only ask for what he wants: the buy price. Some traders always ask for buy/sell quotes whereas others do not.

Paul, the dollar-sign drawing bond analyst, prefers to talk to the same people in order to develop long-term co-operation with counterparts and clients. He had, however, not given any thought to why, so when I asked him to 'become his own sociologist' he said: 'I also want to know why I want to meet people!' We discussed the matter at some length. According to him, meeting someone face-to-face is not only about developing trust for each other, but also helps to 'get a feel' for what the other party does – whether he has a plan, if he seems competent, strategic, and so on. This is important to Paul, as an analyst expected to value companies. He pointed out that meeting someone face-to-face can provide added value in the form of slips of the tongue. I suggested that the expressed need to meet with clients has to do with some kind of cognitive process of developing a feeling of being in the know, developing a frame of reference. Paul misheard me and thought I said 'cumulative process' and agreed enthusiastically: 'Yeah, maybe that's it! A cumulative process of knowledge!' Maybe we can call it a cumulative, cognitive process where repeated face-to-face meetings, in addition to other kinds of knowledge-gaining activities, provide a frame of reference for future contacts and evaluations of received information (cf. Thrift, 1996: 213ff.). The more you meet with someone, the surer you become of your ability to correctly evaluate information coming from that person (whether that is in fact the case or not, is another matter).

Not everyone likes entertaining, however. Alex, a proprietary trader at a large bank in London, is one of them: 'Why should I spend time with loads of East-End brokers I don't like? Lap dancing and that shit! I'm simply not interested.' Alex is a proprietary trader in charge of his desk at his bank. He is thus high up on the status ladder. A couple of other proprietary traders, Stewart and Richard, shared the same views of entertaining and said they tried to avoid doing too many deals using brokers:

> R: We don't want that kind of relationship [entertaining-kind] with brokers, because then you become committed.
> A: What do you mean by committed?
> R: Well, they expect something. For example, if a friend gives you a present you're expected to give one back.

So, Stewart and Richard rarely go out with brokers but when I asked if they have met the brokers they do use, Stewart said: 'Yeah, I *know* them all!' Some of the brokers, traders, and analysts I met during fieldwork emphasized, in a mantra-like manner, the importance of entertaining, face-to-face interaction, and personal networks in order to exchange information. Others said that it is not enough to have access to certain information – you need to know *how* this information can make you money, that is, you need to know how this particular piece of information is going to be interpreted by other market participants (see also Abolafia, 1996: 24; Hägglund, 2000, 2001). It is only when you can predict how others are going to act, that you can work out what to do in order to make money (cf. Beunza and Stark, 2004). Thus, although far from everyone applied this kind of reflexive reasoning (cf. Lowry, 1984: 33), most brokers, traders, and analysts I met agreed that entertaining and meeting face-to-face was important for business.

Learning on the job

Brokers, traders, and analysts-to-be, to a large extent learn on the job. Official credentials such as licenses to broker and trade together with higher formal education only take the novice so far. Generally speaking, the higher formal education a trader-to-be has, the less tedious tasks he has to start with, but it is on the job that they learn to talk the talk and to walk the walk, and they learn this by participating in work practices both inside and outside of the office.

They learn what to do in a fragmented fashion that does not follow what is on paper, a straightforward sequence of quoting followed by broking or trading. This fragmented way of learning on the job, of becoming 'experienced', provides the apprentice broker and trader with a first sense of structure in relation to the workings of 'the market' in general, and trading floors in particular (cf. Lave and Wenger, 1991). They thereby slowly learn what brokers, traders, and analysts are supposed to be like.

There are, however, different paths to become a broker or trader. In London two groups crystallized: 'the Hooray Boys' and 'the Essex Lads'. Brokers and traders mainly used the terms in a derogatory manner when talking about others, and not when describing themselves.[6] The so-called Hooray Boys had a higher level of education (often public school), came from a prosperous background, and often lived around South Kensington/Knightsbridge/Chelsea – a very central and expensive area of London. This was also where the non-British traders and brokers tended to live. The so-called Essex Lads, in contrast, had less formal education, came from a less prosperous background, and usually lived in the suburbs towards Essex where they had been brought up – an area often associated with the working class. According to the brokers and traders themselves, this polarization is also visible in the instruments they trade: Hooray Boys work on the stock market, whereas the Essex Lads work on the foreign exchange market. I did not come across such a marked polarization in New York or Stockholm, but there too, the foreign exchange market was often associated with those brokers and traders who came from a working-class background and had had less formal education.

Nevertheless, regardless of educational background, most brokers and traders I have worked with often referred to having 'a feel for the market' or 'a gut feeling' when they explained how they know what to do. For example, when I asked Ron, the board boy who became head of the desk, what that means, he replied that he knows what to do because he has experience. Knorr Cetina and Bruegger (2000: 159) state in passing that 'feeling for the market' is 'a kind of pattern recognition capacity programmed on long experience of the market'. These authors leave it at that, but it remains an interesting issue *what kind* of experience we are talking about. Experience is obviously important when 'forming a view on the market' (cf. Bruegger, 2000), but it is not any old experience that counts – it is largely experience acquired on the job. Brokers and traders gain experience through participation, by taking part in specific work practices on and off trading floors.

Modes of market knowing and knowledge distribution

As suggested above, financial market knowledge is acquired in different arenas. For the broker, trader, and analyst-to-be it is not a matter of acquiring a fixed structure of knowledge. Instead, they acquire an increased access to legitimate participation roles in these arenas. They move from being a newcomer and apprentice, to becoming an old-timer, master, and expert. Actual work practices – such as going to watch table dancing, talking at a morning meeting, and calling clients – guide and discipline the newcomers' manoeuvring in the financial market field and turn them into legitimate actors. Through increased participation they both absorb and are absorbed into certain ways of doing, talking, and thinking (Lave and Wenger, 1991). Work practices are slowly turned into their own habitus as they move from newcomer to old-timer.

I argue that learning how to manoeuvre in the four arenas of trading, research, sales and entertaining, as described above, develops into financial market knowledge. It is in these domains that we should look for how one achieves a 'feel for the market'. 'A feel for the market' is a kind of non-verbal knowledge based on ideas of participation, 'gut feeling', and first-hand experience. It appears distinct from an articulated kind of knowledge, which can be accessed in, for example, research reports, in financial text books, and at morning meetings.

Fredrik Barth (1989) has discussed modes of knowing in terms of a conjurer/initiator mode of knowledge versus a guru-kind of knowledge. At first sight, his categorization seems to fit perfectly with financial market knowledge. On the one hand, we have the slightly mysterious conjurer/ initiator knowledge that cannot be taught, only learned through experience, that is, through actual encounters with 'the market'. It is a kind of embodied knowledge that brokers, traders, and analysts learn by engaging with the market, by broking and trading, by watching the screen, the volume and speed of trading, hour after hour, in order to work out what the market, and other market participants, are going to do next. The market is treated as a living, acting, and re-acting organism, and in order to understand the market, a trader has to tap into its very essential being. This knowledge is rarely analyzed by brokers, traders, and analysts themselves. Even if not kept as a secret, it is neither widely shared, nor openly discussed. The broker/trader/analyst-conjurer can turn the uncertainty created through the mystification of the market to his own advantage, by systematically spreading distorted information to others – information that is difficult to both control and verify.

On the other hand, there is the kind of knowledge that is characterized by the apparent objective reproduction of facts. The gurus of the trade, the experts, offer explanations, instructions, and examples. This kind of knowledge is not dependent on presence in the same manner the embodied kind of knowledge is – a trader does not have to be present when a research report is produced in order to understand what the report says. It is knowledge that a trader can retrieve from memory at a later stage and verbally share with someone else (cf. Barth, 1989). This kind of knowledge consists of matter-of-fact financial facts, accounted for through apparent objective quantifications and measurements based on financial theory.

Are we dealing here with two distinct types of knowing that can be linked to the social and educational backgrounds of brokers, traders, and analysts? Does not the cunning, street-wise deceiver and 'bullshitter', known as the Essex Lad, seem especially well-equipped to play the part of the conjurer with its embodied knowledge, whereas the formally educated Hooray Boy better masters the guru role with its articulated knowledge? This neat fit does not, however, hold up under further examination. The guru–conjurer distinction is more problematic and less clear-cut than suggested by Barth. Before I discuss this further, let me say something more about the asymmetries of knowledge distribution among brokers, traders and analysts.

Financial market knowledge is asymmetrically distributed among these market actors. These asymmetries are linked to their respective situated positions in the world, that is, to their varying perspectives and horizons (Hannerz, 1992). A trader's perspective is closely related to his earlier experiences and engagements in life. The perspectives of brokers, traders, and analysts come in various arrangements, and account for much of financial market dynamics (cf. Hannerz, 1992). For example, it can be of the kind: *He thinks he knows what they think*, as when traders try to work out the perspectives and interpretations of others. Take, for instance, Stewart, a proprietary trader in London who pays a lot of attention to on- and off-screen charts and calls himself a contrarian.

A contrarian trading strategy is one in which the trader forms a view on what other important market actors will do in the future and then tries to go the opposite way in order to make money. According to Stewart, really useful market knowledge is word-of-mouth from sources that 'know' – meaning people who are the actual original source, or are very close to the source of a certain piece of information.

Or, take Derek who is a successful proprietary bond trader working at a large American investment bank where he and his colleagues take large risks in trading and also make a lot of money, which in turn gives them very high status on the trading floor. Derek has a complementary kind of experience to fall back on when working as a trader. He used to work for a central bank and claims he has certain insights into the decision-making processes at work in such financial institutions. Derek makes 'evaluations of the market' (for example, trying to predict whether the central bank, of this or that country, will raise the interest rate or not), by trying to think about the different variables the central bank representatives themselves focus on when making such a decision. Thereby, Derek argues, he knows what the bank representatives will do before they actually do it.

The perspectives of brokers, traders, and analysts can also be of the kind: *I know they know what I know*, as when Stewart says he does not read research reports, or any other kind of distributed news, since 'everyone' has access to this, which makes the pieces of information less value adding. Another alternative is: *He thinks he knows that his broker's other client knows something*, as in the situation where Robert, the broker, tries to get his clients to trade. Or: *I know they don't know*, which has to do with information for the authorized few through the use of passwords, Intranets, privileged access, and insider knowledge. The problem of prediction together with the expected systemic deceit, contribute to actual and imagined symmetries and asymmetries in knowledge distribution, which, in turn, play an important role in organizing financial markets. In this uncertain environment, brokers, traders, and analysts spend much energy trying to out-think each other.

Although there are qualitative variations in how we know and learn things, the guru–conjurer distinction can only be of use if we remember that they are *ideal* models. True, it seems plausible to argue that the research arena is mainly characterized by a guru-kind of knowledge; the entertaining arena by a conjurer-kind, and the sales and trading arenas, to a higher degree than the previous two, combine the two modes of knowing. The link between modes of knowing and social and educational background is, however, harder to establish.

In other words, there is not a perfect match between asymmetries in knowing and differences in education. Although the formally educated may be more familiar with, and comfortable with, the guru-kind of knowledge, they also emphasize the need to have a feel for the market. It is, further, not uncommon that brokers and traders with less formal education learn on the job how to use economic models and formulas. Brokers, traders, and analysts value these two kinds of knowing differently, but the differences do not seem to follow educational patterns. If anything, the material collected in the course of the fieldwork points to the importance for 'everyone' of developing a feel for the market, through engaging with the market.

Further, the defining characteristics of the two modes are not as rigid as Barth (1989) suggests. For example, written research materials can hide more than they reveal, and to master the mysterious market can be interpreted as the sign of a true guru, instead of that of a conjurer. The mystical and the rational exist side by side, but what is perceived as guru-knowledge by one, may well be viewed as conjurer-knowledge by another, depending on where one is positioned. The boundary between what is guru and what is conjurer is simply blurred most of the time. Also, brokers, traders, and analysts employ, to a varying degree, both ways of knowing. To be aware of how other market actors employ these modes can be a way to affect the actions of others. Knowing about knowing hence becomes a technique used to out-think others.

Notes

1. This text is part of the doctoral dissertation *On and Off the Trading Floor: An Inquiry into the Everyday Fashioning of Financial Market Knowledge* (Hasselström, 2003), and I would like to thank the Bank of Sweden Tercentenary Foundation for making the study possible.
2. The majority of fieldwork, consisting of semi-structured conversations with brokers, traders and analysts, together with observations on and off trading floors, was conducted in Stockholm, London and New York in 1998 and 1999. All names have been changed to preserve anonymity.
3. A junk bond is a high-yielding, high-risk bond.
4. In the United States, a 'lap dance' refers to a dance that includes varying amounts of contact between the dancer and the customer, whereas a 'table dance' involves no such contact (Frank, 2002). In London, most brokers, traders, and analysts referred to the no-touch dancing as lap dancing.
5. Warren Buffet is a renowned American large-scale investor.
6. Due to a wider recruiting of people with diverse backgrounds in the 1970s and 1980s, together with a fair amount of non-English brokers, traders, and analysts

working in London, these two categories are not as distinct as they used to be (Thrift, 1996: 245ff.).

References

Abolafia, Mitchel. 1996. *Making Markets: Opportunism and Restraint on Wall Street.* Cambridge: Harvard University Press.

Barth, Fredrik. 1989. 'The guru and the conjurer: transactions in knowledge and the shaping of culture in Southeast Asia and Melanesia'. *Man* 25: 640–53.

Beunza, Daniel, and Daniel Stark. 2004: 'Tools of the trade: the socio-technology of arbitrage in a Wall Street trading room'. *Industrial and Corporate Change* 13: 369–400.

Bourdieu, Pierre, and Loic Wacquant. 2001. 'NewLiberalSpeak: notes on the new planetary vulgate. Commentary'. *Radical Philosophy* 105.

Bruegger, Urs. 2000. 'Speculating: work in financial markets'. In H. Kalthoff, R. Rottenburg and H.-J. Wagener (eds), *Ökonomie und Geschellschaft, Jahrbuch 16 – Facts and Figures: Economic Representations and Practices.* Marburg: Metropolis Verlag, 229–55.

De Goede, Marieke. 2001. 'Discourses of scientific finance and the failure of long-term capital management'. *New Political Economy* 6(2): 149–70.

Dilley, Roy. 1992. 'Contesting markets: a general introduction to market ideology, imagery and discourse'. In R. Dilley (ed.), *Contesting Markets: Analyses of Ideology, Discourse and Practice.* Edinburgh: Edinburgh University Press. 1–27

Eriksen, Thomas Hylland. 2001. *Ögonblickets Tyranni: snabb och långsam tid i informationssamhället.* Falun: Nya Doxa.

Fligstein, Neil. 2001. *The Architecture of Markets: An Economic Sociology of Twenty-First-Century Capitalist Societies.* Princeton: Princeton University Press.

Foucault, Michel. [1982] 1997. *Ethics: Subjectivity and Truth.* Volume One, edited by P. Rabinow. New York: The New Press.

Frank, Kathryn. 2002. *G-Strings and Sympathy: Strip Clubs and Male Desire.* Durham and London: Duke University Press.

Geertz, Clifford. 1973. *The Interpretation of Cultures.* London: Fontana Press.

Hägglund, Peter. 2000. 'The value of facts: how analysts' recommendations focus on facts instead of value'. In H. Kalthoff, R. Rottenburg and H.-J. Wagener (eds), *Ökonomie und Geschellschaft, Jahrbuch 16 – Facts and Figures: Economic Representations and Practices.* Marburg: Metropolis Verlag, 313–37.

Hägglund, Peter. 2001. *Företaget som investeringsobjekt: hur placerare och analytiker arbetar med att ta fram ett investeringsobjekt.* Stockholm: EFI, Stockholm School of Economics.

Hannerz, Ulf. 1992. *Cultural Complexity: Studies in the Social Organization of Meaning.* New York: Columbia University Press.

Hasselström, Anna. 2003. *On and Off the Trading Floor: An Inquiry into the Everyday Fashioning of Financial Market Knowledge.* Doctoral dissertation, Department of Social Anthropology, Stockholm University.

Hertz, Ellen. 1998. *The Trading Crowd: An Ethnography of the Shanghai Stock Market.* Cambridge: Cambridge University Press.

Knorr Cetina, Karin, and Urs Bruegger. 2000. 'The market as an object of attachment: exploring post-social relations in financial markets'. *Canadian Journal of Sociology* 25(2): 141–68.

Knorr Cetina, Karin, and Urs Bruegger. 2002a. 'Global microstructures: the virtual societies of financial markets'. *American Journal of Sociology* 107(4): 905–50.

Knorr Cetina, Karin, and Urs Bruegger. 2002b. 'Inhabiting technology: the global lifeform of financial markets'. Paper prepared for *Current Sociology*.

Lave, Jean, and Etienne Wenger. 1991. *Situated Learning: Legitimate Peripheral Participation*. Cambridge: Cambridge University Press.

Lépinay, Vincent. 2002. '*Finance as circulating formulas*'. Paper presented at the New York Conference on Social Studies of Finance, Columbia University and the Social Science Research Council, 3–4 May, 2002.

Lépinay, Vincent. n.d., *Patchwork of Formulas: Rhythms, Vareties and Strengths on Financial Markets* (unpublished manuscript).

Lowry, R. P. 1984. 'Structural changes in the market: the rise of professional investing'. In P. A. Adler and P. Adler (eds), *The Social Dynamics of Financial Markets*. London: JAI Press Inc.

Millo, Yuval. n.d., a. 'Talking about risk: risk assessment methods as communicative media in financial markets' (unpublished manuscript).

Millo, Yuval. n.d., b. 'Safety in numbers: the regulatory formation of index-based derivatives' (unpublished manuscript).

Muniesa, Fabian. 2000. 'The case of price discovery automation in the financial markets. In H. Kalthoff, R. Rottenburg and H.-J. Wagener (eds), *Ökonomie und Geschellschaft, Jahrbuch 16 – Facts and Figures: Economic Representations and Practices*. Marburg: Metropolis Verlag, 289–312.

Muniesa, Fabian. 2002. '*Reserved anonymity: on the use of telephones in the trading room*'. Paper presented at the New York Conference on Social Studies of Finance, Columbia University and the Social Science Research Council.

Norberg, Peter. 2001. *Finansmarknadens amoralitet och det kalvinska kyrkorummet. En studie i ekonomisk mentalitet och etik*. Doctoral Dissertation. Stockholm: EFI, Stockholm School of Economics.

Porter, Theodore M. 1995. *Trust in Numbers: The Pursuit of Objectivity in Science and Public Life*. Princeton: Princeton University Press.

Preda, Alex. 2002. 'On ticks and tapes: financial knowledge, communicative practices, and information technologies on 19th century financial markets' (unpublished manuscript).

Shore, Chris, and Susan Wright. 1997. 'Introduction'. In C. Shore and S. Wright (eds), *Anthropology of Policy: Critical Perspectives on Governance and Power*. London: Routledge, 3–39.

Thompson, Victoria. 2000. *The Virtuous Marketplace: Women and Men, Money and Politics in Paris, 1830–1870*. Baltimore: Johns Hopkins University Press.

Thrift, Nigel. 1996. *Spatial Formations*. London: Sage.

Zaloom, Caitlin 2003. 'Ambiguous numbers: trading technologies and interpretation in financial markets'. *American Ethnologist* 30(2): 258–72.

Zaloom, Caitlin 2004. 'The discipline of the speculators'. In A. Ong and S. Collier (eds), *Global Assemblages: Technology, Politics, and Ethics as Anthropological Problems*. London: Blackwell. Chapter 14.

8
Culture, Ideology and the Financial Market: Examining Pension Plan Reform in Sweden

Monica Lindh de Montoya

Pension plans and pension reforms are becoming increasingly discussed topics in the press and in political debate in the industrialized West. In part this is a result of demographic trends; as the large postwar 'baby-boomer' generation begins to reach pension age, birth rates in these countries are falling, making current state programmes untenable in the long term. France and Austria have recently passed unpopular reforms after intense protests,[1] and both Italy and Great Britain are currently in the process of re-evaluating and reforming their programmes; a process fraught with political dangers, and therefore both slow and inadequate.[2] In Italy, pensions already absorb 14 per cent of GNP, yet few voters are willing to support major 'corrections.' In the United Kingdom, pensions costs consume 5 per cent of GNP, a figure that is expected to rise to near the current Italian level.

In the USA pensions are also a pressing concern because of the huge losses suffered by many investors with the overall fall in stock prices beginning in the year 2000, and the economic mismanagement and failure of huge companies such as Enron, Tyco and Worldcom, where many employees held much of their pension savings in the form of company stocks. Also, some companies' pension plans, long assumed to be secure, are now proving to have been based on unrealistic calculations regarding workers' life expectancy and retirement age, causing payouts to be slashed drastically.[3] Additionally, fraudulent practices in mutual fund management companies are just coming to light.[4] Thus there are several reasons for many of those employees counting on state, or company pension plans for their retirement to feel concerned.

While some European countries are in the beginning of a pension debate, Sweden is in the position of already having reformed a very generous and reputedly unsustainable system. The visible and debated part of this reform involved bringing 'the market', in the guise of the stock market, into the state pension system, albeit in a limited way. In November 2000, all working-age Swedes over the age of 16 who were employed and had earned at least 8,700 Swedish krona (Skr) during the year, or had previously been employed, were given the opportunity of choosing a maximum of five of a total of over 460 mutual funds in which to invest 2.5 per cent of their accumulated state pension compensation. The success of the funds they choose will be reflected in the size of the pensions they receive upon retirement.

The fact that this peaceful and well-organized shift of a large amount of state-managed pension funding into the market occurred at a time when stock markets were buoyantly rising probably played a part in making it a politically acceptable move. The timing also helped focus citizens' attention on this market-based aspect of the reform, while the more crucial cuts in the national pension programme were carried out in a much less publicized manner. Long in coming, the reform grew out of the economic necessities and rhetorical trends of the times, and was the upshot of a political battle carried on more in committees than on the street. It was a political compromise that was viewed as a defeat by some political parties, but was hailed as a visionary new way of creating wealth and security by others. For most Swedish citizens, however, the reform appears to have been a tiresome and confusing exercise that aroused considerable anxiety and scepticism, but which, once carried out, seems to have been largely forgotten.

This chapter makes some observations about the pension plan reform, as it was carried out in Sweden in the last years of the twentieth century. I will discuss why and how the reform was carried out, how it was conceived, staged and presented to the public, and the expectations of some of the financial market actors. I will consider the strengths and weaknesses of the idea of using the 'market' in the form of stocks and funds as part of pension planning, and take a look at the structure of current Swedish participation in the stock market, and what it means for popular participation in the pension reform's mutual funds. Finally, I will make some more general comments on the concept of providing for old age.

From state to market

Pension reform in Sweden has been concerned with two issues: cost and responsibility. Only twenty years after being instituted in 1960, the 'pay as you go' system was judged to be impossibly expensive to maintain in the long term. From the 1980s a slow and politically sensitive process of investigation and recommendation began, in which insurance experts, administrators, and civil servants working for The National Social Insurance Board, the *Riksförsäkringsverket* (RFV), and a series of parliamentary committees examined the impact of the system, devised new alternatives, made recommendations, and finally implemented a new plan. The process was a reflection of what is happening in Europe in general: economic and demographic growth is not keeping pace with the needs of the ageing population, while advances in nutrition, medicine and lifestyle mean that people are living longer. Consequently, new ways are being sought to provide for an aging population, and people are being made to understand that they must expect less. European countries are seeking to implement reforms by increasing the number of years that must be worked to qualify for full benefits, by switching any indexation from wage inflation to price inflation, by increasing the retirement age, as well as by increasing mandatory contributions and reducing benefits.[5]

Secondly, in Sweden the reform is part of a gradual de-linking of the welfare state from some of the areas in which it once guaranteed its citizens protection from the cradle to the grave. Once world-famous for its extensive social welfare programme, Sweden has found it necessary to repeatedly cut the extent and size of benefits, a process which is, in the public mind, most readily associated with the deep, disturbing economic crisis that the country suffered at the beginning of the 1990s, with unacceptably high unemployment, soaring interest rates, and speculation against the national currency which caused substantial losses and a large fiscal deficit (see Peebles, this volume). A part of the cure for the economic downturn involved the downsizing of the public sector. Some public employees laid off at this time were encouraged to start their own companies offering the same services, and a number began to work for 'flexible labour' companies who hire out employees, such as Manpower and Poolia (Garsten, 2002). Private companies now compete for contracts to deliver many of the services such as transportation, care of the elderly, and some medical services that the state used to regard as being its own responsibility. A number of public services have been completely privatized and others have been curtailed or have become more expensive for the users, while, conversely, other services such as telecommunications have become cheaper following the ending of state monopolies. Thus, socioeconomic and political changes are taking place via an increasing dependence on market mechanisms, or market solutions. 'The market' is increasing its influence on citizens' lives at the expense of the state. The trend towards private alternatives along with – or in place of – public services is often framed rhetorically in terms of returning the freedom of choice to citizens, as widening possibilities, and as making people responsible for their own futures. Here, market-based solutions are both touted as opportunities for personal enrichment (such as in privatization, entrepreneurial solutions, and fund investment), and increasingly recommended and instituted as a model for the organisation of the public sphere.

Thus, Swedes are gradually moving from communal solutions to more private, market-based initiatives, a transition involving some public debate, and, eventually, a new general consensus about how individual and communal responsibilities should be formulated. The increasing medial attention given to the country's situation in the global financial market, and widening participation of the population in financial investment can be seen as a part of this growing market discourse, and is also something that, in its turn, influences the discussion. While some reforms, such as those in medical services, were politically couched in the language of 'making savings', that is, looking for cheaper, more efficient solutions, working a bit harder and cutting the slack, other reforms were phrased in the language of 'personal responsibility', and 'the right to choose'. This line of argument maintained that people should not be cosseted, and that they are perfectly capable of, and should be, actively making strategic decisions about their futures. By extension, this choice-making opportunity is a right that state hegemony in the social services sector wrongly denies citizens.

The rhetoric of pension reform played into both of these ways of understanding unpopular political reforms. The state could not afford to maintain the current pension system, so savings had to be made, and it was up to people to seize the chance to begin to provide more for their own retirement.[6] Political parties to the left pointed out that Sweden was really not too poor to provide its citizens decent pensions for its citizens, and that everything depends on the priorities that are agreed upon. It is not my purpose here to discuss priorities, the 'real' extent of the need for reform, or to debate the merit of its implementation; all political movements have an idealistic/rhetorical/ideological face as well as a realistic/negotiable/practical face. What is interesting to note is that despite occasional sour expressions and comments on events from some smaller parties, there was, in practice, broad support for the reform among the leadership of the country.

The background of the reform

In his critical discussion of the pension reform, Scherman (2000) describes its background. The concept of general pensions arose in Europe at the end of the nineteenth centurys[7] and came into operation in Sweden in 1913, when a general pension was instituted from the age of 67.[8] The pension provided was, however, meagre. The *folkpension* or 'peoples' pension' was instituted in 1935, and improved in 1948, but even then it still represented only 20 per cent of an average industrial salary (Nilsson, 1998: 11). In 1960, the 'ATP' system[9] was instituted, an economic arrangement under which current workers have the obligation to pay the fees to finance the pensions of past workers. Since this system depends upon the existence of a sufficiently large proportion of economically active people to pay for the pensions of past generations of workers, it is, in principle, a contract between past and future generations. When it became obvious that the ATP system was not financially viable due to increasing life expectancy rates and a slower than expected demographic increase, a parliamentary committee was organized to examine the financial problems the system would face in the coming decades. In 1990 this committee delivered its report, which presented alternative solutions but did not make any recommendations.

In 1991, RFV presented a proposal for reform that would lower pensions in an egalitarian way, and would make active use of the national pension funds (*AP fonderna*). It did not include any investment in mutual funds, however, which was a demand of the conservative parties, and was therefore largely ignored by legislators. A second parliamentary committee was constituted in 1991 to develop concrete suggestions for a new pension system.

Three years later their work culminated in a legislative decision to implement a more robust system, which would take account of future economic and demographic changes in the country. Lindqvist (2000) recounts how the reforms, including the introduction of a mutual fund investment scheme, were agreed upon by five of the seven parties in the government, and then hurried through the legislature to make sure that pension reform would not be one of the issues of the 1995 elections. In 1996, however, when the social democrats held an extra congress and internal consultation on the reform within the party, party activists soundly criticized it. Nonetheless, the party elite refused to bring the reform up on the political agenda again.

Basic elements of the new system were a pension that was based on the total income made during one's working life (40 years), the age at time of pension, continuous contributions to the system, and the obligation of the individual to place part his pension capital in mutual funds. This parliamentary decision formed a point of departure for the final design of the reform, which was to be carried out by an 'implementation committee', consisting of representatives of the major political parties in the country (Scherman, 2000: 5).

The reform was planned to begin in 1995, but was gradually pushed forward in time. The final plan was first approved in detail in 1998. There was a broad political majority for a dual concept: first a general pension that will be available to all citizens, which, secondly, is complemented with a second pension based on the ones' total working-life income.[10] What is new and somewhat controversial in the reform is that for the first time, part of the pension fee – 2.5 per cent of the total yearly payment of 18.5 per cent of ones' salary – must also be placed by all employees in their own mutual fund account (Premium Pension Account, *premiepensionskonto*) which makes up the third part of the three-tiered pension. When the reform was implemented, it was this part of the reform that received nearly all the media attention. However, as Lindqvist (2000) points out in an article, the bulk of peoples' future pension income will still be provided by 'pay-as-you-go' vehicles; a low but guaranteed general pension, which will come to all citizens, the (*garantipension*), and the income pension, tied to lifetime earnings (*inkomstpension*). Lindqvist's article is deeply critical of the manner in which the social democratic party ignored grassroots party cadres' opinions and hurried the reform through the political process despite lack of members' support. He also points out how the new system betrays party ideals by, for example, hurting women, who often spend less time in the paid workforce due to family needs. The new pension plan is set up so that one receives either the guaranteed pension or the income pension – whichever is more favourable – plus a mutual fund pension. Lindqvist notes that in practice, most women, and perhaps around 40 per cent of the population, are likely to receive only the guaranteed pension, due to periods of study, unemployment, and part-time work when they have not been earning a full-time salary. He indicates that the changing nature of work today, where people change careers, go back to school, take time off to pursue personal goals, and aspire to early retirement make it increasingly unlikely that people will work full-time for 40 years and earn full benefits. In addition, the reform has many in-built 'brakes' on the size of pensions. This includes the manner in which they are indexed to salary increases, and, for example, the fact that as the pool of pensioners grows, the pool of money available (which can also be affected by acute state expenses) will be divided among more participants, reducing the size of the guaranteed pension. This, says Lindqvist, is the real impact of the reform: a new system for calculating benefits (based on 40 years' income, instead of the best 15 years) which is unfavourable for women and other part-time workers, as well as a series of 'brakes' which reduce the size of payouts as the pool of pensioners grow, or as state finances suffer stress. These are the changes that will have an effect on peoples' futures, much more than the highly publicized mutual fund investment aspect, which involves a relatively small portion of the total pension contributions.

Yet, as I noted above, due to the prevailing economic climate at the time of the reform, the 'market' aspect was what received nearly all of the public attention. Indeed, none of the political parties involved had anything to gain through public scrutiny of the broad-based agreement, and this may explain their low profiles and near silence on the reform as it was implemented. Lindqvist (2000) and Scherman (2000) both note the lack of public or political debate on the new scheme. The supposed excitement and responsibility of investing part of 'one's own' state pension in the successful funds being publicized by banks and fund managers completely dominated the information in the media.

The task of informing the public about the reform was primarily carried out by the labour unions and by market players, although newspapers and magazines also published articles on how best to choose ones' funds, and there were some television programmes related to the reform, or to the stock market in general. Choice was emphasized as being very important; citizens were repeatedly urged to make a choice, and not to leave their money to be managed by the state-run pension fund. Yet when, on the eve of the deadline, several key politicians, including the Economic Minister, were asked how they had chosen to invest, they replied that they believed that the state could do as good a job of fund management as any of the private companies, and that they would therefore leave their money with the state. As an observer of the panorama, one could sense differing private opinions regarding the broad party compromise, hovering somewhere, beyond speech.

Swedes as shareholders

We see, then, how the financial market-oriented aspect of the reform overshadowed other structural changes that are likely to have a far greater impact on the size of peoples' pensions in the long run. For most of the Swedish population the concept of saving for the future in stocks or funds was not a novel one. As the reform, and the obligations it would place on individuals and households, produced more media interest during 1999 and 2000, interesting things were happening in the financial markets, which were also receiving increasing attention. Stock markets were booming, a factor that had a substantial influence on the atmosphere in which the reform was carried out, and that also made supporters of the new scheme believe that it would be met with substantial interest.

While Swedes maintained traditional bank savings accounts, their longer-term savings were already being funnelled into the stock market, either through investment in stocks or through the stock funds (mutual funds) run by banks and brokerages. The low interest rates paid on savings accounts and the long period of the stock market boom witnessed in the industrialized West were two important reasons for this situation. Another factor was the introduction of new financial instruments made popular over the last 25 years,[11] including a wide variety of funds in which individuals can save gradually and have their savings invested by financial experts according to predetermined parameters. This is stock market investing made simple and – supposedly – more secure. The low interest rates, surging stock markets, and innovative new funds together resulted in a situation in which banks encouraged clients to invest their long-term savings in funds. Swedes have long been enthusiastic investors in individual stocks, in part because of the country's industrial base of well-established, multinational, listed companies, such as Ericsson, Asea Brown Boveri (ABB) Volvo, Electrolux and Astra-Zeneca. More recently, the Swedish stock market has also been characterized by a growing share of high-tech companies oriented around the growth of medical research and communications technology, including the Internet. In the last decade, reporting on the financial market has expanded, and by the end of the 1990s, even the evening tabloids offered stock-market advice at least once a week. Monthly magazines dedicated to 'managing personal wealth' began to appear, and the media featured articles about, and analyses of the new Swedish Internet and communications companies, foreign markets, and the probable future of Ericsson, the largest and most influential company on the Stockholm Stock Exchange.

Individual investors are also encouraged and aided by the continuing technological advances in information systems. Powerful personal computers have become relatively inexpensive, and it is now easy to obtain efficient and inexpensive Internet trading accounts and real-time stock quotes at relatively low prices. At the end of the 1990s, accounts with Internet stockbrokers were rising rapidly in Sweden, according to an article in a Stockholm morning newspaper noting that such accounts were increasing by 1,000 per day, and that providers were having a difficult time keeping up with demand.[12] Internet data transfers and easy-to-use software for the technical analysis of stocks also provide tools for enthusiastic individual investors, making it possible for novices to track stock performance in sophisticated ways. Information is easy to access both in the traditional media and on the Internet, and information is not only available about the local market, but also about markets abroad, thereby opening new arenas for investors.

These developments are, in turn, reflected in social life. When I carried out research on individual stock investors in Stockholm between 1998 and 2001, a number of people I interviewed described their interest and participation in the stock market as something that they needed to do in order to maintain and develop social skills – to be 'in' on what is going on in the world.[13] Participants in some of the classes I attended offered by *Aktiespararna*, the Swedish shareholders' organization, said they invested the time and effort to take a course on stock investment not only in the hope of economic gain, but also to learn enough about the market to be able to participate actively in conversations about stocks – both among friends and with colleagues at work. General knowledge about the financial market was, then, gradually becoming a part of an educated person's expected conversational repertoire. Stocks and funds were being discussed socially and in the workplace, and in a few jobs, particularly those in the technology and communications sector, people watched their portfolios daily on their computers, and might even trade stocks while at work. Several people with their own companies, such as independent consultants and accountants, indicated that they had become involved in the stock market partly because they worked from home and were able to keep in touch with what was going on in the marketplace during the day.

This focus on financial markets eventually made a broad segment of the population feel that they needed a higher level of competence in managing their own financial affairs. Peoples' private economies no longer only involved administrating one's monthly income well enough to pay all the bills, taxes and put away some savings; but had come to include choosing funds for long and short term savings, funds for the children, and sometimes managing a stock portfolio, perhaps an inherited one. But how widespread is really stock ownership and trading in Sweden, and how do individual investors go about selecting stocks? What does participation look like, and how do investors go about making sense of the market? Although recent years have seen more research in the social sciences on stock markets (Abolafia, 1997; Hasselström, 2003; Knorr Cetina and Bruegger, 2002) and investors (Gyllenram, 1998; Hartwig, 2002; Hertz, 1998; Lindh de Montoya, 2002a; Lindqvist, 1999), still relatively little is known about how individual shareholders think about their investing activities. Regarding Sweden, we do know the general outlines of proportion of shareholders, and their level of activity.

At the end of December 1999, before the mutual fund reform was implemented, a poll undertaken by a Swedish market research agency estimated that 66 per cent of all Swedes age 16 or over owned stocks. Some owned stocks in several different forms; in individual companies, in stock funds, and perhaps through their place of work or participation in a stock-picking club. Listed companies were owned by 36 per cent, and mutual funds by 54 per cent; and 28 per cent owned foreign stocks either directly or through a fund. Five per cent of all shareholders owned stocks through their place of work (Temo, 2000). These figures represented a substantial growth in ownership compared with figures recorded in previous years.

However, according to a poll of 1650 people conducted by pollster Temo a year later, in the last week of December, 2000, 80 per cent of all Swedes over age 16 owned stocks in one form or another. Certainly stock ownership had swelled again, as can be seen from Table 8.1[14] accounting for the percentage of the population aged 16 or over that held stocks in various forms.

The largest and most recent increase in total stockholders (80 per cent in 2000, up from 55 per cent in 1998, and 66 per cent in 1999) can in part be attributed to the pension reform; as placement in mutual funds through the scheme took place in November 2000, those who chose stock funds for the first time through the reform thus augmented the numbers of stock investors. But some commentators give the reform credit for the increase in stock-based savings in general, because it

Table 8.1 Shareholding in Sweden, 1985–2000

Year	Listed stocks	Stock funds	Total
1985	12	9	29
1990	18	24	34
1995	26	34	53
2000	41	55	80

Note: The totals also include other types of stockholdings, and can be lower than the sums because many investors own both stocks and funds.

focused Swedes' attention on their future pensions, and many may have decided to take individual action to improve their financial futures, investing in stocks or funds independently. The public offering of a part of Telia, the national telephone monopoly, in the spring of 2000 also probably encouraged shareholding, since the shares were heavily advertised by the government as a 'peoples' stock' and were presumed to be a safe and reliable investment.

What, then, do shareholders do with their shares? An examination of shareholders registered at the central stock registry (*Värdepapperscentralen*, VPC) in 1997 shows that of those investing in individual stocks, 72 per cent did not carry out any transactions in 1997, and 14 per cent carried out only one transaction. Nor did small investors tend to spread their risks: 61 per cent owned only one stock, and 16 per cent owned two.[15] The Temo poll carried out in December 2000 contains information about the frequency of stock trades, indicating that 59 per cent of those owning stocks made no trades during the year. An additional 20 per cent had made one or two transactions. Only 10 per cent bought or sold more than six times a year, and of these, 2 per cent were the most active, with 21 or more transactions in 2000. Although activity had increased since 1997, these numbers still indicate a great deal of stability in investors' holdings. The numbers in the Temo poll carried out at the end of 2001 (**Modig, 2002**), a year in which stock values fell drastically, revealed a decrease in the number of trades: 66 per cent of those interviewed had not bought or sold any stocks during the year, 9 per cent had made one trade, 6 per cent had made two. There was also a decrease in stock ownership across the board (from 80 per cent to 77 per cent), although the owners of specifically pension plan related funds increased slightly, by 4 per cent.

The Temo poll for the year 2000 also tells us something about the value of the stock investments held. Thirty-one per cent of stockowners' holdings totaled 20,000 crowns or less (at last tax submission).[16] Slightly over another third (35 per cent) had holdings valued between 21,000 and 250,000 crowns. One in ten had over 250,000 invested in stocks (and of these, one per cent had more than two million crowns invested). Almost a quarter of those polled did not know, or declined to say, how much their investments were worth; the poll notes that most of those in this group were women, or people with less than a high-school education, which might indicate that sums were small (men tend to own more stock than women). Not surprisingly, people over 65, and the highly educated tend to have larger sums invested.[17]

The available data are not detailed enough to gain a very precise picture of the diverse forms of ownership within the stock market. But it does appear that while stock ownership is broad, only small segments (not necessarily the same segments) of the stock-owning population have substantial amounts of money invested in this form of savings (10 per cent with 250,000 crowns or more in 2000), and/or are relatively active in trading stock or fund shares (21 per cent with more than two trades a year; 10 per cent with six or more, 2 per cent with 21 or more).

One also notes that most Swedish stock investors save in a few stocks or funds, although perhaps today there is more diversification than in 1997, when 77 per cent of the shareholding population held only one or two different stocks. Regarding levels of activity, an active 10 per cent of the 80 per cent of the total stock-owning population 16 years or older (5,714,135 in the end of 2000) would be 57,141 people nationwide, or a sum roughly equal to the population of the municipality of Gotland, a Swedish island just off the eastern coast of the mainland. One can surmise that the majority of Swedes, although they do save in stocks and funds, are not very actively involved in the stock market in their everyday lives. And one might then further wonder how likely it is that a pension plan with a focus on fund acquisition and trading is likely to spur them to greater activity?

The research director at the Stockholm Stock Exchange (*Stockholmsbörsen*), Leif Vindevåg, feels that Swedish households should be encouraged to save in stocks over time, since individual stockowners reduce the volatility of the market, balancing the large volume, more short-term trades of institutional investors.[18] While Swedes own more and more stock, households' percentage of the total market value of the stock market has decreased, due to the increase in the number, and the size of the companies listed on the exchange. In the fall of 2000, Leif Vindevåg was of the opinion that the pension reform would have a positive impact upon the business climate in the country, because it would make the general population more aware, and concerned about what makes stock market rise and fall.[19] Because people would be anxious to see their pension funds rise, they would have a greater tendency to support pro-business policies. In this, Vindevåg was voicing the hopes of many in business and financial sectors, particularly those to the political right. In conservative political circles, there are those who would also like to see a future increase in the percentage of funded pension capital.

Implementing the reform

Two years after the reform, there is little indication that the reform has had any larger impact on peoples' opinions regarding national economic policies. Indeed, most indications are that citizens made their fund choices and then put the decisions behind them. Although it is possible to change pension funds without paying taxes or fees, there is little indication of active trading, and the agency responsible for the funded part of the pension reform, the Premium Pension Authority (*Premiepensionsmyndigheten*, PPM), has noted that rather than mounting another campaign encouraging people to be active regarding their pension funds, they need to make economy (both personal and national) mandatory subjects taught in schools.[20] Making use of the economic power of markets to provide for the future is a good idea; for in this way the industry and prosperity of the society at large contribute to pension income, as countries and economies grow. However, it has proven difficult to interest citizens in these funds, and to keep them interested. In part, this may have to do with the anxiety produced by change, the information that people were given about how to select funds, and with the kinds of funds that the major Swedish banks marketed to their clients.

PPM, the agency implementing the mutual fund part of the reform, labour unions and the press in general encouraged people to approach their fund choices in a common-sense, methodical manner. Much of the discussion in the daily press concerned the managers of particular popular and successful funds, fund sizes, and the fees charged. It was noted repeatedly that particular funds' success depended on their talented managers, and that successes might not continue if the manager left. The size of funds was also important, the larger the fund, the more difficult for it to make gains through trading. And fees were pointed out to be very important; over time, high fees could cut into earnings significantly. Here, then, were three criteria for the well informed to consider.

The information sent out by the pension authorities and the labour unions carried instructions to simplify the decision-making process by dividing it into different stages. First, people should consider how much of their allotment to dedicate to stock funds, and how much to interest bearing funds. Here, they should take their age and years until retirement into consideration, as well as their feelings about risk. When this was decided, people were directed to choose the orientation of funds – regional funds, branch funds, or more general world, or global stock funds. After making this decision, people were directed to choose between individual funds and managers, and fees in the sectors of their choice. Overall, the brochures stressed the need for diversification between low-risk and riskier investments, and that it was better to choose as many funds as permitted, and not put all one's money with one manager. Major banks developed specific funds in hopes of attracting clients. Reasoning that many people would feel quite confused over what to choose, yet that many would have basically the same requirements regarding the funds that they would hold over time, some banks organized so-called 'generation funds' that people could choose depending on when they were born. People born in the 1950s would choose the 50s fund, and those born in the 1980s would choose the 80s fund, which would invest more aggressively, since they had many years left until retirement. Such funds were advertised as the easy, one-stop way to make the big decision, and had the weight and legitimacy of the banks behind them.

Considering, then, that people had supposedly taken the time and mental energy to ponder risk, diversification, fund managers, fund sizes, and fees, or decided to give their bank a vote of confidence with a generational fund, it seems improbable that they would return to the angst-inducing decision-making process repeatedly, checking on their funds' development and making strategic changes. Probably only people who are interested enough in funds and shares to belong to the already market-active percentage of the population would do so.

Embedding choices in daily life

One problem with inspiring sustained interest in mutual funds is their anonymity, and the difficulty with which they are 'embedded' in the larger scheme of peoples' private lives (Granovetter, 1985). My research on shareholders (Lindh de Montoya, 2002b) shows that people tend to, consciously or unconsciously, look for a connection between their investment and their daily lives, and conceptions of themselves. They try to tie in choices with their practical knowledge and concrete perceptions of the world. Often, people invest in things they know about. For example, among my interviewees, a hospital administrator bought shares in companies offering medical care services, an IBM employee invested in companies with which he had business dealings and which he felt were responsible business partners; a manufacturer of dental equipment bought stock in firms that develop new dental technology. And in general, people commonly own stock, or are offered options in the companies they work for, and invest in companies whose products they enjoy or admire. One can also embed choices with a regional or nationalist bias: one Swedish investor of Polish origin only bought stock in Polish companies, and a Swedish immigrant in the United States, faced with the all the companies on the United States exchanges, began by choosing 'good, solid, Swedish companies'.

Another way to give foundation to one's choices is through the study of particular stocks. Very active investors who use technical analysis look for companies that act in predictable ways, and buy and sell on the signals they read in the charts or the 'feeling' or intuition they gain after following the company intently over a long period of time. Some may base decisions in part on the flow of chat about stocks in online discussion rooms. People thus deal in stocks that they have invested time and effort in learning about. One can argue that fundamental investing is based on similar mechanisms of embedding; on analyzing the history and financial statistics of the company, or 'fundamentals', and deducing its prospects for the future – a process some investors call 'doing one's homework'. The real work involved in such company studies seems to make people more inclined to invest in them: I found that sometimes members of stock-investing clubs bought their first stocks independently soon after the club decided against buying a stock that they had researched and liked. People find 'good stocks' and 'strong companies' among those in which they in fact have some non-economic investment or stake, a fact which may also explain many peoples' reluctance to sell their stocks even when they begin to lose money, since by then they have far more than a merely economic investment in them.

It could be argued that with all the surprises in stock markets, and the multitude of theories, professional opinions, information, and speculation about the performance and future of companies and funds available in the media, people will find the input they need to justify decisions they make on a more emotional basis. However, this is not how individual investors generally see it. The investors I interviewed were convinced of the basically scientific and rational basis of their choices, and believed that the search for information, honest dealing, and a viable personal strategy are very important for their success. They want to make the 'right' decision, and are convinced that choice matters (Lindh de Montoya, 2002b).

Mutual funds, however, are not stocks. They are ever-changing collections of stocks – investors seldom know exactly which ones – and are identified in more generic ways: by activity such as region or branch, by the firm offering them, and, possibly, by manager. They do not live the very public lives of major listed companies. Their products are largely invisible; and their managers usually faceless. This makes them anonymous, and much less easy to identify with. It is interesting to see how advertising attempts to deal with this anonymity. Funds are abstract economic constructions; and advertising must work to embed them somehow within the familiar social world of the prospective investor.

In the autumn of 1998 a typical advertisement for Swedish funds at one of Sweden's four major banks showed photos of smiling white-haired pensioners (in one case buying postcards in the sun), pictured the needs of children – in the form of vacations and computers – and portrayed basic consumer luxuries, such as a sports car, and a traditional red-painted, lakeside summerhouse flying the Swedish flag. These images represent unambiguous, generalized desires, within the reach of an average Swedish working-class family. These benefits are now also obtainable through investment and the dynamic growth of capital. Particular images, here the family through generations and the traditional country summer home with the flag, are used to make investing concrete, and to signify it as responsible action. The unfamiliarity and uncertainty of placing hard-earned savings in a financial instrument subject to occasionally rapid gains and losses is offset by the everyday and familiar, and with the added reassurance of the flag. Another brochure from the same bank advertising European funds symbolizes ideas about unity via a group of European flags, and security through depictions of the well-known products of international companies, such as tyres and mobile phones.

The advertising designed to encourage people to invest their allotted shares of pension money in the funds run by various banks and insurance companies at the end of 2000 was similarly revealing. The most dramatic advertisements were two huge images covering the surface of two entire high-rise buildings. One portrayed a woman in her thirties reflecting over a cup of coffee: 'I can't resist *Folksam* (a large insurance company) funds because of their low fees'. The other was a hazy image, taken from above, of an older woman and child – presumably grandmother and grandchild – dancing on a red and white tiled floor. Only the name of the firm offering the funds was inscribed above. These are only two of many possible examples of advertising where companies, rather than approaching investors on a logical and rational level, tried to appeal to the emotional and everyday, or to hopes for the future.

Thus conceptions of the life one wants to live in older age, ambitions for one's offspring, and the role one wants one's country to have in Europe's economic future can be equally salient when one makes financial decisions. Expectations or 'embedders' are not made explicit in the information about a stock or fund, where focus is on the financial history and potential of the fund; rather, they lie concealed in the images, not the figures; in decoys placed beyond the boundaries of our rational thought. Peoples' reflections concerning the market and their actions within it are oriented not only by the rationality that seeks to maximize profit above all, but equally by a complex web of social factors; a desire to participate, somehow, in a potentially profitable new venture, and to obtain the social skills and acceptance that come with this participation. Banks and fund companies play on this need for inclusion, as well as on other social configurations, such as the needs generated by ageing, family responsibilities, and the individual's desire for excitement and a sense of taking charge of his economic future. These, in turn, mesh with the processes of the state, as it deregulates and cuts down on commitments to, and investments in, community. The many actors in the financial arena – from investment banks to analysts to hardware and software vendors – all seek to entice or persuade the individual to deposit money in their hands, and use the techniques developed within advertising to do so (see Moeran, this volume), playing on various emotions and needs, and drawing on the knowledge produced by the financial community itself. The individual, seeking solutions, searches for information, and embeds his financial decisions in some sort of logical framework that tends to have more to do with his own highly particular economic resources and personal world of knowledge, than with the logical constructions of investment experts.

Back to the future?

As noted above, the Swedish pension reform has been criticized as being unlikely to provide adequately for a substantial portion of future pensioners. The mutual fund choice component is a wild card that may or may not live up to expectations, depending on how markets perform and how nations conduct their finances. It has failed to capture the imagination of the population, and although over time it may grow more popular, that is more likely to be a reflection of a nationwide growth in interest and activity in the stock market in general, rather than in the pension solutions per se. But what might a different future hold, and how might the provisioning of old age otherwise reasonably be undertaken?

Pension plans can be constructed and adjusted in any number of ways. Basing them in part on the growth of markets is not unsound. As populations grow, so does economic activity and innovation. Participation in stock funds is participation in this growth, and although stock markets rise and fall, in the long term they have always risen. Long-term, well-diversified participation is the key. Today Sweden provides substantial child support to families. Perhaps, along similar lines, the state might invest a certain sum for every new citizen that is born, possibly into a basket of index funds from around the world. This investment could be accessed at age 60, for example. Such a system could provide a pension component that would be equal for all citizens, recognizing the fact that everyone has the same basic needs as they age, regardless of their previous occupation; it would be a way to use the long-term growth potential inherent in market activity to provide for citizens in a more egalitarian way than at present. Its ability to provide would, however, be dependent on how Sweden manages its finances, because high inflation, for example, destroys such savings.

I would suggest, too, that a reasonable future pension strategy would be to take a more holistic and diversified view of life and earning in general. Past decades, perhaps especially in Sweden, have been marked by the coming-of-age, or perfection of modernization. The state has divided up citizens' lifespans into different productive stages and provided for each – childhood, education, productive years, pension. It is assumed that the majority of the population will be employees, living off a salary for about forty years, and later off a pension. Conceptually, the pension is tied, historically and practically, to a particular economic model that is undergoing a transformation. As lifestyles change, lifespans increase, and production begins to take on new structures and rationalities, these solutions come into question, not only because they are becoming increasingly unviable from an economic point of view, but also because they are tied to certain assumptions about peoples' needs and potential, which are also in flux. The pension solution ceases to fit the lives we lead. Career paths look quite different now than in the 1950s, involving much more change. Telecommunications and knowledge-based enterprises have the potential to incorporate people into the workforce in novel and useful ways both in youth and old age.

Perhaps the future will bring us lifelong working lives, where work, being easier to integrate with lifestyle and family needs, does not begin and end at more-or-less specified ages, but varies in scope and intensity as long as health and energy allow, or until economic means make it unnecessary. Such a future could certainly bring increased financial recognition of the unpaid work of women. People might, from an early age, plan 'post-pension' income-generating strategies, such as running small businesses, taking occasional short-term jobs, perhaps becoming more involved in education and in providing for the needs of the coming generation; strategies that they can combine with their own personal interests, hobbies, concerns and capabilities. Life after full-time work might ideally encompass multiple income streams, some entrepreneurial, some philanthropic, others the result of savings made both inside and outside a formal pension system. Owning one's own home would probably become a central strategy. Thus, thinking more about 'the market' and how to participate in it is part of such a solution.

In many ways, 'the third age' in European industrial countries could come to resemble that in less developed areas, where the older generation participates more fully in the productive work of their locality, and of families. Governments have many possibilities for providing opportunities and incentives through, for example, taxation schemes, education, and subsidies. Lifelong work, as capacity permits, would certainly require a different way of living, a re-conception of ageing, and greater investment in preventive medicine and lifelong learning. But taken seriously, as a goal rather than a necessity, it is more likely to improve quality of life than reduce it.

There are already indications of some movement in this direction. Many who are able to are making mid-career changes, opting for work that is more rewarding, and it is often work that they can carry on beyond pension age. The media carry many stories of people who drop out of high-pressured, stress-filled jobs to earn less but live longer, more happily. A re-evaluated 'quality of life' is likely to be the call of the future – and it may well not include a mandatory pension age, or a mandatory pension. The way to move forward is to generate a discussion, at a national level, about ageing and provision; a conversation that openly examines and reflects upon how people want to live, and how they propose to get there. Providing for old age concerns us all, involves far more than saving and investing, and means more than securing a decent pension. It is too important a matter to simply leave in the hands of politicians and committees. For here, as always, as we sow, we reap.

Notes

1. See 'The crumbling pillars of old age', *The Economist*, 27 September 2003, pp. 71–4.
2. See 'Berlusconi burlesque', *The Economist*, 11 October 2003, and 'Poor, old, confused', *The Economist*, 9 October 2003, online.
3. See 'Failed Pensions: A Painful Lesson in Assumptions', *The New York Times*, 12 November 2003.

4. See 'The scandal spreads', *The Economist*, 11 October 2003, p. 81; and 'Perils in the savings pool', *The Economist*, 6 November 2003, online.
5. See 'The crumbling pillars of old age', *The Economist*, 27 September 2003, pp. 71–4.
6. These arguments paralleled those used in other parts of Europe, such as Thatcher's UK, where reductions were also being made in social programmes.
7. One of the first 'pay-as-you-go' pension systems was introduced in 1889 by Otto van Bismark, Germany's chancellor. At the time the average life expectancy was 48, the retirement age 70, and the active workforce was much greater than the number of retirees (see 'The crumbling pillars of old age', *The Economist*, 27 September 2003, pp. 71–4).
8. Scherman points out that at the time, the average life expectancy was 55 years, while today it is 80 years, and the average age at pension is currently between 59 and 60.
9. ATP stands for *Allmän tilläggspension*, meaning general added pension. With this reform, pensions began to be linked to employees' incomes; those who earned more would receive higher pensions.
10. In the former ATP system, the 15 best years of income (of 30) are the basis for the size of the additional pension.
11. Peter Bernstein's *Capital Ideas* (1992) contains an interesting description of how the ideas behind today's mutual funds originated and became such important vehicles for mass investment.
12. See *Svenska Dagbladet*, 10 October 1999.
13. This research project was one of four in the research programme 'Cultural models of the market: trust, risk and social change' held at the Department of Social Anthropology at the University of Stockholm between 1998 and 2001. The programme was funded by the Bank of Sweden Tercentenary Foundation, and my project also received financial support from the Handelsbanken Research Foundation (*Handelsbankens forskningsstiftelser*).
14. This table is compiled from statistics collected by Sifo (1985–90) and Temo (1991–2000). They are based on interviews with a representative selection of the Swedish population, from which percentages have been extrapolated. The complete poll (year 2000) is called *Åtta av tio svenskar äger aktier* [Eight of ten Swedes own stocks], and is available at www.temo.se.
15. See *Dagens Industri*, 9 March 1998. *Småsparare sover* [Small investors asleep].
16. The Swedish crown (*krona*) is, at the time of writing, valued at roughly 7.3 to the US dollar, but has varied between 6 and 10 to the US dollar within the last ten years.
17. Older people who have invested over the years profited the most from the long rise in stock market values; and the highly educated presumably have well-paid jobs and are consequently able to save more.
18. See *Svenska Dagbladet*, 7 April 1997. *Hushållens börsägande borde öka* [Households' shareholding should increase].
19. Personal communication, Autumn 2000.
20. See *Dagens Nyheter*, 3 April 2003. *PPM söker regeringshjälp* [PPM seeks the government's help].

178 Culture, Ideology and the Financial Market

References

Abolafia, Mitchell. 1997. *Making Markets: Opportunism and Restraint on Wall Street.*
Cambridge, MA: Harvard University Press.
Bernstein, Peter. 1992. *Capital Ideas: The Probable Origins of Modern Wall Street.*
New York: The Free Press.
Dagens industri. 'Småsparare sover' [Small savers are sleeping]. 9 March 1998.
The Economist. 2003. 'The crumbling pillars of old age'. 27 September, 71–4.
The Economist. 2003. 'Berlusconi burlesque'. 11 October, 38.
The Economist. 2003. 'Poor, old, confused'. 9 October, online: http://www.economist.
com/printedition/displayStory.cfm?Story_ID=S')8(.PA%5B%20%23%40%22%
2C%0A.
The Economist. 2003. 'The scandal spreads'. 11 October, 81.
The Economist. 2003. 'Perils in the savings pool'. 6 November, online: http://
www.economist.com/displayStory.cfm?Story_ID = S')8(%24RA3%22%20P%
20L%0A.
Garsten, Christina. 2002. 'Flex fads: new economy, new employees'. In I. Holmberg,
M. Salzer-Mörling and L. Strannegård (eds), *Stuck in the Future: Tracing 'The New
Economy'.* Stockholm: Bookhouse Publishing AB, 237–61.
Granovetter, Mark. 1985. 'Economic action and social structure. The problem of
embeddedness'. *American Journal of Sociology* 91(3): 481–510.
Gyllenram, Carl-Gustav. 1998. *Aktiemarknadens psykologi, eller Vad styr upp- och
nedgångarna på börsen? [The Psychology of the Stock Market, or What steers the rise
and fall of the bourse?].* Stockholm: Rabén Prisma.
Hartwig, Kurt. 2002. 'Magic and the market: a case study of Warren Buffet and
shareholders of Berkshire Hathaway'. In U. Kockel (ed.), *Culture and Economy:
Contemporary Perspectives.* Aldershot: Ashgate Press, 89–98.
Hasselström, Anna. 2003. *On and Off the Trading Floor: An Inquiry into the Everyday
Fashioning of Financial Market Knowledge.* PhD dissertation, Department of
Social Anthropology, Stockholm University.
Hertz, Ellen. 1998. *The Trading Crowd: An Ethnography of the Shanghai Stock Market.*
Cambridge: Cambridge University Press.
Knorr Cetina, K. and U. Bruegger. 2002. Global microstructures: the virtual societies
of financial markets. *American Journal of Sociology* 107(4): 905–50.
Lindh de Montoya, Monica. 2002a. 'Looking into the future: anthropology and
financial markets'. In J. Cohen and N. Dannhaueser (eds), *Development Beyond
the 20th Century: A Critical Discussion in Economic Anthropology.* Lanham, MD:
University Press of America, 241–64.
Lindh de Montoya, Monica. 2002b. 'Constructing shareholders: images of individual
investors in Stockholm'. In Ullrich Kockel (ed.), *Culture and Economy: Contemporary
Perspectives.* Aldershot: Ashgate Press, 71–88.
Lindqvist, Mats. 1999. 'Igår var vi slösare. Idag är vi sparare. Etnologiska reflek-
tioner kring en privatekonomisk mässa' [Yesterday we were wasteful. Today
we save. Ethnological reflections about an economic exhibition]. In *Kulturella
Perspektiv* 1999 (1): 25–38.
Lindqvist, Sven. 2000. 'Pensionstjuvarna. Eller hur 258 miljarder försvann ur
pensionsfonderna' [The Pension Thieves. Or how 258 billion disappeared from
the pension funds]. *Ordfront*, vol. 5/2000, 24–35.

Modig, Arne. 2002. *Aktieägandet I Sverige. December 2001* [*Shareholding in Sweden. December 2001*]. Aktiefrämjandet: Temo.

The New York Times. 2003. 'Failed pensions: a painful lesson in assumptions'. 12 November 2003.

Nilsson, Pia. 1998. *Din framtida pension* [*Your future pension*]. Stockholm: Sellin & Partner.

Scherman, K. G. 2000. *Den Nya Pensionen. En reform med stora problem* [*The New Pension. A reform with big problems*]. Stockholm: Sveriges Pensionärsförbund.

Svenska Dagbladet. 'Hushållens börsägande borde öka' [Households' shareholding should increase]. 7 April 1997.

Temo. 2000. 'Två av tio svenskar äger inga aktier' [Two of three Swedes own no stocks]. Online: http://www.temo.se/genomfordaprojekt/.

9
The Crown Capitulates: National Currency and Global Capital in the Swedish Currency Crisis[1]

Gustav Peebles

[I]n fact it [money] has its name (nomisma) because it is not by nature, but by the current law (nomos), and it is within our power to alter it and to make it useless. (Aristotle, *Nichomachean Ethics*, Book V, Chapter 5)

Introduction

Aside from the literature in economics, the social sciences have mostly neglected the study of modern currency crises. Instead, they have focused more strictly on the connections between currency and group morality. Scholars have thus foregone the opportunity to attach this relationship to some of the ways in which currency attains and retains value on the international marketplace, and then how these revaluations impact the lives of the people involved. This phenomenon, though ever-present in the functioning of national currencies, becomes most obvious during currency crises. These crises provide us with particularly vivid instances in which to witness the intertwining of markets and moralities (see Garsten and Lindh de Montoya, this volume).

During a crisis, the standard conflation that lies at the heart of money is laid bare. Money is many things to many people (as some excellent ethnographies have shown us, for example, Parry and Bloch, 1989; Comaroff and Comaroff, 1990; Hutchinson, 1992; Znoj, 1998; Akin and Robbins, 1999), but in this essay I want to think of it as a conflation of national currency and capital (cf. Hart, 1986).[2] Conflation is a better word than 'combination', for it denotes how the combination is forgotten in everyday life; it also felicitously evokes both inflation and deflation, whose mercurial interrelations are one of the central foci of monetary policy. It is vital to recognize this conflation, in order to understand how discourses and rhetoric surrounding the national aspect of money can impact its price and even hide the shifting ownership of the capital of which it is also comprised. Conversely, as the Swedish crisis informs us, when the economic value of a currency deteriorates, the national unity that the currency indexed can undergo a similar fate. Gregory (1997) tackles a similar issue, when he points out that as states wax and wane in power, we find that their currency experiences a similar fate; perhaps currency is one material index of the power that Gregory considers essential to a new 'quality theory of money'. As he writes, 'There is no natural tendency for metallic standards to oust others... rather, there is a cultural tendency for those with power to impose their standards of value on others with different standards' (Gregory, 1997: 257). The shifts in power that are indexed by the Swedish currency crisis stand as testimony to Gregory's assertions; Sweden's ability to determine the value of value (Harvey, 1996) disintegrated at that moment.

By studying Sweden's 1992 currency crisis, I would like to add to the frequently heard claim that capital ruthlessly breaks down barriers (Marx and Engels, 1978; Harvey, 1990) by asserting that national currency serves to build them. This side of money is often neglected, for so often people use the terms 'capital', 'currency', and 'money' interchangeably. However, during currency crises, money is clearly broken down into its component parts – capital and currency. Thus, Zelizer's (1994) concern with separating out various currencies from one another must be taken to the global level. National currency is not capital. It is the nation-state's attempt to represent and concretize capital. By representing it, the nation-state hopes to capture and control it, to keep it confined within its borders.[3] Capital, meanwhile, is manifestly abstract and global (or at least, these days, beyond the national), as Adam Smith recognized: 'No part of it [capital] can be said to belong to any particular country, till it has been spread as it were over the face of that country, either in buildings, or in the lasting improvements of lands' (Smith, 1976: 445).

Anthropological techniques can teach us as much about currency as they do about the ways in which people value any object. Capital, as Marx never tires of informing us, is fickle and vampyric. It (as Marx sees it, capital becomes a thinking subject) judges every situation based on the potential for profit. Currency, however, is often judged based on metonymical[4] ties to nation-states and communal values that have very little or nothing to do with 'rational' prices, as I hope to show in this chapter.

The Swedish currency crisis serves as an excellent springboard from which to analyze all currency crises. Because it was one of the first of the recent wave, and was so well documented, it can tell us much about the currency crises we witnessed throughout the 1990s. The Swedish currency crisis had many effects, some of which I hope to document here; while others fall outside my purview. Most importantly, however, I want to emphasize the ways in which ideas about the nation played a role in determining the value of the Swedish krona (which means 'crown' in Swedish, thereby evoking the connection to the country qua royal kingdom). While some of the structural details were replicated globally, some elements of the Swedish crisis were indeed unique; in particular, we will see the ways in which a strong valorization of national 'solidarity' had a dramatic impact upon the way in which the Swedish crisis differed from others in Europe.

In other regards, however, Sweden's situation is not at all unique. Aside from the many other European countries that experienced currency devaluations in 1991–2, the last few years have witnessed the devaluation of many Southeast Asian currencies, just as many Americans are well aware of the collapse of the Mexican peso and the Brazilian cruzeiro; in 2001, the Turkish lira joined the club of tumblers. Many of the ways in which those currencies' values were negotiated are reminiscent of the value-negotiation of the krona. For example, the people of South Korea were widely reported in the news to have rallied around the won and made substantial personal sacrifices (such as turning in gold family heirlooms) in an effort to restore its 'health' and value (Pollack, 1997: A1). Understanding the crisis of the krona in 1992 can shed light on this complex but recurrent phenomenon. Currency crises stand as one of the premier sites from which to study the impact of the global on the local (Comaroff and Comaroff, 1992). Overnight, we are told, global capital markets eviscerate the economic value of a national currency, often leaving local families with only half the savings that they had the night before. Yet, as we shall see, this economic value has not simply evaporated, but has merely shifted elsewhere. National currencies, I hope to show, are often configured in such a way so as to produce crises of representation that necessarily cause the redistribution of capital between public and private hands.

In order to tell this story I begin with a general history of the day-to-day oscillations of the krona's economic value during the currency crisis in Sweden. After detailing the events that led to the krona's eventual devaluation, I conclude with a more general approach to understanding currency crises. For, as the years go by, monetary policy is becoming more and more of a prominent international (and even colonialist, cf. Gregory, 1997, for the historical antecedents of this) issue and a popular tool for many governments and world institutions (such as the World Bank and the International Monetary Fund). Hence, we find the recrudescence of 'currency boards' and other monetary measures that bring with them the potential to incite more crises – crises that will assuredly (as they always have) allow vast quantities of economic value to change hands. In many ways, the currency crises in Europe in 1992 marked the end of one important facet of modernity. It was at that time that an assemblage of non-colluding global market players managed to prove to national governments that their lengthy hegemony over currency value had ended. The monopoly that governments had wielded over currency during the modern age (and therefore, largely, money in general) had been eclipsed. Governmental hubris since 1992 has been manifestly tamed, and ever since we have heard much of the ascendancy of markets over these newly chastened governments (cf. Leyshon and Thrift, 1997).[5]

Furthermore, currency crises illuminate the fact that countries seemingly fighting over the value of their money are often negotiating other things simultaneously, in and through the national currency and their battles with the global market, which is often made to seem foreign, as though Sweden itself has nothing to do with this market. This is the side to currency crises that is not discussed in the economics literature, and is precisely what allows an analytic inroad into the meanings of the 'national' that materialize in an otherwise highly abstract money.

Part I: the crisis

Determining the instigating factors of the story of the 1992 devaluation of the Swedish krona is probably impossible. Certainly some distant historical factors played a role in its fall, such as the disintegration of the Bretton Woods accord in 1973, which allowed currencies to float freely (James, 1996: 224). In addition, Sweden's past proclivity to devalue its currency, such as in 1981 and 1982, greatly contributed to the crisis (*Dagens Industri*, 1990a; Wibble, 1994: 38). New laws and international agreements to free up the circulation of capital across national boundaries also played a role (cf. Corden, 1994: 113). Other experts emphasize the central role of the reunification of Germany, which forced up interest rates in Germany and in turn led to considerable turbulence in European currencies in the fall of 1992 (Dennis, 1998: 144, 150). Several books do a good job of laying out other aspects of the lengthy history, and I will rely on them here. One book, *Att Leda Sverige in i Krisen (To Lead Sweden into the Crisis)* by Carl Hamilton and Dag Rolander, focuses on the contribution of the government's economic policy to the crisis. Memoirs from Sweden's central bank, the Riksbank, Governor at the time (Bengt Dennis) and the Minister for Finance (Anne Wibble) also provide personal histories. In short, it is evident from the literature that multiple factors played a role in the fall of the krona.

October 1990

Though the factors that instigated the crisis may be debatable, its timing is less so. The krona began experiencing significant turbulence on the international currency markets around October 1990. At that time, Sweden had been combating a recession and a broad swathe of people operating in the currency markets were beginning to fear that the Swedish government would resort to a devaluation in order to bolster economic growth and the competitive advantage of export industries. Consequently, international traders began to put pressure on the krona, and Sweden experienced a major capital outflow. The Swedish financial daily, *Dagens Industri (Industry Daily)*, attributed this 'acute currency crisis' to various rumors of a devaluation, particularly one reported in the *Wall Street Journal* that week (Sundling, 1990a).[6] Whatever the immediate cause, it became clear to the Swedish government and central bank that the rumours needed to be countered, in order to quell the speculation. As a response, the Swedish government, central bank, banks, industry, labour unions, and newspapers committed to an astonishingly unified front in favor of a hard-currency policy. Everyone believed that the crucial factor was convincing the outside world that they could have faith in Swedish money, despite past habits.[7] 'Confidence' became the buzzword.

Though this hard-currency policy was generally uncontested, the means to achieve it were vigorously contested. *Dagens Industri* began a series during October entitled 'The Sick Krona' that constantly agitated for Sweden to tie itself to the European Exchange Rate Mechanism (ERM).[8] The newspaper touted Britain's recent successful entry into the system with headlines such as 'The pound shows the way to ERM for the krona' and 'The cure against inflation' (Fahlen, 1990; *Dagens Industri*, 1990b). The latter article brought metaphor into play, in line with the name of the series. The krona was alleged to be sick, and the ERM provided the cure. The article queried 'when will Sweden swallow the medicine?' (*Dagens Industri*, 1990b).

The newspaper clarifies its agenda to the public via its utilization of metaphor, and, crucially, personification. Fernandez (1986: 8) describes metaphor as 'a strategic predication upon an inchoate pronoun (an I, a you, a we, a they) which makes a movement and leads to performance'. In the case of the Swedish krona, the newspaper takes an ordinarily quite mundane object (already metonymically tied to the nation-state), and embodies it with life, with all its concomitant fragilities and potential ailments. Considering the krona's metonymic attachment to the state, it would clearly behoove all Swedes to work toward its cure, recovery, and well-being. The 'Sick Krona' articles stand as an instance within a long-standing discourse of convincing Swedes that the European Community (EC) and its institutions will cure many ills, but like many cures, it might demand a bit of pain in return.

Of course, counter-discourses also came to the fore. One of the strongest and best positioned to propagate an alternative approach to the krona crisis was the central bank Governor, Bengt Dennis. He maintained a different opinion about how confidence in the Swedish krona could be restored and its value maintained. In the years that followed, Dennis emerged as the staunchest defender of the strength of the currency, and put his belief into practice frequently. Indeed, the story of the krona's rollercoaster ride could be read (and, indeed, often was read) as a battle between Dennis and the market. Instead of following the moves of Europe's other central bankers during a time of general turbulence, he set a unique course for Sweden's economy. Perhaps more than anyone else involved in the crisis, he believed in the power of the nation-state, and in the power of the words he uttered as its representative.

In response to the speculation on the krona, Dennis raised interest rates in October in order to alert the market that Sweden was committed to defending the value of the krona. Economically speaking, such a move was intended to tighten the liquidity in the economy, making it more worthwhile to hold the krona relative to other currencies, and thereby stem the tide of capital flight; it also conveyed the message that Sweden would not slip back into what the market considered to be its poor record of maintaining currency value. This tactic may also slow an economy that appears to be heating up, or, in the case of Sweden, cripple an economy trying to move out of a recession. Thus, the sacrifices necessary to defend the krona immediately became apparent. This did not deter Dennis. His operative metaphor for the currency was not a body prone to sickness or health, but rather, a stream of liquid that could be manipulated through governance.

After looking at many quotes by Dennis, some of which will follow below, it is evident that one of his primary strategies for building confidence involved making authoritative claims that the currency was secure not because of Sweden's sound economic situation, but because of Sweden's collective defence, and that the Riksbank was behaving as a responsible steward. If repeated often and assertively enough, Dennis seemed to think market players would start to believe him; it also appears that he may have thought, correctly, that his exhortations would nurture and sustain the vital unified front. Further, Dennis' performative utterances did, in fact, constantly impact the value of the currency.[9]

Given the history of central banking in Sweden to 1992, Dennis would have good reason for making this assumption. During the modern era, central banks did exercise a profound amount of influence over the value of their currencies, and the market often abided by the rates set by the central banks.[10] Dennis openly stated that the primary means to defend the currency was to cultivate confidence abroad, but he denied that this had anything to do with establishing a formal tie to the ERM. Instead, he felt that the government needed to put forth a fiscally responsible plan for expenditures and revenues: 'The problem lies in economic policy', and thus not in monetary policy (Yamdagni, 1990). This statement marks the beginning of Dennis' effort to present a united front to the market. It was also a means of deflecting responsibility away from his office and placing the onus on elected officials to act in accordance with Dennis' own policies. By asserting that his own house is in order, any future problems with the krona could be attributed to others. His comments can be viewed as a not-so-subtly veiled threat that serves as an inducement for these officials to fall into line with his own actions and to establish a unified position with which to confront the market.

On the same day that these comments were made, the government called a press conference to assert, following Dennis, that the situation would be reversed once the new economic package was released the following week. The promises of reductions in government spending and business taxes assuaged the many people working in the markets. On 20 October the front page of *Dagens Industri* expressed its relief, with a headline that read: 'Finally calm on the market' (*Dagens Industri*, 1990c). This is the first evidence of Sweden's willingness as a democratic nation to make collective sacrifices in order to defend the national currency. Government policy and Riksbank rhetoric were coming together.

The business community voiced its discontent with the government plans, but for the most part the currency remained stable in the days following the announcement of the future plan. This stability was attributed to the government's promises to engage in membership talks with the European Community (EC) and not exclusively to the government's economic plan. Thus, such negotiations became the new demand of the market players. One author (Sundling, 1990b) writes, 'Now what counts is that the government gives us a date for an entrance to the EC, anything less and the market will not be satisfied'. Two elements of this quote are interesting for the purposes of this essay. Firstly, the market is now personified. This speech tactic occurs frequently in the newspaper *Dagens Industri*. By personifying the market, an exceedingly complex entity with countless different interests becomes monolithic; this personification sets up the possibility for a metaphoric showdown between the personified market and the personified krona.

Secondly, the fact that the market was calmed whenever Sweden voiced an interest in the EC indicates that people who work in the markets had a tendency to equate the EC with monetary fortitude and fiscal integrity. Throughout this study, it will become clear that the status of the krona was often intertwined with the fiscal policies of other nations that were seemingly analogous to Sweden. As a nation, Sweden was not viewed in isolation, exclusively upon the merits or faults of its own policies; instead, people assessed its position and future trajectory based on the perceived strength of its links with other nations. In many ways, the series of events surrounding the krona can be seen as a long struggle over Sweden's identity – would it remain part of Scandinavia, that 'anachronistic' island of social democracy, or would it become associated with the free trade zone known as the EC?

May 1991

The Swedish government clarified its position on this question six months later. On 17 May 1991 Sweden tied itself unilaterally to the ERM, abandoning its former basket weighted towards the dollar.[11] Having asserted an association with the new Europe, the Swedish press thought the krona's troubles were over. 'This measure now definitively closes the door to all devaluations' writes *Dagens Industri* in its staff editorial (*Dagens Industri*, 1991a).[12] The blindness of this claim reveals just how strongly people believed that the mere association with Europe would be a panacea. In fact, since the krona was tied unilaterally, Sweden could not depend on the aid of other central banks in the ERM in the case of speculatory threats, as true members of the ERM could. Additionally, the Swedes only allowed themselves a stringent 1.5 per cent floating band around the ECU, which was around half that permitted in the case of other countries (Fahlen, 1991).[13] Nevertheless, the bold move restored the market's confidence in the krona, and capital started flowing back into the country (*Dagens Industri*, 1991b).

November 1991

Despite the initial enthusiasm, the honeymoon proved to be short-lived. Just as Sweden was successfully building an image of itself as European, its strategy was undermined by the devaluation of the Finnish markka. Its neighbour's move suddenly reminded market players of Sweden's position in Scandinavia, instead of focusing on its connection with Europe. Worried traders set their sights on potentially similar problems in Sweden, and the pressure they exerted forced the central bank to raise interest rates substantially, in an effort to disassociate itself from Finland's devaluation (Wallen, 1991).[14] Both Prime Minister Carl Bildt and Dennis claimed that Sweden would soon enter the ERM as a full member, another move to disassociate itself from Finland (*Dagens Industri*, 1991c). Apparently these interventions, coupled with assertions of European-ness, alleviated the situation, for the next day the krona was up again (Sundling, 1991).

At about this time, claims emerged in the press that only foreign traders were betting against the krona. The market threat was perceived as a foreign threat, even though later studies have shown that many Swedish market players profited handsomely from the crisis. However, a national tendency to bet in favour of the krona should not be completely discounted. One banker I spoke with explained that her colleague upbraided anyone who tried to make money on krona trades, believing that profiting on the national currency's struggles was immoral. But even less emotional aspects of the citizen – state nexus could impact people's behaviour during the crisis. One trader bluntly stated that 'if the government promises something, then we assume it will abide by its promise', so he trusted the government when it said the krona would not be devalued. This opinion about government is, needless to say, far from a universal opinion – many American traders would find it 'laughable'; rather, it reflects a common strain within Swedish society to believe in what is called 'the strong state'. The press desperately grasped onto this belief, and in so doing promoted the idea that external forces were maliciously aiming to harm Sweden. Via the national attachment of currency, battle lines were drawn in the national press that did not correspond with market reality.

June–September 1992

In Autumn 1992 the European currency markets were exceedingly volatile. By August heavy speculation had occurred against several currencies in the ERM, most famously, the lira and the pound (Corden, 1994: 113); many attribute the infamous June 2nd Danish 'no' vote on the Maastricht Treaty as the instigating factor to the general European currency turbulence that fall.[15] Dennis writes matter-of-factly that the Danish no vote over a political matter impacted economic ones: 'The Danes' no to the Maastricht Treaty broke the positive trends in the Swedish interest rate market' (Dennis, 1998: 33). Sweden's proximity to Denmark – geographically, culturally, and politically – led many in the market to again look at Sweden more critically, as though it were no different than Denmark (Dennis, 1998: 33).

After some oscillations, the real trouble began just prior to the so-called Black Wednesday, 16 September 1992, when the pound and the lira fell out of their ERM bands after speculative assaults. Once again, the story begins, at least partially, with Finland. On 5 September *Dagens Industri* reported rumors of a new Finnish plan to devalue its currency. By the 8th, it had indeed allowed the markka to float, and it lost 14 per cent of its value. On 9 October *Dagens Industri*'s front page read: 'Finland's crisis is ours' (*Dagens Industri*, 1992a). Apparently, in the morning hours alone, worried 'foreign' traders handed in 15–20 billion kronas (circa 3–4 billion dollars) in the fear that Sweden would follow Finland. Dennis responded by hiking interest rates substantially again, to 24 per cent, thus arresting the flight from the krona (Fahlen, 1992a). Dennis argued that 'We think that this hike will suffice for giving us respect within the market. And if anyone still questions the Riksbank's commitment, then they will come to understand who is the strongest' (Magnerot, 1992). At about the same time, Wibble and Bildt came out with a joint statement concurring with Dennis that 'The uncertainty that has occurred after the Finnish decision can only be met with decisive measures, for which there can be no boundaries' (Dennis, 1998: 44). The crisis continued to be personified, and indeed, the metaphors even became bellicose. The front page of *Dagens Industri* on 10 September flashed: '1–0 to Dennis' (*Dagens Industri*, 1992b) following his new hike of rates to 75 per cent. Dennis boldly threatened the market by stating, 'We can pile on more of the same thing. *There is no boundary for a central bank*. We have barely begun to use the weapons arsenal that we have at our disposal. This is a signal to the market. No one, no one should doubt the Riksbank's determination to defend the krona' (*Dagens Industri*, 1992b and 1992e; emphasis mine). Several reports mention that the Riksbank and its chief were becoming more and more respected abroad. One headline in the paper christened Dennis 'The tough guy who steers Sweden', while another personified the state itself: 'Sweden fights like a man' (*Dagens Industri*, 1992d). The newspaper also reported that Swedish investors had been buying the krona in massive quantities to strengthen it; they were

betting against a devaluation. A cartoon showed 'Mother Sweden' vac-
uuming up Swedish currency all over the European continent (*Dagens
Industri*, 1992c). Dennis' strong assertions, the actions of the press (and
its favorable portrayal of Swedish traders), together created the image of
the formidable unified front that kept the krona stable; all of Sweden
was successfully caricatured as a housewife dutifully cleaning up after
a group of irresponsible and thankless guests. Dennis' use of the first
person plural and the personifications of the country point to the collectivity behind his actions; Swedes could fend off these attacks as a group.
Furthermore, the national currency was thought to be protected by the
national community, its value allegedly guaranteed by a government
and a unified front that would never lose to an anonymous market.

500%

Round two in the standoff occurred about a week later, following the
general chaos on Wednesday 16 September. The krona was bet against
in much the same manner as were the pound and the lira, but while
other central banks yielded to the market, Dennis refused to waver. While
Britain and Italy fell out of the ERM, Dennis hiked rates to an unheard
of 500 per cent, essentially freezing bank activity and, thus, much of
the rest of the economy. He stated, 'This is not a rate level that will be
permanent. But if one lets the speculators win, then it is permanent for
the economy' (*Dagens Industri*, 1992f). Asked about the possibility of a
devaluation, Dennis defiantly explains, 'Not in those conditions that I am
working toward. There are two conditions. The first is that the political
system falls into line behind the stable exchange rate policy. The other is
that the market understands that there exist no boundaries for the central
bank' (Altan and Jonsson, 1992). Dennis made sure that the international
market grasped his belief in the lack of boundaries for central banks, for
at a press conference he stated in English, 'The sky's the limit' (Stenberg
and Örn, 1996a: A6; Dennis, 1998: 137).[16]

Stating this in the wake of Britain's and Italy's failures seems quite
audacious on Dennis' part. It certainly appears that Dennis truly believed
in the power of the nation-state to stand up against the whims of global
capital; he felt that his words and deeds, coupled with those of the
government, could withstand any attack. *Dagens Industri* supported this
belief when it wrote that 'In this situation the Swedish Riksbank stands
out as the only truly solid rock in the currency storm. . . . He [Dennis]
has not for the blink of an eye in the slightest statements strayed from his
line – the krona shall not be devalued' (Fahlen, 1992b). The market also
seems to have respected the Swedish response, for the currency survived

the fierce September round of speculation. (Dennis (1998: 56) refers to 17 September as 'one of the most chaotic days in the financial system's history'.) An article from 19 November 1992 argues that the krona withstood the September attacks because of the unified front presented by all the Swedish participants in the crisis, led by Dennis' unyielding defense (Fahlen, 1992c).

Britain's Chancellor of the Exchequer, Norman Lamont, was asked if the Bank of England could have responded in a similar manner to Sweden, by also instituting a 500 per cent rate rather than allowing its currency to float. He retorted, 'Yes, but we use common sense' (Stenberg and Örn, 1996a: A6). Here we clearly see the impact of culture on monetary policy. At this point in the crisis Sweden remained staunchly committed to a national community that must be protected from the mercurial and fickle inclinations of the global market. Guided by the social democratic state's foundational moral imperative – solidarity – Sweden maintained this commitment by sustaining a broad unified front; government policy demanded sacrifices out of its citizenry to defend the national currency that British and Italian citizens did not have to make despite similar conditions.

One of the primary practical upshots of the confrontation between the Swedish unified front and the market was the so-called 'crisis packages' that the government presented in an effort to prove to the market that it was matching the Riksbank's tough monetary policy with equally tough fiscal measures. To make the government's commitment to a smaller public sector more transparent, two packages were pushed through in September. The first cut back on holidays and sick days, raised the retirement age, lowered housing subsidies and increased taxes on gas and tobacco (Hamilton and Rolander, 1993: 70). The second crisis package cut back on employer contributions to social welfare, compensated for with increased taxes and further cutbacks in government services (Stenberg and Örn, 1996a: A7; Dennis, 1998: 88–96).

The government in power at the time was a minority government, so it needed the support of the opposition Social Democrats. The pressure on the krona was significant and frightening enough that the opposition agreed to these two back-to-back trimmings of the welfare state. *Dagens Nyheter*, one of the major daily papers in Sweden, wrote 'Currency chaos and 500 per cent interest rates drove forth a *unique* crisis agreement between the government and the opposition in order to save the krona's fixed exchange rate' (Stenberg and Örn, 1996b: A7; emphasis mine). The support of the Social Democrats for the cutbacks stands as testimony to the importance with which Swedes viewed the stability of their currency, and to the remarkably broad constitution of the unified front. For the Social Democrats, the cutbacks meant dismantling parts of the cherished welfare state that they had worked so long to build, and considered the pride of their nation and party. Wibble goes so far as to say that 'in a word, the Social Democrats signed on to a very conservative policy' in agreeing to the crisis packages (Wibble, 1994: 33). Clearly this coalition served as evidence that Sweden was committed to a stable krona. The market retreated as long as the central bank, the government, industry, and Swedish economists were all operating cohesively, vehemently defending the representational power of the krona.

The Crisis Climax: October–November 1992

Things went well for the embattled krona for most of October. The crisis packages were well-received by the market; interest rates fell back to the more manageable 20 per cent range (but still high), and the krona strengthened. Dennis jubilantly declared that September's 'test' had allowed Sweden to show the world exactly how committed it was to the establishment of a stable currency. He went on to say that 'Never has the potential for long term growth been greater' (*Dagens Industri*, 1992 g). The test was a communal ritual. While proving to the market that Sweden could create a unified front, the test also in part created the unified front, by having Swedes go through a collective process of sacrifice that distinctly set them apart from the rest of the European nations that had tumbled out of the ERM in September.

Several commentators comment on the incredible state of silence given the state of the country's finances, and the questionable nature of its monetary policy. *Dagens Nyheter* (Stenberg and Örn, 1996a: A6) wrote four years later that

> In October and the beginning of November there is no public criticism of the fixed exchange rate. No one wants to say that the emperor is naked, that the golden thread that politicians and the Riksbank have spun around the currency is an illusion. The only thing heard is the Riksbank's and the government's constant promise that they will defend the fixed exchange rate until the last drop of blood.

The newspaper goes on to cite the chief of the Confederation of Swedish Industries, who stated that 'There was a taboo in the Swedish public sphere. No one was allowed to question monetary policy. The weaker the position of the krona became, the harder it became to question the policy' (Stenberg and Örn, 1996a: A7). Hamilton and Rolander (1992: A4), in an op-ed piece published three days before the currency floated, claimed that 'The defense of the krona is so taboo-laden today that no independent economist or actor on the market wants to openly reveal what they all actually realize, which is that the krona must be let go.' Dennis informs us that even the forest industry – customarily an export industry that heavily favours devaluations – stood behind the unified front. Karl Ohlson, the Chief Financial Officer of a major forest company, stated on 18 September 'of course we should defend the krona' (Dennis, 1998: 68).

These quotes indicate the united front that Sweden presented, but it is also interesting that in a relatively free and democratic society one encounters such a degree of conformity in the public sphere.[17] According to Hamilton and Rolander, rigorous economic criticism of Swedish policy came from abroad.[18] Additionally, the taboo that *Dagens Nyheter* and Hamilton and Rolander discuss reveals the manner in which cultural values play a role in the market negotiation of price. Both comments underscore the point that many people agreed that the government policy was wrong, but no one dared to admit it in public. Perhaps in this instance respect for the government or fear of splitting the united front (and conceivably 'injuring' the nation) leads to a remarkable silence.

Hamilton and Rolander go further, and argue that only the big companies recognized the flaws in the policy in time, and managed to escape the problems of the krona's crash; indeed, having guessed the correct outcome, they exploited the situation for profit: 'What happened was a socialization, in an orderly fashion, of the coming devaluation losses' (Hamilton and Rolander, 1993: 71–2). According to this analysis, Swedish tax money was utilized to save Sweden's largest multinational companies while many individual investors and small companies went bankrupt.

Explaining how this could occur, one informant pointed out to me that often only certain large companies even have the possibility of 'hedging' their currency risks with futures contracts.[19] Due to the commission costs it can be quite an expensive endeavour, and therefore not worth the risk that the hedging process itself involves. Thus, the large companies that made money from the crisis may not even have done so intentionally; they were merely prudently insuring their investments in a fairly standard manner. By contrast, smaller companies could not afford this sort of insurance. This further attests to the power of national currency – it places certain groups at the mercy of government policy while other groups are wealthy enough to 'buy themselves out' of this (often economically detrimental) governmental control. In other words, national currency structures economic decisions in a discriminatory way: beneficial, self-interested behaviour is only available to the wealthiest of actors in the business world.

Post-crisis fallout

Be that as it may, the government, then run by Carl Bildt and a center-right coalition, stated on 18 November that a new 'crisis package' was about to be announced because of renewed pressure on the krona. Bildt's package planned on further lowering the employer taxes, a policy to which the market responded well. Since it was a minority coalition, Bildt needed the support of the opposition Social Democrats to pass the package; in short, he needed to remobilize and rejuvenate the unified front. He called the opposition leader, Ingvar Carlsson, at 2 a.m. on 19 November to ask for his support. A few hours later the Confederation of Swedish Industries announced that it was in favour of a floating krona. Then came a meeting between Carlsson and Bildt. As Carlsson left the meeting, the press asked him his opinion on Sweden's stable krona policy. Carlsson neglected to answer the question. By not responding, market players believed his party had abandoned the policy (Sundberg, 1992; Ekbom and Tulin, 1992; *Dagens Industri*, 1992i). Soon afterwards, after both reserve interventions and even a rate hike failed to stem the flow of money from the krona, the Riksbank announced that the currency would float (Moore and Whitney, 1992: A11).

Oddly enough, on 19 November the currency markets were actually fairly calm at the beginning of the day. Informants explained to me that many people working in banks had no forewarning at all of the currency's fall and that everything appeared quite normal that morning: partially they had put their trust in the government and partially they were the victims of a lack of information. Though one woman had been watching the krona's ups and downs closely (because her son was studying abroad in England), she was caught completely unaware when the krona floated. By ducking out of the ERM and letting their currencies float at an early stage, the British and the Italians saved untold billions from rushing out of their reserve coffers, whereas the Swedes unloaded all of the country's reserves (and then some more) to defend the krona, to no avail. In the end, the krona fell anyway, Sweden lost billions in reserve money, ran up debts with other central banks from which it borrowed, and the currency speculators and big Swedish companies walked away with the windfall. On that day, the Swedish krona lost more than 10 per cent of its value (Moore and Whitney, 1992: A11), and even more in the months that followed. Aside from the public money lost in the episode, the value lost to the krona also had a considerable impact upon individual lives. One woman (over) dramatized its impact by discussing her newfound inability to travel outside of Sweden because of the fall in the value of the krona. She told me, 'We've become a developing country.' This statement testifies to a national currency's ability to build obstacles to actual physical movement, as this person felt newly imprisoned by her currency.

Dagens Nyheter assessed the financial damage of the currency collapse four years later. The newspaper argues that the largest Swedish companies gained money at the taxpayers' expense. In his book, Dennis claims that it is impossible to tell who gained specifically from the crisis. In the individual sense, he is telling the truth: we don't know the specifics of who reaped the harvest doled out by the Riksbank.[20] Yet what he fails to note is the obvious point that the money began as public money and ended up as private money.

According to a series of articles (Stenberg and Örn, 1996a, b), the Swedish banks and larger companies were the ones who actually instigated the currency flow out of the krona.[21] Yet ultimately George Soros and other infamous speculators are blamed by the general public for the final rush against the currency. This claim regarding the involvement of Swedish multinationals was largely absent in the media at the time of the crisis. Instead, the currency crisis was constructed in national terms, and then the responsibility for the fall could successfully be portrayed as a question of national identities and boundaries.

Part II: metonymic money and boundaries

Given the significance of national attachments (for example, in choosing a currency basket or in influencing market players' opinions) to the process of currency value-determinations, it is interesting to consider the implications of a currency and its metonymic ties to the nation-state. As previously mentioned, for much of modern financial history, governments have been able to exert a profound influence on the economic value represented by their currencies. The metonymic attachment serves to symbolize who has control over the value of the currency; this symbol in turn signals to the market who governs its value determination – that is, who the market should listen to and trust when considering the placement of capital. In an exhibit discussing the previous power of American states (as opposed to the federal government) to issue American dollars, the Swedish National Museum of Monetary History claims that 'When others control the currency it is almost always a sign of weakened state power'. After some countries in Europe have exhibited a lack of power to control the value of their currencies, we also find that many of these countries surrendered the metonymic attachment that they previously enjoyed with regard to their currencies. The new currency appearing on the European horizon, the Euro, is metonymically attached to a different, larger state, governed from Brussels and Frankfurt (the location of the European Central Bank). One of the primary goals of European Monetary Union (EMU) is to broaden state power in order to eclipse the power that the market has exhibited over smaller currencies in the determination of value (Leyshon and Thrift, 1997: 113–15). Many of the proponents of EMU whom I have spoken with in Sweden constantly assert that EMU will allow Europeans to return to the days when they controlled the value of their currencies, rather than remaining at the whim of the market.

This metonymic tie between national currency and the state also contributes to the creation of boundaries. These boundaries then play an integral role in the construction of the world economy. Indeed, the discipline of macroeconomics, it could be argued, is fixated (and founded) upon the value of national boundaries, focusing as it does on Gross National Product, trade surpluses, national debt, and the like. These boundaries confer a sense of 'home', where the currency 'belongs', and the only place where it can ultimately be redeemed for something else – either a commodity such as labour-power, or another currency traded from the central bank's reserves. In short, the state is the guarantor of its value. Since the issuing of money has often become the prerogative of the modern state, it is a significant way in which the state power apparatus imposes notions of boundedness and group unity.

Additionally, a particular morality becomes attached to money (cf. Zelizer, 1994; Znoj, 1998) in this manner. Because money is metonymically tied to the state, it can become morally incumbent upon citizens of that state to behave in a manner that protects the national money – at least in the case of Sweden, where sacrifices for the general good of the state are seemingly expected. Thus, many Swedes sought to deny or scorn involvement in 'speculating' against the krona, and to blame foreign elements for its fall. It was subjected to 'attacks' from abroad, and the country had to unify in order to 'restore the currency's health'. Wibble explains that while the crisis was under way she received many personal letters and phone calls 'from people who appreciated the defense of the krona and the politicians' ability to gather in unity during hard times. For a short time there was a real national gathering' (Wibble, 1994: 31–2). Dennis likewise details the wrath of citizens against those who they saw to be 'traitors': 'The Volvo Workshop Club in Gothenburg demanded that the traitors be brought forth and the Union of Insurance Workers #49 in Östergötland wanted to know which businesses had speculated in the Swedish devaluation. They wanted to know 'so that we are not forced against our will to buy their products' (Dennis, 1998: 323). In these ways and others, it becomes clear that the krona was viewed as sacrosanct during the crisis (cf. Brantlinger, 1996). The strong taboo against defaming it also testifies to the fact that the attachment between money and states can create sentiments around currencies that are separate from their use as mere units of exchange-value. It is as though the krona, within certain groupings, carries a sort of Maussian *hau* (Mauss, 1990) that binds the group together via a spirit infused in the object.

Furthermore, as the krona met the harmonizing effects of increased international trade, Swedes also had to reassess their commitments and loyalties to various structures and groups; the fixation on maintaining currency value (itself a cultural choice among various options) eroded. The krona, up until and during the crisis, represented and indexed the faith that many Swedes had in their government. It was also a vehicle through which they asserted their faith; it was the instrument around which the nation could rally in order to present a unified front and a strong belief in itself as a group. Similarly, the currency served as the vehicle for the government to assert its faithfulness; defending a strong krona would prove government trustworthiness. I was told by one informant that he believed that the currency crisis marked the transfer from a previous faith in governmental leaders to one in business leaders (though this may not have been a society-wide belief). Substantiating this claim, a new proverb entered into the lexicon during the crisis, which asserted 'It's the market that counts, not the government' (personal communication). Other variations of this include 'the tyranny of the market' (cf. Karlin, 1992) and 'Now it's money that steers' (cf. Wallner, 1992).[22]

Conclusion

In short, national currency serves as one of the primary symbolic mediators between the nation (including the citizenry) and the market in capitalist systems. It clothes economic value with a history and an identity, both of which are not *a priori* necessary to economic value's functioning. As such, it is worth noting the ways in which national currency (or any form of currency) aids in the construction of boundaries, while the economic value that it is meant to represent is famous for destroying or disregarding boundaries.

But precisely because of this paradox inherent within currency (see Hart, 1986), the value of the krona ultimately fell. Where this value went is an important consideration in this analysis. In terms of specific trajectories, the monetary resources lost by the central bank apparently accrued to foreign speculators and the larger Swedish companies. But the number of kronas in circulation did not change at the same moment that the krona lost 10 per cent of its value. Anne Wibble, when asked how much money was lost in defending the krona, responded, 'it is not as if society has lost those coins. We have them in Swedish kronas, whereas before we had them in foreign currency' (Hamilton and Rolander, 1993: 73). Though Hamilton and Rolander complain that this comment is but a deft and hollow attempt to deflect criticism, there is nonetheless some truth to it; Wibble is playing upon the usual conflation of money and economic value. Whenever a country complains of a 'currency outflow', they are neglecting to point out that the home currency is rushing into the country to pay for the outflow. However, after a certain point in time, such as in a period of currency revaluation, the currency undergoes what Marx (1990: 314) calls a 'metempsychosis' of value. Economic value that originally existed in the krona has suddenly been socially transferred elsewhere. Money, in the form of national bills, is not lost, but instead economic value is moving from one national currency to another. Economic value flows from one currency into some other currency or commodity, fleeing the boundaries set by national currency.[23] Economic value 'clings' to currency, but only tenuously; it defies currency's attempts to enclose it within national boundaries.

This ability of currency to confer a sense of national control over, and identity with, economic value via metonym also then conceals other aspects of the metempsychotic movement of this value. A discourse of protecting the unity and prestige of the national currency, in this instance, concealed the fact that many Swedish players walked off with sizable portions of the national reserves in their pockets. The predominant discourse focuses upon an opposition between foreign and national, rather than, for example, other oppositions such as class differences that may also be present in the movements of the krona or the simple opposition between public and private money. The fact that national money carries other values (in particular, a variety of 'national values' that bind a group together) beyond its mere economic one is precisely what creates the conditions necessary to redistribute economic value along the trajectories illuminated here. The Swedish currency crisis, like virtually all subsequent currency crises, effected a massive transfer of wealth (as capital) from the 'average taxpayer' who fills the government's coffers to the balance sheet of some of the world's wealthiest people and corporations.

Notes

1. This chapter has been greatly aided by the thoughtful and discerning critiques of Susan Gal, Christina Garsten, John Kelly, Keith Hart and Monica Lindh de Montoya. An early version of it also benefited from the instructive comments of many listeners at an American Anthropological Association conference. Much editorial assistance came from Stephanie Rupp. The research for the chapter was supported by a NSF Graduate Student Fellowship and by the MacArthur Foundation. I would like to thank these organizations and interlocutors for their many efforts and encouragement.
2. In this chapter, the terms 'capital' and 'economic value' will be used interchangeably.
3. Here, however, it is worth noting the commentary of Cohen (1998), who points out that with increased cross-border transactions, some prominent currencies are now competing globally for 'market share'; in other words, they are not necessarily exclusively interested in keeping their currency confined within national borders. However, the opposite remains generally true for Cohen's so-called 'plebeian currencies', which comprise most of the world's currencies.
4. For a very illuminating anthropological study of the role of metonymy – parts standing for wholes – in social life, please see Durham and Fernandez (1991).
5. Devaluations had occurred before, but the magnitude of the 1992 crisis was unparalleled and it led to the break-up of the European Exchange Rate mechanism, which instigated, in turn, a new commitment to a then foundering and still Panglossian belief in the Euro (see below).
6. All translations from the Swedish are mine throughout the text.
7. In her memoirs, Wibble (1994) explains her reasons for mounting a rigid defence of the fixed exchange rate. She personified the market, as something with a memory that needed to be contended with on those terms: 'The market has a long memory, it never forgets which countries try to devalue themselves out of problems' (Wibble, 1994: 34). She further states that Belgian government officials with whom she had consulted told her that with the market, 'old sins are never forgotten' (Wibble, 1994: 34).
8. The ERM is one part of a broader agreement known as the European Monetary System, established in 1979. Its short-term goal was to reduce the hazards to business transactions of fluctuating currency values in Europe's increasingly integrated economies, and to keep down inflation by tying currencies more intimately to the consistently anti-inflationary policies of Germany's Bundesbank. In the long term, it also evolved into a sort of testing (and training) ground for the future European Monetary Union (EMU), the title of the then-planned single currency project of the European Union. In short, participant countries in the ERM agree to keep their currency values in a narrow band revolving around the basket of their currencies known as the European Currency Unit (ECU). In agreeing to tie one's currency to the ECU, a country then takes on the obligation

to not devalue without approval from all members of the agreement. To combat any market attempts at devaluations, countries are additionally obliged to aid each other in marketplace intervention; to support a flagging currency, the central banks will often jointly purchase the currency in order to reestablish its value on the market.

9. Just as Alan Greenspan's comments have an impact on the market, currency traders of course judge their strategies partly on the statements made by central bank chiefs. This is especially true in fixed-exchange rate regimes.

10. For example, for years the French government abided by what it called the 'franc fort' policy – the 'strong franc' policy. This policy attempted to keep the franc in line with the German mark, occasionally at tremendous expense to the government and to the dismay and frustration of many economists. This policy is usually attributed to national pride to see France's currency as strong as Germany's, and is thus excellent evidence of the impact of cultural practices and beliefs on currency value. But it also attests to the fact that, given enough resolve, a state could determine market valuations of national currency.

11. A 'basket' is a manner in which a country fixes the value of its own currency by attaching it to the value of a mixed 'basket' of other currencies that it holds in reserves.

12. If one wanted to become a successful currency speculator, these are the sorts of comments to look for when seeking the impending doom of a currency; such rigid comments seem to universally presage currency devaluations.

13. A floating band around a currency value means that the Swedish central bank will allow the krona to fluctuate within this band prior to defending its price with any interventions. It could drop up to 1.5 per cent, or rise 1.5 per cent, and need not be exactly in line with the basket ECU. However, this is a particularly stringent band; many floating band currency regimes intentionally have broad bands, in order to minimize any necessary commitments to intervene. With such a stringent band, Sweden is announcing to the world that it is committed to a very particular currency price. Whenever it falls above or below this price, many in the market know that there exists potential to take advantage of the constraining policy. And again, it is important to recall that Sweden was only unilaterally tied to the ERM, so other central banks were not committed to defend Sweden's stringent band.

14. The fact that blocs of national currencies often fall or stand together is a phenomenon that has been christened 'contagion'. Discussing the potential risks of globalization, The *Economist* writes (6 December 1997: 89): 'The risk of "contagion", when a crisis in one country leads the market to change its view of prospects in others, is a further complication, as recent events in Asia have emphasised' (emphasis mine). In the instance above, regarding the relationship between Sweden and Finland, the market could become 'worried' because some of the people operating within the market are protecting their investments, rather than necessarily believing that the currency is overvalued in the same manner as Finland's. Instead, their moves are a way in which to hedge against the risk that Sweden might be in a position similar to Finland's, an opinion generated at least partially by proximity, stereotypes and alleged commonalities. In my opinion, this attests to the significance of the national identity of currencies when negotiating their value. Economic game theory

tries to explain these sorts of motives and moves, thereby acknowledging that currency movement may not always be related exclusively to 'economic fundamentals'.

15. Following the Danish vote, France swiftly announced that it would hold a referendum, thereby placing all the co-operation on a high wire for months and increasing the instability of the ERM (Dennis, 1998: 3).

16. Indeed, Dennis was not allowing any notion of 'boundary' guide his own thinking. Dennis explains in his book that in March 1983 the French government attempted a defense of the franc with a 1,000 per cent interest rate. Dennis and Wibble both discuss in their books the hidden fear they harboured that 500 per cent would not suffice to stem the flows of currency. Dennis says openly that he briefly considered and discussed a 4,000 per cent rate with his colleagues (Dennis, 1998: 55; cf. also Wibble, 1994: 28).

17. This trait has often been noticed in Sweden. Daun (1996: 86), for example, writes that 'Sweden . . . has the reputation of having a political culture in which sharp conflicts are generally avoided whenever possible.' Elsewhere (1996: 105) he writes, '[Swedes] each want "to play the same melody" with the same rhythm and in the same key.' Daun of course has myriad critics (see, for example, Linde-Laursen, 1995; O'Dell, 1998), and this is not to endorse the entirety of his work, merely to add context to Hamilton and Rolander's claim.

18. Complaining bitterly of the unfair reception given to a homegrown utopian theorist, a Swedish historian complained of this same problem long ago: 'The Swede in general has a hard time, or is completely incapable of recognizing personal labor . . . before it has been properly exclaimed, preferably by foreigners' (Henriksson-Holmberg, 1913: 215–16).

19. By locking in exchange rates at a future date via futures contracts, hedging assures a business that future market fluctuations will not impact its own position, that is, businesses can buy future kronas (or any currency for that matter) at a rate that is fixed today. This, perhaps needless to say, is a form of betting: you don't know whether the currency you bought in the future will end up costing either more or less than you assumed. But by 'hedging', you have locked your company into a predictable price for the currency so that if it then becomes too expensive, you still have your guaranteed amount of kronas, settled at the price you thought reasonable at an earlier date. But as with all betting, someone always loses: if you guessed that the currency would go up in the future, then you have gained, because you are buying it at a cheaper price and can turn around and sell it immediately on the market for its current value. In this instance, the person on the other side of the contract loses money, for he has to sell you the currency at the agreed-upon cheaper rate rather than selling it at the current market rate. As one currency trader explains bluntly, 'foreign exchange is a zero-sum game (Pardee, 1994: 166).

20. Dennis provides us with a comparison that puts the amount of money spent on the krona's defence in perspective. He informs us that between September 1992 and June 1993 'the Swedish state answered for . . . a fifth of all debt undertaken by state and suprastate borrowers on those markets. The World Bank was number two, with 10 percent' (Dennis, 1998: 45). This refers to the amount of money that Sweden borrowed on the world markets during this period.

21. It would be interesting to investigate further whether these multinationals have 'less' of an ideological or cultural commitment to, and investment in, the nation-state than other companies and citizens, given their transnational business dealings. This is certainly the folk wisdom, as evidenced in debates over NAFTA and the like. As Adam Smith posited long ago: 'A merchant, it has been said very properly, is not necessarily the citizen of any particular country. It is in a great measure indifferent to him from what place he carries on his trade; and a very trifling disgust will make him remove his capital, and together with it all the industry which it supports, from one country to another' (Smith, 1976: 444–5).

22. A worker who made this latter statement elaborated upon it by stating, 'Where does it lead if a few finance men sit somewhere and steer the world? This is anarchy. Money steers' (Wallner, 1992). The Swedish word for steers, 'styrs', probably translates better as 'runs', in the sense of 'running a country or a business'.

23. It is important to note that there are ways in which to retain this economic value within the bounds of the nation-state. So-called 'capital controls' disallow substantial outflows of national currency, which thereby manage to keep the capital in the country, for no one can trade the currency outside the country. However, the use of such capital controls as policy measures is viewed with increasing scepticism.

References

Primary sources

Altan, Pär and Göran Jonsson. 1992. 'Valutakaos drev fram chockräntan'. *Dagens Industri*. 17 September, p. 8.

Danielsson, Annika. 1992. 'Hårdingen som styr Sverige'. *Dagens Industri*. 10 September, p. 44.

Dagens Industri. 1990a. 'Devalveringsjubileum med samma siffror'. 8 October, p. 6.

Dagens Industri. 1990b. 'Kur mot inflationen'. 9 October, pp. 14–15.

Dagens Industri. 1990c. 'Äntligen lungt på marknaden'. 20 October, p. 1.

Dagens Industri. 1991a. 'Bättre sent än aldrig'. 18 May, p. 3.

Dagens Industri. 1991b. 'Ränteraset'. 21 May, p. 1.

Dagens Industri. 1991c. 'Räntorna snabbt nedåt'. 19 November, p. 41.

Dagens Industri. 1992a. 'Finlands kris är vår'. 9 September, p. 1.

Dagens Industri. 1992b. '1–0 till Dennis'. 10 September, p. 1.

Dagens Industri. 1992c. 'Comic strip'. 10 September, pp. 12–13.

Dagens Industri. 1992d. 'Sverige slåss som en karl'. 10 September, p. 13.

Dagens Industri. 1992e. 'Riksbanks Bengt Dennis fires interest rate cannon'. 10 September, p. 13.

Dagens Industri. 1992f. 'Natt-Svart: Sista chansen rädda kronan'. 17 September, p. 1.

Dagens Industri. 1992g. 'Dennis sätter punkt för oron'. 8 October, p. 33.

Dagens Industri. 1992h. 'Budgetchocken'. 24 October, p. 1.

Dagens Industri. 1992i. 'Last ditch effort failed to stem the tide'. 20 November, p. 10.

Dennis, Bengt. 1998. *500%*. Stockholm: Bokförlaget DN.

Ekbom, Christer and Lars Tulin. '1992. Bildt vädjade förgäves'. *Dagens Industri*. 20 November, p. 6.

Fahlen, Olle. 1990. 'Pundet visar vägen för kronan till ERM'. *Dagens Industri.* 8 October, p. 29.

Fahlen, Olle. 1991. 'Kronan knyts till ecu'. *Dagens Industri.* 18 May, p. 28.

Fahlen, Olle. 1992a. 'Dennis hästkur'. *Dagens Industri.* 9 September, p. 6.

Fahlen, Olle. 1992b. 'Belöningen blir stor om Riksbanken segrar'. *Dagens Industri.* 18 September, p. 32.

Fahlen, Olle. 1992c. 'Små sprickor i enigheten om fast kurs för kronan'. *Dagens Industri.* 19 November, p. 35.

Hamilton, Carl and Dag Rolander. 1992. 'Låt kronan flyta!' *Dagens Nyheter.* 16 November, p. A4.

Hamilton, Carl and Dag Rolander. 1993. *Att Leda Sverige in i Krisen.* Stockholm: Norstedts.

Karlin, Björn. 1992. 'Regeringen tappade kontrollen'. *Dagens Nyheter.* 3 September, p. A4.

Magnerot, Dan. 1992. 'Räntehöjning ska ge respekt'. *Dagens Nyheter.* 9 September, p. C1.

Mårdbrant, Christer. 1992. 'Kallsinnig reaktion i Bryssel'. *Dagens Industri.* 9 September, p. 9.

Moore, Stephen and Glenn Whitney. 1992. 'Sweden decides to float Krona after speculators drive it down'. *Wall Street Journal.* 20 November, p. A11.

Sundberg, Maria. 1992. 'Räntan rasade 5 procent'. *Dagens Industri.* 20 November, p. 5.

Sundling, Mattias. 1990a. 'Ny Räntechock'. *Dagens Industri.* 13 October, p. 34.

Sundling, Mattias. 1990b. 'EG-Optimism'. *Dagens Industri.* 27 October, p. 38.

Sundling, Mattias. 1991. 'Kronan upp, räntan ned'. *Dagens Industri.* 20 November, p. 44.

Wallen, Mosse. 1991. 'Finland devalverar'. *Dagens Industri.* 15 November, p. 10.

Wallner, Jacques. 1992. 'Någon boom blir det inte'. *Dagens Nyheter.* 20 November, p. C1.

Wibble, Anne. 1994. *Två Cigg och en Kopp Kaffe.* Stockholm: Ekerlids Förlag.

Yamdagni, Nalini. 1990. 'Räntan 17 Procent'. *Dagens Industri.* 19 October, p. 6.

Secondary sources

Akin, David and Joel Robbins, eds. 1999. *Money and Modernity: State and Local Currencies in Melanesia.* Pittsburgh, PA: University of Pittsburgh Press.

Aristotle. 1992. *Nichomachean Ethics.* In Michael Morgan (ed.), *Classics of Moral and Political Theory.* Indianapolis, IN: Hackett Publishing Company, 235–381.

Brantlinger, Patrick. 1996. *Fictions of State.* Ithaca, NY: Cornell University Press.

Cohen, Benjamin. 1998. *The Geography of Money.* Ithaca, NY: Cornell University Press.

Comaroff, Jean and John Comaroff. 1990. 'Goodly beasts, beastly goods: cattle and commodities in a South African context'. *American Ethnologist* 17(2): 195–216.

Comaroff, John and Jean Comaroff. 1992. *Ethnography and the Historical Imagination.* Boulder, CO: Westview Press.

Corden, W. Max. 1994. *Economic Policy, Exchange Rates, and the International System.* Chicago: University of Chicago Press.

Daun, Åke. 1996. *Swedish Mentality,* translated by Jan Teeland. University Park, PA: Pennsylvania State University Press.

Daun, Åke. 1993. 'Nationalism and internationalism in Sweden: toward a new class society?' *Ethnologia Scandinavica.* 23: 1–10.

Durham, D. and J. W. Fernandez. 1991. 'Tropical dominions: the figurative struggle over domains of belonging and apartness in Africa'. In J. W. Fernandez (ed.), *Beyond Metaphor: The Theory of Tropes in Anthropology*. Stanford: Stanford University Press, 190–212.

Economist. 1997. 'Bearing the weight of the market'. *The Economist*. 6 December, pp. 88–9.

Fernandez, James. 1986. *Persuasions and Performances*. Bloomington, IN: Indiana University Press.

Frykman, Jonas and Orvar Löfgren. 1987. *Culture Builders: A Historical Anthropology of Middle-Class Life*. New Brunswick, NJ: Rutgers University Press.

Gregory, Chris. 1997. *Savage Money: The Anthropology and Politics of Commodity Exchange*. Amsterdam: Harwood Academic Publishers.

Hart, Keith. 1986. 'Heads or tails? Two sides of the coin'. *Man* 21 (4): 637–56.

Harvey, David. 1990. *The Condition of Postmodernity*. Cambridge: Blackwell Publishers.

Harvey, David. 1996. *Justice, Nature and the Geography of Difference*. Cambridge, MA: Blackwell Publishers.

Hayek, Friedrich. 1976. *The Denationalisation of Money*. London, England: Institute of Economic Affairs.

Henriksson-Holberg, Gustaf. 1913. *Socialismen i Sverge: 1770–1886*. Stockholm: Axel Holmströms Förlag.

Hutchinson, Sharon. 1992. 'The cattle of money and the cattle of girls among the Nuer, 1930–83'. *American Ethnologist* 19(2): 294–316.

James, Harold. 1996. *International Monetary Cooperation Since Bretton Woods*. New York: Oxford University Press and Washington, DC: International Monetary Fund.

Leach, E., and J. Leach, eds. 1983. *The Kula: New Perspectives on Massim Exchange*. New York: Cambridge University Press.

Leyshon, Andrew and Nigel Thrift. 1997. *Money/Space*. New York: Routledge.

Linde-Laursen, Anders. 1995. *Det Nationales Natur: Studier i dansk-svenske relationer*. Lund, Sweden: Historiska Media.

Malinowski, Bronislaw. 1984. *Argonauts of the Western Pacific*. Prospect Heights, IL: Waveland Press, Inc.

Marx, Karl and Friedrich Engels. 1978. 'The Communist Manifesto'. In Robert Tucker (ed.), *The Marx-Engels Reader*. New York: W.W. Norton and Co, 473–500.

Marx, Karl. 1990. *Capital*. Volume 1. Translated by Ben Fowkes. New York: Penguin Books.

Mauss, Marcel. 1990. *The Gift*. New York: W.W. Norton.

Munn, Nancy. 1986. *The Fame of Gawa*. Durham, NC: Duke University Press.

O'Dell, Thomas. 1998. 'Junctures of Swedishness: reconsidering representations of the national'. *Ethnologia Scandinavica* 28: 20–37.

Jonathan Parry and Bloch, Maurice. 1989. *Money and the Morality of Exchange*. New York: Cambridge University Press.

Pardee, Scott. 1994. 'A trader's view of the foreign exchange market'. In David Colander and Dewey Daane (eds), *The Art of Monetary Policy*. Armonk, NY: M.E. Sharpe, 161–9.

Pollack, Andrew. 1997. 'Frugal Koreans rush to rescue their rapidly sinking economy'. *New York Times*, 18 December, p. A1.

Shell, Marc. 1993. *Money, Language, and Thought*. Baltimore, MD: Johns Hopkins University Press.

Simmel, Georg. 1991. *The Philosophy of Money*, translated by Tom Bottomore and David Frisby. New York: Routledge.

Smith, Adam. 1976. *An Inquiry into the Nature and Causes of the Wealth of Nations*, edited by Edwin Cannan. Vol. 1. Chicago: University of Chicago Press.

Stenberg, Ewa and Gunnar Örn. '1996a. Kronan hade inte skuggan av en chans'. *Dagens Nyheter*, 1 November. pp. A6–7.

Stenberg, Ewa and Gunnar Örn. 1996b. 'De spelade bort sexton miljarder'. *Dagens Nyheter*, 3 November, pp. A6–7.

Zelizer, Viviana. 1994. *The Social Meaning of Money*. Princeton, NJ: Princeton University Press.

Znoj, Heinzpeter. 1998. 'Hot money and war debts: transactional regimes in Southwestern Sumatra'. *Comparative Studies in Society and History* 40(2): 193–222.

Postscript

Postscript

10
Homo Mercans and the Fashioning of Markets

Christina Garsten and Anna Hasselström

Introduction: the trouble with markets

As recent social science research has shown, *l'ésprit du capitalisme* penetrates deeply into everyday lives of people (Boltanski and Chiapello, 1999). We live by the understanding that markets have no feelings, that they can, in bearish times, strike fear into the heart of the toughest trader and overthrow politics by their whims, that markets are, in essence, populated by greedy, self-interested individuals. At the same time, liberal economics is grounded on the assumption that free markets will, eventually, 'transform selfish individual behaviour into benevolent social outcomes' (Robertson, 2001: 55). By a wave of the invisible hand, a leap from positive to normative economics will be accomplished. Neither of these two market images has proven to be completely true. Rather, relations and interconnections between the social on the one hand, and the economic, on the other, are complex and constantly negotiated. Just when contemporary mainstream economic theory has solidified around the assumption that the market is all about simple pursuit of self-interest, there have emerged in the world of corporations and politics declarations about the motivational and normative complements of capitalism. Some corporate leaders advocate 'corporate social responsiblity', 'corporate citizenship', or even 'corporate religion' as new ways of conceptualizing the role of the corporation in society. The idea that the invisible hand of the market will work to 'the benefit of all' is here applied on a global basis.

But as businesses are becoming large-scale economies, we are left with a fragmented political authority with limited means with which to fashion markets. Alternative arenas for power play open up as new economic and political actors fight for *their* right to define the state of the world we live in. The power of globalizing markets highlights the ways in which the nation-state is now made the recipient of market transactions with their own inherent logic, accentuating the need to understand how markets are fashioned, that is modeled, shaped and governed.

The discourse around the fashioning of markets reflects a growing concern with what has been called 'the limits of government' and the power of market dynamics (Power, 1997: 52). Speaking to a widening divide between polity and economy, the concept of audit has slipped its moorings in finance and accounting, and acquired an expanded meaning. Contemporary society is to a large degree an 'audit society', or 'audit culture' (Power, 1997; Strathern, 2000), in which new practices of governance are being put to work. It also suggests that individuals and organizations alike are being subject to new types of managerial control, whose goals and practices may differ from those of state agencies (Martin, 1997; Miller and Rose, 1990; Rose and Miller, 1992). Business corporations and other market actors are active promoters of such techniques and ideas of control, ranging from evaluation procedures to the fostering of enterprise culture and a commitment to corporate accountability standards.

In this context, a number of concepts, such as 'accountability' and 'transparency', have been turned into key tropes with a social presence of a new kind (see also chapters by Garsten and Micheletti, this volume). The idea of accountability may be seen as a response to demands on rendering financial transactions and global business activities credible. The ethos of accountability embraces individual actors as well as collectivities, and also extends beyond markets, to universities, state agencies, and international aid. It implies new links and partnerships between organizations in different domains (see, for example, Marcus, 1998). Accountability is where finance and ethics meet (Munro, 1998). Yet, while the idea of accountability may render business more credible, it is not always clear to whom individuals and organizations are to be accountable, nor what the wider webs of values in which accountability is embedded look like (Garsten and Hasselström, 2003).

Likewise, the notion of transparency is increasingly brought into discussions about how economic life should ideally be conducted. As a concept, it embraces ideas of clarity, openness and justice, and tends to appear in many different social contexts involving change (see, for example, Stirrat, 1992). In the financial markets, it is often used in reference to information; for example, that information should be freely shared, comprehensible, and reach all actors at the same time. Transparency of operation is everywhere endorsed as an outward sign of integrity. And audit endorses transparency as one of its aims, making procedures visible and available to outside enquiry and, hence, generally more 'ethical' (Strathern, 2000: 292). Yet, in markets where profits often depend upon exclusive information, it remains an ambiguous concept, malleable, and open to interpretation. But all demands of transparency that make certain relations and processes more visible, divert attention away from others – the transparency involved is hence always of a selective kind.

Accountability and transparency are key tropes in the narratives that guide the fashioning of global markets. The challenge for corporations is to meet demands for accountability and transparency, to bear some responsibility for the effects of their activities on the social, natural, and political environment in which they operate, and to provide a degree of openness to the public eye. We are now seeing the beginnings of change in this direction as damage to reputation and external public pressure force a sharper perception of human rights onto the corporate agenda.

Around these tropes directed at control and supervision of market forces a vast collection of individuals and organizations with divergent interests are gathered. And as the stock market flickers with anxiety about the effects of military interventions, terrorist threats or currency rates, and stakeholders are on the lookout for corporate misbehaviour, we may wonder: How are contemporary markets fashioned? Who are the actors involved in the fashioning of markets? How is market value conceived and negotiated among actors? We wish to take up on the discussion on the fashioning of markets by introducing the idea of *market man* as a way to understand the contemporary construction of markets and market actors, and by discussing the ways in which market man is entangled in market processes.

Compared with *Homo Economicus, Homo Mercans* has a greater repertoire of alternative actions to choose from. *Homo Mercans* also calculates, but, it is not always predictable what kind of calculation *Homo Mercans* uses – it is not necessarily always an instrumental one.

Economic man – or market man?

If the idea of the contemporary global market economy entails an increased scale of transactions across the world, an organizational landscape of translocal corporations, and a great deal of financial flux, it should also entail a new conception of its actors. Who are they? Which skills, competences, and personal characteristics are most desirable? And what kinds of practices and social interactions characterize their whereabouts? Based on our studies in financial markets, flexible labour markets, and in the area of corporate social responsibility (CSR)[1], we wish to tentatively sketch the idealized characteristics of market actors and what these involve in terms of a transformation of our selves, of our professional work identities, and of how we valorize relations as well as commodities.

The notion of the 'enterprise culture' may provide a useful starting point here. Enterprise culture, as it has been outlined by Miller and Rose (1995), suggests a distinct set of ideals concerning production and the identity of the worker that aligns ideals of individualism to neo-liberal political visions. Here enterprise means not simply an organizational form, but rather an image of a certain mode of activity that could be applied equally to organizations, to individuals within organizations, and to persons in their everyday existence. The political vocabulary of enterprise promises a new identity for the individual. It has contributed to the putting to work of new strategies of governing the workplace, in which order is to be achieved through individuals working upon and disciplining themselves, to become entrepreneurial, flexible, employable, and socially competent. As Miller and Rose (1995: 455) put it: 'The political vocabulary of enterprise established a versatile set of relations among a critique of contemporary institutional forms, a program for the revitalization of economic life and national power, and an ethics of the self'.

In the free-market ideology, notions of the enterprising individual, the indulging consumer, and the competitive market actor, together come to form something of a new semantic cluster, mobilized in policy-making as well as employment advertising. For management doctrines as well as political visions, enterprise culture has created space for the development of a variety of programmes and a series of deregulations aimed at reinvigorating individual initiative and infusing vitality into the labour market. In a Foucauldian sense, these managerial doctrines and political visions may be seen as political technologies, or vehicles through which new forms of power are formed and put in place. In this sense, the enterprise culture makes up a powerful set of technologies.

The notion of enterprise culture leads us to see the extent to which the market is becoming a mobilizing metaphor in the make-up of actors in the contemporary global market economy. While we are familiar with the notion of 'economic man' of neo-classical economics, we are just becoming acquainted with a new version of it – that of 'market man' (*Homo Mercans*). While this is certainly not a new invention (humans all over the world have always been involved in trade and economic trans-actions), market man enters the stage as a model for thought and action in the global economy. Market man is:

an individual oriented towards market transactions. He or she is embedded in a discourse that places prime value on the marketability of goods and services as well as skills, competencies, manners and attitudes. Market man is taught to think in terms of financial transactions, value him- or herself as a product in the market, and take the idea of enterprise as a mode of action. Moreover, he or she is flexible, autonomous, self-reliant, and disciplined...the sort of person contained in the market model is the true or valid person, the standard against which other notions of the self are measured, and usually found wanting. (Garsten, 2002: 243)

In Foucault's view (1979), the process of normalization lies at the heart of how modern power operates: the 'normalizing gaze...establishes over individuals a visibility through which one differentiates them and judges them'. To be a market man is, in the global market economy, the normal way of being. To begin with, let us make clear that assuming that *Homo Mercans* is always greedy or evil is just as problematic as assuming that all 'globalization' is bad (Hannerz, 1996). Market man is neither good, nor bad, by definition. *Homo Mercans* is an individual who makes informed choices.[2] He comes in various versions and is brought forth by different collective settings. The intents and effects of his actions need to be understood as situated in local settings of sociomaterial interaction.

What, then, sets *Homo Mercans* apart from his older relative *Homo Economicus*? Whereas *Homo Economicus* is always guided by neo-classical formal rationality (thereby constantly being on the lookout to maximize his utility), the rationality of *Homo Mercans* is differently situated. He draws heavily on neo-classical economics, but is differently entangled in sociomaterial and temporal relations compared with economic man, who always tends to rationally calculate the most beneficial alternative (cf. Nelson, 1998). *Homo Mercans* is, moreover, not an actual person, but rather a dimension thereof. He is a way of being in the world dependent on the setting, and is rarely, if ever, totalizing. *Homo Mercans* is not forever set in his ways; his actions are open-ended without being random. He thereby escapes the essentializing gaze. For starters, he is not always sure of exactly what it is he needs to maximize. He is faced with making choices, but reaching a decision is not the straightforward, automatic affair it is for *Homo Economicus*. The road from A to B is, in the world of *Homo Mercans*, a road of uncertainty and insecurity. He has do deal with overflowing and competing framings, alongside negotiations and interpretations with others, as well as, with himself (Hasselström, 2003).

Market man is forged out of the interplay between different technologies: technologies of production, which allow us to transform and manipulate things; of sign systems, which allow us to use meanings, symbols or significations; of power, which directs the conduct of individuals; and of the self, which allows us to affect our way of being so as to reach a certain state of being (Foucault, [1982] 1997). These technologies are, to a large part, directed at measures of profitability, measures of achievement, which provide the standards against which *Homo Mercans* evaluates himself and others (cf. Porter, 1995).

The technologies by which market man is made up are visible in ongoing transformations of the labour market (see, for example, Garsten and Jacobsson, 2004). Neo-liberal doctrines suggest that present-day organizational restructurings and global competition call for 'new career paradigm' employment principles (Arthur *et al.*, 1995). These principles are said to offer a basis for shared understandings in modern, frequently tacit, employment contract arrangements. One important aspect of these shared understandings is that the exercise of freedom also implies greater responsibility for the consequences of choices, so that freedom from bureaucratic constraint must be balanced by a commitment to so-called 'market discipline' (DeFilippi and Arthur, 1996). This value asserts that work performance should be assessed in terms of its market-based outcomes, and that workers must cultivate skills that are valued by the marketplace. Such a perspective is a clear example of the kinds of message that circulate in labour markets and society in general, and according to which the individual is encouraged to take responsibility for his or her career development. It exemplifies the ways in which individuals are taught to exercise self-control and self-discipline.

That the best way to get along successfully in the labour market is to exercise self-discipline was a storyline often told in Garsten's studies of temporary employees. 'Discipline, discipline, discipline is the key', one informant explained. She was a middle-aged, experienced woman, who had entered the temporary staffing sector somewhat reluctantly, but had gradually become content with her situation. 'But it takes a lot of work', she said, 'before you get experience and self-discipline enough to get the hang of it'. Temping involves a great deal of personal responsibility and market discipline. As a temp, one is responsible for representing the agency well, being on time, meeting the expectations of the client, and fitting in with the social environment. Since normally the employer will not be close by to exert control over the temp, he or she needs to be self-disciplined. Temps, then, to some degree collaborate with their employers and clients in disciplining themselves. Hence, they contribute to the 'making up' of the flexible temporary employee as a market man (Garsten, 2002). In Hasselström's studies of financial actors (2003), it was also evident that certain aspects of the sociomaterial setting of financial markets discipline brokers, traders, and analysts into being instrumentally rational, into being maximizers of financial profit. In some sense then, they become quite like economic man – not because it is in their nature but since they *cannot* be anything else in that setting (cf. Callon, 1998, 1999). Take for example, a situation in which a trader's boss is breathing down the trader's neck wanting better results, because the boss' boss is breathing down *his* neck, expecting competitive profit calculations, to display in the upcoming comparison of gains and losses between trading desks. In such a case, the trader might decide to use a broker he is not obliged to, and actually dislikes, but thinks is better than the one he is obliged to, and likes. The trader can then try to justify the decision to himself, his broker, and his colleagues, by formatting it as being about business after all.

The idea of market discipline also goes hand in hand with the notion of an 'audit culture' or 'audit society' (Power, 1997; Strathern, 2000). These notions draw our attention to the increased tendency of making organizations, people, and practices auditable by putting in place practices that ensure comparability, transparency, and possibilities for evaluation. The rationality of audit culture, as it manifests itself in the making up of market man, is that it facilitates the management of large numbers of people by making every individual acutely aware that his or her conduct and performance are under constant scrutiny. Market discipline is part and parcel of the schemes of government that seek to establish and make operable the market man identity.

Model *of*, model *for*: the double character of the market

The market as model gives meaning and objective conceptual forms to our world by fashioning the world, as well as by being fashioned by it (Geertz, 1973; see also Lien, 1997). The market works, in other words, both as model *for* and as model *of* the world. For actors in flexible labour markets, in financial markets, in transnational business corporations and elsewhere, the market provides a conceptual tool for ordering the world and a device for the structuring of their own thoughts and actions. For market man, the market works both as a model *of* and a model *for* the world.

As a model, the market is made up of sets of symbols. Symbols are here understood as 'any object, event, quality or relation which serves as a vehicle for a conception' (Geertz, 1973: 91), that is, the meaning of the symbol. The model *of* makes people, objects and relations visible and apprehensible by modeling physical relationships (Geertz, 1973). The market as model *of* gives us clear and general ways to perceive the world, ourselves, and the relations in between. Specific situational contexts offer certain symbols for our use, but do not limit the usage, which can be both creative and open-ended and lead to new discoveries. This in turn can lead to a change in representations of the model *of*. In the model *for*, the relations between symbols fashion people's thoughts and actions. The market as model *for* provides us with basic mental dispositions. The model *for* dimension also carries a possibility for change. People act from within sociomaterial templates that fashion our reality. However, we cannot always count on co-operation from this reality. Sociomaterial patterns are created in specific situational settings and every attempt to use these patterns in other settings will look slightly different. There is no guarantee that the result is the desired one. This discrepancy between pattern and setting opens up for change of the model *for* the world. An alternative when we experience this cognitive dissonance is to keep the *for* image but change our behavior to better fit the model. Market man is aware of this duality within his being – sometimes he reflects over it, sometimes he does not. Compared with *Homo Economicus*, *Homo Mercans* has a greater repertoire of alternative actions to choose from, and he knows that others do to, which adds to his, somewhat, fragile and anxiety-ridden existence (Hasselström, 2003).

He is also part, however, of an environment in which things, people and relations are individualized, fairly stable, durable and reliable entities. It is a world where many, but not all and not for ever, objects, responsibilities, rights and obligations are 'clearly mapped out and can be intersubjectively recognized' (Slater, 2002: 238). *Homo Mercans* also calculates – stability, durability, and reliability (and hence some degree of predictability), guaranteed by legal frameworks, make calculation possible. But, it is not always predictable what kind of calculation *Homo Mercans* uses – it is not necessarily always an instrumental one. In the world of *Homo Mercans*, technologies of individuating cannot always predict market practice.

Take the following example of how the calculations of financial actors involve both relational, instrumental and financial components (Hasselström, 2003): The idea, on this particular trading floor in the City in London, is that the traders should tell their colleagues when their respective clients are doing large deals that might affect the foreign exchange market. Large deals, rumours, and news are supposed to be distributed to all traders on the floor via the internal speaker system – something which does not, however, always happen. For example, Martin occasionally withholds information, especially the kind that could benefit Toby, whom Martin, for some reason, dislikes. A possible explanation behind this dislike is that this particular trading floor is run by traders with working-class backgrounds who, with little formal education, have managed to reach high positions. Martin himself started, but never finished, a university degree. Toby, on the other hand, is a so-called rocket scientist, with a PhD in mathematics – somebody others either admire or despise. He uses several mathematical formulas when trading. Next to Toby sit a couple of other traders with working-class backgrounds. They claim they trade more on gut feeling than by using formulae. Martin likes these two, and is more than happy to pass information on to them hoping that will generate future business. If Martin had chosen to nourish his relationship with Toby a bit more, he would probably make more money out of it, but he chooses not to do so. Martin mixes both financial and relational components in his decisions on how to trade, and the decision is thus dependent on situational judgements. Market transactions are in this case disentangled, in the sense that goods, buyers, sellers, and infrastructures to transact are provided through various kinds of individuating technologies. The transactions are, however, also re-entangled through the relations between traders, where likes and dislikes, having to do with settings outside the actual trading floor, are important. In this sense, the event can be defined as a market transaction, not due to formal calculation, but due to the particularities of the dual process of particular disentanglings and re-entanglings. The notions of entanglement and disentanglement are useful here in that they allow for an understanding of the movement 'away from or closer to the market regime' (Callon, 1998: 19).

It could also be argued that Martin *is* in fact displaying instrumental rationality within this particular sociomaterial setting. Since working-class traders are in charge on this particular trading floor, siding with them might be the most instrumentally long-term rational thing to do. As Callon suggests there is, in attempts at framing, always a degree of over-flowing. In Callon's words (1998: 17), 'there are always relations which deny framing'. The notion of market as model *for* opens up for other criteria than those directly related to market value to enter into the judgement.

Corporate leaders who engage in corporate social responsibility often operate with the market as a model *of* reality. Social and environmental concerns are, through the corporate business lens, viewed as externalities that may impinge on the market value of their products, should they be connected to the actions of the organization. With the market as model of reality, social issues and environmental hazards may then come to be perceived of as externalities that need to be dealt with, through CSR activities. They are then reframed and internalized. To adopt a code of conduct or standard aimed at enhancing social accountability is done by using the market as model *for* reality. A code of conduct, a standard, or a CSR project of some sort then comes to function as a symbol that directs attention and interpretation in particular ways.

This double character of the market as model *of* and model *for* the world makes it dynamic and facilitates change in relation to how we represent the world (Sewell, 1999). The two dimensions of the market as model can be disconnected from each other, opening up for critical reflection of any dimension separately or both dimensions at the same time.

The making of things 'economic'

Callon (1998) states that market transactions comprise a dual process of entangling and disentangling. Our take on this is that we are dealing, mainly, with entanglings and disentanglings of relations between people and things.[3] Various entanglings and disentanglings result in the framing of relations as, for example, 'social', 'cultural', or 'economic'. If a relation is framed as being an economic relation, it follows that people and things involved also become 'economic', and vice versa. That is, the persons involved in the relation take part in 'economic activities' and make use of 'economic objects'. Once defined as 'economic', once certain relations are formatted as internal, or external, to the activity taking place, certain things can be said and done, while others are ruled out. The disentangling involves formatting some relations as being external to a particular transaction or activity, that is, as not belonging to the same framing, which means that these relations are irrelevant for how things should be organized, understood, and acted upon. Re-entangling takes place when relations that were previously seen as being external, are re-incorporated into the activity in question.

This is, however, the ideal version, and does not account for the fact that people engaging in market transactions are differently situated, and will thereby apply different sociomaterially based perspectives on the world. The ability to frame, or to re-frame, relations is asymmetrically distributed among people – some are better positioned than others to do this. Furthermore, all framings involve negotiations, contestations, and misunderstandings, as well as discrepancies between what people say, do, and say they do.

A trader at a trading desk exchanges a thing in a commodity state (a share) for another thing in a commodity state (money), making use of various technologies, such as computer-based trading indices, formulae, and research reports. These technologies help make the commodity, the transactors, and the exchange visible. The particular formatting of people (as traders and brokers), objects (as financial instruments) and relations (as buyers and sellers) involved, frame this as an economic event (as a market transaction), based on assumptions developed, partly, out of the same specific sociomaterial settings these brokers and traders are part of (Hasselström, 2003).

It is, however, only through grounded accounts that we can say something about the actual configurations at play in various settings. Or put differently, that we can see if, and in that case how, so-called pure 'economic' relations are entangled and disentangled from relations between people and things, that in other settings would be referred to as 'social' or 'cultural'. In financial markets, brokers, traders, and analysts use more or less 'pure' forms of formal calculation. Sometimes there is a shared idea that 'we are quits once the formal transaction has taken place', sometimes rights and obligations stretch beyond the actual formal exchange of financial instrument and money, and sometimes the transactors are not in complete agreement over what constitutes the transaction (Hasselström, 2003).

The sociomaterial settings that financial markets are part of, make these 'pure' and 'impure' calculations possible. In order to be of use, the idea of calculation, as suggested by Callon (for example, 1998) will have to be able to accommodate these settings. Through specific kinds of disentangling and re-entangling in relation to market transactions, people occasionally and momentarily display capacities to formally calculate. However, since transactors often are differently positioned, it is not always easy to agree on *when* they are quits (Slater, 2002) – that is, on what further kinds of reciprocity, or renewed interaction, should count in a particular transaction, as the examples from above show.

So, when trying to account for market transactions we should not ignore that market exchanges disentangle some relations, people, and objects in ways that has consequences for how people act and think about themselves, and their place in the world. But market exchange is simultaneously re-entangled in other relations, people, and objects, which means that humans are not fully embracing the instrumental rationality associated with *Homo Economicus* (cf. Slater, 2002). Transactions in which individuating technologies are used as means of both disentangling *and* re-entangling are better accounted for if we use the model of *Homo Mercans* to think with. That *Homo Mercans* in any particular situation temporarily displays instrumental rationality has to be, in each case, empirically accounted for, and not a priori assumed (Hasselström, 2003).

Financial brokers, traders, and analysts manoeuvre in settings partly characterized by institutionalized practices and technologies directed at anonymity. Alongside these disentangling dimensions of financial market knowledge, brokers, traders, and analysts are busy re-entangling their relations, often by making use of the same information and communication technologies that dissociate market transactions (cf. Zaloom, 2003). Although both disentanglings and re-entanglings are often aimed at making money, that is not necessarily *always* the only result, or the only aim – not all action seems to be directed at maximizing monetary profit.

In a similar vein, corporate leaders may disentangle dimensions of the social and environmental consequences of their activities and treat them as belonging to a market regime. This, in turn, may lead them to re-entangle dimensions of them in a changed conceptualization of the interrelations between market and society, and the responsibilities of market actors. It has, for example, been recognized that corporate social responsibility may prove profitable in the long run, even if the short-term costs are high. An exerpt from the website of Business for Social Responsibility, a US-based business association aimed at promoting CSR, exemplifies the combination of bottom line and business with universal ideals: 'There is a growing body of data – quantitative and qualitative – that demonstrates the bottom-line benefits of socially responsible corporate performance.' Examples are then given of how socially responsible business practices may eventually lead to improved financial performance, reduced operating costs, and enhanced reputation with the public as well as within the business community, increasing a company's ability to attract capital and trading partners (www.bsr.org/BSRResources). The CSR area abounds with examples of how market transactions involve the disentangling and re-entangling of products and people that are situationally negotiated and defined and in ways that allow for different logics to operate simultaneously (Garsten, 2003).

The making of a market transaction

We can account for this dual process of disentanglings and re-entanglings of people, things and relations, by considering how *markets are fashioned* in everyday practice. A focus on *fashioning* involves looking at how markets are modelled, shaped and governed. To understand this process, we first need to say a few more words about what sets a market transaction apart from any other kind of transaction.

Radin (1996: 6) states that: 'Universal commodification is a conceptual scheme, a worldview. The language in which this conceptual scheme is couched is the rhetoric of the market: supply, demand, price, opportunity costs, production functions, and so on.' Market rhetoric is, basically, the discourse of commodification. Along these lines, we agree with Slater when he states that a market transaction is characterized by a separative technology where objects are 'materially and conceptually, disentangled from their context as discrete and transactable things, items that can be passed from one context to another as property' (Slater, 2002: 238). We may also agree with Callon (1998: 19) when he argues that a market transaction is what happens when a person, thing, or relation is turned into a commodity, and a buyer and a seller is construed. In order to become a commodity, a buyer, or a seller, certain ties between the things in question and other objects and people, have to be cut.

Commodification entails the putting into place of a conceptual scheme. As for financial markets, the entities broker, trader, and analyst (and client) have to be produced as different professional categories. This is sometimes managed through formal education, but learning on the job, and thereby through direct experience of the market, is more important. For instance, a broker learns ways that are supposed to get traders to trade all the time, a trader learns how to interpret the market (as well as the brokers trying to get him to trade) prior to trades, and analysts learn how to produce material that traders and brokers use when forming a so-called view of the market (Hasselström, 2003). Temps on flexible employment contracts likewise learn to think of themselves as 'products', as 'brands', the market value of which may vary depending on the needs of the client organizations, the supply of temps to choose from, and the particular skills, attitudes and competencies of the temp. Temps are continuously tested, evaluated and classified to facilitate the ordering of them into categories according to market criteria (Garsten and Turtinen, 2000).

Other entities that have to be produced as separate, distinct 'things' in the world of financial traders are, for example, investment banks, brokerage houses, management teams, trading floors, and back-offices handling the paperwork emanating from trading and brokerage. Further, the commodities also need to be construed as things, as financial instruments, or products, that are identifiable, measurable, and, of course, exchangeable. These are made visible, thereby construed, for instance on computer screens, through computer software, on paper print-outs, on balance sheets, in research reports, and in formulae calculating risk and value. The logic of calculability and visibility supports the creation of a conceptual scheme of commodification, and, hence, the fashioning of markets as models *of* and models *for*. It facilitates the making up of market man as the central actor in the fashioning of markets. This making of commodities, buyers, and sellers, we may add, relies heavily on national and transnational regulations and standardizations of various actors, obligations, and rights, regulations that function as political technologies in the fashioning of markets.

A commodity is, then, to a certain extent de-contextualized, dissociated, detached, and disentangled. But we need to modify this statement slightly by adding that in order for disentangling to take place, there must be re-entangling. For example, when a trader has to decide how to repay the broker who provided him with information that helped him make money, he can do this by using the same broker for his next trade, which would generate commission for the broker. But the broker might place a higher value on the information he 'added' to the trader, and will therefore expect the trader to turn to him for more than just the one future deal. The broker will hereby try to extend the initial exchange between him and the trader into the future; whereas the trader might want to call it quits at an earlier stage. Disentangling the transaction in terms of being even becomes a matter of negotiation, one that demands a degree of re-entangling.

A market transaction is hereby better characterized by specific disen-tanglings and re-entanglings of things, relations, and people (or dimensions thereof) in the form of property, made possible by various kinds of individuating technologies. These processes of disentangling and re-entangling fashion – or perform – the collective interaction between transactors (cf. Slater, 2002). The concepts of framing, formatting, externality, and overflow allow us to focus on how this is done, and what is included and excluded in the temporary agreements and contest-ations between actors taking part, directly or indirectly, in the market transaction (cf. Callon, 1998). They can account for how the boundaries of market transactions are negotiated, in terms of, for example, deciding what the rights, responsibilities, and obligations involved in a transaction are – or should be.

For instance, say a multinational company is announcing a possible relocation from one country to another, justifying its decision by referring to more favorable tax laws. Those either unwilling or unable to relocate are laid off. The fate of these people as individuals (or of those securing a job in the other country), is not part of the calculation a trader makes when deciding how to interpret this news into possible gains or losses *for him*. The workers' feelings about this possible move are turned into an externality in the trader's formatting of this particular trade. He might reflect over it, but it will, most likely, not play a part in his decision to trade. Through a particular kind of dissociation and re-association of people, objects, and relations from the networks in which they are given a certain meaning, they become calculable. But they are also given partly new meanings, and the process of turning an object into something that can be calculated is not always predictable. The ways this can be done are many and sometimes contradictory (cf. Slater, 2002: 248). In order to be of use, the concept of calculativeness has to be more open-ended and it has to allow 'for the fact that actors are part of inter-secting networks simultaneously internal and external to different frames' (Slater, 2002: 243).

An example of this is the trader who had to decide the appropriate pay-back to the broker who fed him useful information. As suggested above, the framing of this transaction is not always straightforward. The trader and the broker might disagree as to how to measure and value the information exchanged. Calculating the transaction hereby also involves agreeing what to include and exclude in their exchange. These negotiations are not only part of the relations between brokers and traders. Exchanges of information and deals *between* traders also display the same uncertainties in relation to how to format particular market transactions.

Disentangling and re-entangling, as opposed to calculation, can better account for so-called impure market transactions lacking in instrumental rationality, and for reflexive action among transactors, as well as for the overflowing that occurs. Instead of assuming that calculation, in the form of instrumental rationality, takes place and use disentangling to account for its (stable) emergence, disentangling and re-entangling can be used to account for various ways of calculating without assuming instrumental rationality. We can thereby better account for the fact that some actors will actively try to *de*stabilize market transactions as well as stabilize them (Slater, 2002: 243). One way of doing this is for a broker, or a trader, to invoke different framings associated with friendship, on the one hand, and business, on the other hand, into the transaction. The technologies of individualization fashion market trans-actions in ways that are, to some extent, independent of our perceptions of the same (Slater, 2002: 243). 'Things', such as shares of a company, are made visible, distinct, and measurable. This is important and should not be ignored, whether we approve of this or not. But since certain dimensions of market transactions are less stable, less agreed upon and more contested than others, market transactions are also open to interpretation and negotiation.

Arguing that we should start with a focus on disentangling and re-entangling, and not on calculation, is also based on an a priori assumption that there are such things as disentangling and re-entangling, but this assumption is more open-ended and able to tackle the unexpected, than is the assumption of formal calculation. It is therefore time to bid farewell to *Homo Economicus* and instead welcome *Homo Mercans*.

Market transactions as performative acts

But why should we not leave the definition of what makes up a market transaction to the market actors themselves? Obviously their accounts matter, and it is by looking at what they do, say, and say they do, that we are able in the first place to formulate a temporary definition of market knowledge and market transactions. Based on our studies, we would like to suggest that a *market* is made up of sociomaterial clusters of entangled and dis-entangled relations between people, things, and relations. It is a model *of*, and a model *for*, reality (Geertz, 1973), that accommodates various relations between people and objects. These relations can be labelled as being, for example, 'social', 'cultural', or 'economic'.

In our view, a market transaction is a *performative act* involving at least two parties in actual, or imagined, competition over specific 'things' that are in an exchangeable *commodity state*. The transactors reciprocally affect and influence each other, and so-called pecuniary dimensions – relating to money – play a significant part in the transaction. What separates a market transaction from any other kind of transaction? The category of commodity has often, explicitly or implicitly, been used in opposition to the category of the gift (Gudeman, 2001; Myers, 2001; Thomas, 1991).[4] These are both ideal polar types. In the first, all is exchangeable, in the second, nothing is exchangeable (Kopytoff, 1986). These two modes of transaction exist, but the general concepts of gift and commodity, after being made distinct on a qualitative basis, '[need] to be fractured; not split up, as a partioned essence in a formalistic typology, but instead scattered through the nuances of practice and history' (Thomas, 1991: 26–7).

Let us therefore settle for a very porous distinction on the gift – commodity scale, and simply suggest that in a market transaction, as opposed to in any other transaction, the pecuniary interests should be considerable, but not necessarily totalizing with regards to the relations we decide to study. That pecuniary interests matter cannot be an a priori assumption, but has to be determined empirically. Further, the market transaction should be characterized by a certain amount of disentangling – that is, of an object (thing, person, service, thought, relation) conceptually and materially being turn into a commodity that can be owned and separated from other objects, and transferred between contexts (Barry and Slater, 2002; Slater, 2002). Let us start from there without forgetting that the making of market transactions, the making of commodities, and the making of value is, to varying degrees, negotiated.

A commodity, then, is something that is exchangeable for something else. In order for something to be a commodity, it has to be construed as a thing – materially and narratively – and 'marked as being a certain kind of thing' (Kopytoff, 1986: 64). Instead of thinking of a commodity as being defined by an essential characteristic of certain objects, we should view commodities, and commodification, as taking place in successive, as well as, simultaneous phases – as processes of becoming instead of being. This means that people, as well as all kinds of things, can be defined as commodities at various points of their lives (cf. Appadurai, 1986). Take, for example, the use of trust and friendship among financial brokers and traders. These relations are commodified in the sense that loyalties are forged based on reciprocal rights and obligations that are kept in imaginary ledgers by both parties. This kind of interaction is possible to call upon in relation to so-called pure market exchanges of financial instruments. That is, activities formatted as being about 'friendship' are possible to measure, value, and exchange in transactions between brokers, traders, and analysts. It may be worth noting here that conceiving of a person in market rhetoric is nothing new. Hobbes did so, in stating that 'the Value or WORTH of a man, is as of all other things, his Price, that is to say, so much as would be given for the use of his Power' (Hobbes, 1651, cited in Radin, 1996: 6). In Hobbes' conception, everything about a person that others need, desire or value is a possession that is priced. The Hobbesian person fits the archetype of universal commodification (Radin, 1996: 6–7). People and things hereby all have a *commodity potential*, and, as pointed out by Kopytoff (1986), existing exchange technologies affect the commodification process. As Radin (1996: 13) points out, in the discourse of commodification we may even conceive of human relations as 'sales' with 'prices', even where no money literally changes hands. Hence, it is also along these lines that we are able to understand how social issues, such as human rights and workers' rights, may be conceived of as having a commodity potential, which may be realized by CSR activities.

In order for a thing to be accounted for as a commodity, that thing has to be in a *commodity situation*, that is, in a situation where past, present, or future exchangeability for something else is its significant feature (Kopytoff, 1986). The obvious example of such a situation is when a set of shares is exchanged between a buyer (a trader) on a trading floor in Stockholm, and a seller (another trader) on a trading floor in London, with the help of a London-based broker, making use of various kinds of information technologies directed at financial market exchange.

These situations are not forever set or irreversible, which means that things can move in and out of the *commodity state*. These movements vary in speed – some things move in and out of commodity phases quicker than others. When moving out of such a phase, a thing becomes temporarily de-commodified. For instance, an actual stock certificate, in paper format, from a company that has ceased to exist is no longer a commodity that can be traded in financial markets. It can, however, move back into a commodity state if it, for some reason, becomes a valued collectors' item. A thing can also be formatted as a commodity or not, in the same sociomaterial settings, by different people (cf. Kopytoff, 1986).

To be in a position to commodify, de-commodify, or to restrict com-modification, is to be in a position of power, in a sense that the activities of others are affected. For instance, the inventors of ethical funds have to develop procedures whereby the morally bad is made measurable. In many of these funds, weapons and cigarettes are formatted as being non-tradable things, hence they are de-commodified.

According to Kopytoff, the commodity status of a thing is negotiable (both between persons, as well as within the same person), and always ambiguous, except at the actual moment of exchange when the transactors agree upon the thing as a commodity. It is, however, not always easy for two parties to agree when this 'moment of exchange' actually begins or ends, as was also pointed out earlier in relation to Callon's definition of a market transaction as occurring when transactors close a deal. When brokers, traders, and analysts are engaged in relations with each other that stretch across time and place, and that include various activities, it becomes increasingly difficult to delineate where a particular market transaction ends and another begins. Maybe we are in fact dealing, not with several successive transactions but with one long transaction, punctuated by reciprocal activities.

A thing's *commodity candidacy* refers to whatever the standards or criteria are that define exchangeability in a particular sociomaterial setting. Or put differently, what counts as external, or internal to, a particular situation. A *commodity context*, or framing, is the setting in which the commodity candidacy of a thing is linked to the commodity state of its career (Appadurai, 1986; Kopytoff, 1986). As for financial markets, this refers to the outcome of brokers', traders', and analysts' perspectives towards the perspectives of significant others on what should be included, or excluded, when framing a market transaction.

To recapitulate, a defining characteristic of a commodity is that it is exchangeable in a transaction with something else that is supposed to have an equal value. The making of a commodity hereby involves organizing things in categories of value, that is, to make them alike, in relation to value, to other things in the same category, and different from things in other categories. Commodification hence allows for the measuring of value (cf. Mallard, 1998).

Furthermore, a commodity is something that is exchanged in a market transaction, and a market transaction consists of the exchanging of commodities. Or in other words: exchangeability, as a basic feature, turns something into a commodity, and the exchangeability of commodities, as a basic feature, produces a market transaction, in which the commodity is exchanged. In the case of flexible temporary employment, the exchangeability of the temp, or the work performed by the temp, implies that we are close to a case of commodification. Temp agencies offer temps 'with a guarantee; you pay only if you are satisfied'. Or, one may lease reliable employees; 'Healthy collaborators, whenever you want' (ad campaign for temp agency in Stockholm). In these instances, elements of the temp are given exchange value and are dissociated from context (cf Thomas, 1991).

We would like to think of the circularity of this tentative suggestion, not as an analytical flaw, but as an attempt to account for how people, objects, and relations fashion, and are fashioned by, entanglings and disentanglings we label 'market transactions'. It is an attempt to understand how the market, as a model *for*, and model *of* reality, is actually configured. The specificities of the fashioning of these 'things' have to be accounted for empirically.

Concluding notes

In the wake of the intensified globalization of markets, we fix our gaze at the workings of markets, the underlying assumptions and their performative power. No doubt, the market as a conceptual scheme has 'holding power'. In conclusion, it may be interesting to contrast the great interest and curiosity that social scientists place in markets today to the scorn bestowed upon markets by the nineteenth-century utopian philosopher Charles Fourier, who claimed that:

> the wise men of antiquity never made commerce an object of study; they simply treated it with the scorn it deserves. The masters of the world, the Alexanders and the Ceasars, would have smiled in pity if someone had advised them to subordinate their policies, in today's fashion, to the interests of the dealers in oil and soap. (Fourier, in Beecher and Bienvenu, 1971: 108)[5]

Yet this is perhaps where we still stand today, with the power of globalizing markets resulting in weakened political authority. Hence, the interest in markets should come as no surprise, but as a necessity.

The idea of globalizing markets begs the question: what emerging economic, social, and cultural structures are being put in place? And who are the actors involved in their creation? In the above, we have discussed some aspects of the ways in which markets are fashioned, or modelled, shaped and governed, in situated sociomaterial contexts. Drawing upon our own empirical material from the financial market and corporate worlds, we have discussed the fashioning of markets in everyday practices by introducing the notion of market man (*Homo Mercans*) as an alternative to the rational and instrumental economic man. We suggest that market man is differently entangled in sociomaterial structures and relations compared to economic man, and moves in and out of market understandings more easily. Compared with *Homo Economicus*, he has a greater repertoire of alternative actions to choose from. True, *Homo Mercans* also calculates, but it is not always predictable what kind of calculation *Homo Mercans* uses – since it is not necessarily always an instrumental one. Economic man was introduced as a way of uncovering the pure logic of economic action, as a 'fictional man' ignoring all motives exercising influence on us that are not specifically economic in exercising absolute economic rationality (Blaug, 1994: 56). As such, he was given a prominent argumentative and motivational role in the development of liberal economics (Agevall, 2001: 60–1). Introducing market man as an alternative construct is an attempt to escape the essentialism as well as the motivational dimensions of economic man. It is an attempt to approach 'real' men and women in 'real' sociomaterial contexts – to 'get real' (see also chapters by Lien and Moeran, this volume). Hence, market man is nowhere to be seen as *homo totus*, as a totalizing subject, but as *homo partialis*, as element in the makeup of social identity (cf. Machlup, 1978: 267).

Not only is the market a powerful globalizing force; it also works in everyday contexts as a conceptual scheme and a performative device in our ways of thinking and acting. We have argued in favour of understanding the dual aspects of the market as model *of*, as well as a model *for*, reality. Whereas the model *of* provides an understanding of the organization of the world, the model *for* works as a tool for the direction of action. We have suggested that the logic of *Homo Mercans*, or market man, is a fruitful way to think about and account for the prevalence of contemporary market discourse and practice and the ways in which objects as well as people are shiftingly and continuously drawn into, and cut loose from, the market sphere. It is in acknowledging the partiality of market subjectivity and activity, the shifting and situational nature of entanglement and disentanglement of people and products, that we believe a fuller understanding of the workings of markets may be approached. And in this, we will have to address what Fourier saw as the scorned and faulty system of markets.

Notes

1. This chapter builds on Hasselström's research among financial brokers, traders and analysts in Stockholm, London and New York; and on Garsten's research on the flexibilization of labour markets in Sweden, in the UK and the US, and on corporate activities in the areas of CSR in Europe and the US. We wish to thank the Bank of Sweden Tercentenary Foundation and the Swedish Research Council for funding these projects.
2. *Homo Economicus* is often associated with a masculine kind of rationality and agency – as abstract, detached, objective, and emotionless, whereby the feminine – as concrete, connected, particular, and embodied (Nelson, 1998), as well as the colonial Other, are excluded (Butler, 1992: 12 quoted in De Goede, 2000; cf. Thompson, 2000). *Homo Mercans* also displays many of these assumptions but can accommodate other kinds of rationalities besides this masculine one. We will nevertheless refer to *Homo Mercans* as a 'he' in the text, for reasons of simplicity.
3. We will here simply leave aside the complicating aspect that 'people', 'things', and 'relations' also are labels that format, and are formatted by, the world we live in, and thereby themselves are configured through various entanglings and disentanglings.
4. See also, for example, Parry and Bloch (1989); Mauss [1950] (1990); Miller (1987); Strathern (1988); and Weiner (1992) for discussions on 'the gift'.

5. The text is from the preamble of a manuscript written in 1810 and entitled 'On the Federal Warehouse or the Abolition of Commerce'.

References

Agevall, Ola. 2001. 'Varför homo oeconomicus inte är girig' [Why homo oeconomicus is not greedy]. In G. A. Öygarden (ed.), *Vår tids ekonomism*. Umeå: Boréa, 57–80.

Appadurai, Arjun. 1986. 'Introduction: commodities and the politics of value'. In A. Appadurai (ed.), *The Social Life of Things: Commodities in Cultural Perspective*. Cambridge: Cambridge University Press, 3–63.

Arthur, Michael B., Priscilla H. Claman and Robert J. DeFilippi. 1995. 'Intelligent enterprise, intelligent careers'. *Academy of Management Executive* 9(4): 7–20.

Barry, Andrew and Don Slater. 2002. 'Technology, politics and the market: an interview with Michel Callon'. *Economy and Society* 31(2): 285–306.

Beecher, Jonathan and Richard Bienvenu. 1971. *The Utopian Vision of Charles Fourier*. Boston: Beacon Press.

Blaug, Mark. 1994. *The Methodology of Economics – Or How Economists Explain*, 2nd edn. Cambridge: Cambridge University Press.

Boltanski, Luc and Eve Chiapello. 1999. *Le Nouvel Esprit du Capitalisme*. Paris: Gallimard.

Business for Social Responsibility (BSR). 2003. Online, http://www.bsr.org/BSRResources (visited 31 May 2003).

Callon, Michel 1998. 'Introduction: the embeddedness of economic markets in economics'. In M. Callon (ed.), *The Laws of the Markets*. Oxford: Blackwell Publishers, 1–57.

Callon, Michel 1999. 'Actor – network theory – the market test'. In J. Law and J. Hassard (eds) *Actor Network Theory and After*. Oxford: Blackwell, 181–95.

DeFilippi, Robert J. and Michael B. Arthur. 1996. 'Boundaryless contexts and careers: a competency-based perspective'. In M. B. Arthur and D. M. Rousseau (eds), *The Boundaryless Career*. Oxford: Oxford University Press, 116–31.

De Goede, Marieke. 2000. 'Mastering Lady Credit: discourses of financial crisis in historical perspective'. *International Feminist Journal of Politics* 2(1): 58–81.

Foucault, Michel 1979. *Discipline and Punish*. New York: Vintage.

Foucault, Michel [1982] 1997. *Ethics: Subjectivity and Truth. Volume One*, edited by P. Rabinow. New York: The New Press.

Garsten, Christina. 2002. 'Flex Fads: new economy, new employees'. In I. Holmberg, M. Salzer-Mörling and L. Strannegård (eds), *Stuck in the Future: Tracing the 'New Economy'*. Book House Publishing, 237–61.

Garsten, Christina. 2003. 'The cosmopolitan organization: an essay on corporate accountability'. *Global Networks* 3(3): 355–70.

Garsten, Christina and Anna Hasselström. 2003. 'Risky business: discourses of risk and (ir)responsibility in globalizing markets'. *Ethnos* 68(2): 249–70.

Garsten, Christina and Kerstin Jacobsson. 2004. 'Introduction'. In C. Garsten and K. Jacobsson (eds), *Learning to be Employable: New Agendas for Work, Responsibility and Learning in a Globalizing World*. Basingstoke: Palgrave Macmillan, 1–22.

Garsten, Christina and Jan Turtinen. 2000. '"Angels" and "chameleons": the cultural construction of the flexible temporary employee in Sweden and the UK'.

In B. Stråth (ed.), *After Full Employment: European Discourses on Work and Flexibility*. Brussels: Peter Lang, 161–206.

Geertz, Clifford. 1973. *The Interpretation of Cultures*. New York: Basic Books.

Gudeman, Stephen. 2001. *The Anthropology of Economy: Community, Market, and Culture*. Oxford: Blackwell Publishing.

Hannerz, Ulf 1996. *Transnational Connections*. London: Routledge.

Hasselström, Anna. 2003. *On and Off the Trading Floor: An Inquiry into the Everyday Fashioning of Financial Market Knowledge*. Doctoral thesis, Dept of Social Anthropology, Stockholm University.

Kopytoff, Igor. 1986. 'The cultural biography of things: commoditization as process'. In A. Appadurai (ed.), *The Social Life of Things: Commodities in Cultural Perspective*. Cambridge: Cambridge University Press, 64–91.

Lien, Marianne Elisabeth 1997. *Marketing and Modernity*. Oxford: Berg.

Machlup, Fritz. 1978. *Methodology of Economics and Other Social Sciences*. New York: Academic Press.

Mallard, Alexandre. 1998. 'Compare, standardize, and settle agreement: on some usual methodological problems'. *Social Studies of Science* 28(4): 571–601.

Marcus, George E., ed. 1998. *Corporate Futures: The Diffusion of the Culturally Sensitive Firm*. Chicago: University of Chicago Press.

Martin, Emily. 1997. 'Managing Americans: policy and changes in the meanings of work and the self'. In C. Shore and S. Wright (eds), *Anthropology of Policy: Critical Perspectives on Governance and Power*. London: Routledge, 239–57.

Mauss, Marcel. [1950] 1990. *The Gift: The Form and Reason for Exchange in Archaic Societies*. London: Routledge.

Miller, Daniel. 1987. *Material Culture and Mass Consumption*. Oxford: Blackwell.

Miller, Peter and Nikolas Rose. 1990. 'Governing economic life'. *Economy and Society* 19(1): 469–96.

Miller, Peter and Nikolas Rose. 1995. 'Production, identity, and democracy'. *Theory and Society* 24: 427–67.

Munro, Rolland. 1998. 'Ethics and accounting: the dual technologies of self'. In M. Parker (ed.), *Ethics and Organizations*. London: Sage, 197–220.

Myers, Fred R. 2001. 'Introduction: the empire of things'. In F. R. Myers (ed.), *The Empire of Things: Regimes of Value and Material Culture*. Santa Fe: School of American Research Press, 3–61.

Nelson, Julie A. 1998. 'Abstraction, reality and the gender of "Economic man"'. In J. G. Carrier and D. Miller (eds), *Virtualism: A New Political Economy*. Oxford: Berg, 75–94.

Parry, Jonathan P. and Mavrice Bloch, eds. 1989. *Money and the Morality of Exchange*. Cambridge: Cambridge University Press.

Porter, Theodore M. 1995. *Trust in Numbers: The Pursuit of Objectivity in Science and Public Life*. Princeton: Princeton University Press.

Power, Mikael. 1997. *The Audit Society: Rituals of Verification*. Oxford: Oxford University Press.

Radin, Margaret J. 1996. *Contested Commodities*. Cambridge, MA: Harvard University Press.

Robertson, Alexander F. 2001. *Greed: Gut Feelings, Growth, and History*. Cambridge: Polity.

Rose, Nikolas and Peter Miller. 1992. 'Political power beyond the state: problematics of government'. *British Journal of Sociology* 43(2): 173–205.

Sewell, William. H. Jr. 1999. 'Geertz, cultural systems, and history: from synchrony to transformation'. In S. B. Ortner (ed.), *The Fate of 'Culture': Geertz and Beyond*. Berkeley: University of California Press. 35–55.

Slater, Don. 2002. 'From calculation to alienation: disentangling economic abstractions'. *Economy and Society* 31(2): 234–49.

Stirrat, Roderick L. 1992. '"Good Government" and "the Market"'. In R. Dilley (ed.), *Contesting Markets: Analyses of Ideology, Discourse and Practice*. Edinburgh: Edinburgh University Press, 203–13.

Strathern, Marilyn. 1988. *The Gender of the Gift*. Berkeley: University of California Press.

Strathern, Marilyn, ed. 2000. *Audit Cultures*. London: Routledge.

Thomas, Nicolas. 1991. *Entangled Objects*. Cambridge, MA: Harvard University Press.

Thompson, Victoria E. 2000. *The Virtuous Marketplace: Women and Men, Money and Politics in Paris, 1830–1870*. Baltimore: Johns Hopkins University Press.

Weiner, Annette B. 1992. *Inalienable Possessions: The Paradox of Keeping-While-Giving*. Berkeley: University of California Press.

Zaloom, Caitlin. 2003. Ambiguous numbers: Trading technologies and interpretation in financial markets. *American Ethnologist*.

Name Index

Subject Index

Note: notes at the end of chapters have not been indexed.